Action research for health and social care A guide to practice

Elizabeth Hart and Meg Bond

Open University Press
Buckingham · Philadelphia

Open University Press
Celtic Court
22 Ballmoor
Buckingham
MK18 1XW

email: enquiries@openup.co.uk
world wide web: http://www.openup.co.uk

and

325 Chestnut Street
Philadelphia, PA 19106, USA

First Published 1995
Reprinted 1995, 1996, 1999

A catalogue record of this book is available from the British Library

ISBN   0 335 19262 9 (pb)   0 335 19263 7 (hb)

Library of Congress Cataloging-in-Publication Data
Hart, Elizabeth.
   Action research for health and social care: a guide to practice/
Elizabeth Hart and Meg Bond.
     p.   cm.
   Includes bibliographical references and index.
ISBN 0–335–19263–7 (hbk) ISBN 0–335–19262–9 (pbk)
   1. Action research.   2. Action research–Case studies. 3.   Human
services–Research –Methodology. I. Bond, Meg. II. Title.
   HV11.H349 1996
   361'.0072–dc20

                                                             94–34021
                                                                 CIP

Typeset by Vision Typesetting, Manchester
Printed in Great Britain by St Edmundsbury Press Ltd,
Bury St Edmunds, Suffolk

Contents

Acknowledgements

The collaborative projects upon which this book is based were developed over a considerable period of time and with a wide range of people. We have valued these shared experiences and learnt much from them. We offer our warm thanks to all those who cooperated with us in these endeavours, many of whom, as well as other colleagues, have helped us with the writing of this book. In particular we thank the following. The regional health authority and managers of the district general hospital, sisters, charge nurses and nursing staff who contributed to Case Studies 1 and 2. In preparing Case Study 3 we appreciated the help of Maureen Clark, Dorothy Compton, Audrey Haywood, Cathy Hunt, Edna Pryal and John Sadler. Credits are due to the following for contributions to Case Study 4: Melinda Enoch for her generous voluntary contribution to the running of the project, the community pharmacist for his comments on the draft of the original publication and Des Kelly, the University of Warwick and SCA (Education) for permission to reproduce from *Medication Matters*. Thanks are also due to David Fogg, and to Jenny Lund and Sylvia Hardy for permission to reproduce from their ethical guidelines; to Julie Repper and Pat Walton for help in the diary keeping section; and to John Weeks for material based upon work at the National

Institute for Social Work. All their contributions appear in Chapter 10. We acknowledge too, the support of colleagues at the Department of Nursing and Midwifery Studies, University of Nottingham, Mark Avis, Linda East, Nicky James, Lisa Manning, Anne Marie Rafferty, Julie Repper, Jane Robinson and Shelagh Sparrow, and especial thanks to Ruth Elkan. We thank Alan Prout for helpful comments on an early draft of Chapter 3 and Nick Bond and Alan Hart for support and help throughout.

A note about language and terminology

We acknowledge that in a number of places in this book we have quoted from authors who used the gendered language of their time.

In this book we use the terms 'reflective' and 'reflexive' and as far as possible we have followed their usage by different authors. We recognize that these terms are not interchangeable, although they sometimes appear as such, and that, generally speaking, the term 'reflective' tends to be used in the organizational and professional literatures, while the term 'reflexive' is associated with critical theory. Readers wishing to explore the ideas behind these terms might find it useful to read D. A. Schön's (1983) *The Reflective Practitioner: How Professionals Think in Action*. London, Temple Smith, and L. Harvey's (1990) *Critical Social Research*. London, Unwin Hyman

List of figures and tables

Part I

Action research in context, process and practice

1

Introduction and overview

Our combined experiences of researching and working in health and social care settings over a number of years have led us to recognize the value of action research in helping practitioners, managers and researchers to make sense of problems in service delivery and in promoting initiatives for change and improvement. Through the five case studies in Part 2, which we conducted singly and in partnership with others, we illustrate the scope which exists for front line staff and commissioned researchers to undertake action research projects, and to work collaboratively with clients, users,[1] managers and others towards emergent shared goals. As such we present case studies of instructive failure as well as of success. Although action research is not necessarily the optimum choice in all settings, it is particularly appropriate where problem-solving and improvement are on the agenda. Moreover, the combination of enquiry, intervention and evaluation which powers the action research cycle mirrors the iterative processes employed by professional staff in assessing the needs of vulnerable people, responding to them and reviewing progress. Thus many practitioners will already be familiar with an action research approach, even though they might not explicitly label what they do as such. Within nursing, East and Robinson (1994) have observed that the increasing popularity of action research may be due to its similarities with the nursing process. Another compelling feature of action research is that it may be deployed in small-scale as well as larger enterprises, including single work groups and international organizations (Chisholm and Elden 1993), and can result in the initiation of change at the level of both individual professional practice and organizational structures and processes.

In the following pages we present an argument for action research to be considered as an option by practitioners and researchers in health and social care agencies wishing to improve professional practice and standards of service provision, and by educators teaching research methods to students on health and welfare courses. We do not pretend that action research is ever easy or unproblematic, and we do not ignore its critics. Nevertheless, we do believe that the current ideology of reform and improvement in the health and social care services, along with other related developments, points almost inevitably in the direction of action research. These current developments include growing pressure on professional staff to make use of relevant research findings, to deploy scarce resources effectively, and to be more accountable for their actions. There are also increasing expectations that health and welfare service provision should be both informed by research into the needs of individuals and communities, and shaped by consultation and in collaboration with them (Winn 1990), and that clinicians and managers should be able to use research findings (Peckham 1991). There is also considerable concern that, in the past, the omission of an active dissemination phase from research studies, particularly expensive commissioned projects, has resulted in costly and wasteful dissipation of effort (Richardson *et al.* 1990).

While there is clear acknowledgement, among practitioners and researchers alike, of the potential value of research to inform the work of staff and organizations, there is also a recognition that progress on these fronts is bedevilled by a perceived separation of theory from practice (Wright 1985; Clarke 1986; Hunt 1987; Webb 1989, 1990; Everitt *et al.* 1992; Munn-Giddings 1993; O'Connor 1993). When used in promoting reflexive practice, organizational improvement and learning about research, action research has much to commend it. Although, as Tierney and Taylor (1991: 506) have pointed out, there 'is no one "best" way of bringing research and practice into closer alliance', action research was 'designed specifically for bridging the gap between theory, research and practice' (Holter and Schwartz-Barcott 1993: 299).

The structure of the book reflects the interplay of practice wisdom and theoretical concepts which we believe is the driving force of the action research approach. There are three main sections: Part I considers action research in context, process and practice; Part II consists of five case studies; Part III includes a toolkit, and our concluding comments. Some readers might wish to begin by reading some of the case studies, but for those starting at the beginning of the book Chapter 2 offers an overview of some main developments in action research from the time of the pioneering work of Kurt Lewin in the 1940s in America, through to later developments in organizational change, education, community development and nursing. The chapter traces four broad approaches in action research which have given rise to different orientations: the experimental approach associated with Lewin and his followers; the organizational approach associated with names such as the Tavistock Institute; the empowering approach arising from community development; and the professionalizing approach identifiable in education and nursing. Chapter 3 builds on the preceding overview by defining action research in terms of the four broad approaches outlined in Chapter 2, and in relation to the seven distinguishing criteria. These include the criteria that action research aims at improvement and involvement, is problem focused and context specific, and involves a research relationship in which those involved are participants in the change process. We then present an action research typology (Table 3.1), covering 'experimental', 'organizational', 'professionalizing' and 'empowering' action research types. We consider each of the seven criteria in relation to the four types, and show, for instance, that the meanings of improvement and involvement, and of participation, differ depending upon the type of action research in which they are located. Chapter 4 moves on to consider what is involved in preparing a research proposal. It explores some of the thinking processes involved in making decisions about methodology and modes of research and action in the light of the distinguishing criteria and typology in Chapter 3. Part I thus provides a reference point for issues raised by the case studies in Part II, and underlines the argument that action research involves a subtle interplay between enquiry, action and evaluation.

The five case studies in Part II cover large and small-scale projects in health and social care in which we been directly involved. In reflecting on our experiences in each of these projects, we show, among other things, how our respective roles as researchers and change agents shift and develop over the life of a particular project, and how important it is in action research to pay attention to process, while not ignoring outcome.

Case studies 1 and 2 are interlinked and focus on a project funded by a regional health authority into the management of change in respect of standards of care at a medium-sized district general hospital. Case study 1 provides an overview of the two years of the project from the perspective of the university-based project leader, and uncovers the micropolitics behind the establishment of the project, tensions with senior managers and roles and relationships within the action research team. Case study 2 concentrates on a staff development programme within this larger project, which took place during its second year and involved a group of ward sisters undergoing the change to clinical manager. This case study is an example of a successful action research initiative, which illustrates the way groupwork was used as a vehicle for change and development. For those wishing to undertake a similar staff development programme, groupwork guidelines and further reading are included in Chapter 10, to complement the case study. Both of these case studies relate to broader issues of organizational change and problem-solving.

As an example of practitioner-generated action research, case study 3 explores the successful process of working on shared problems in an action research way with older people in the community. A feature of the case study is its focus on evaluation, highlighting some of the tensions which such projects may encounter in attempting to integrate evaluation of process and of outcome. It also raises issues about working across interprofessional boundaries, including the possibility that health and social care professionals may feel threatened by projects which are successful in empowering otherwise isolated individuals to work together on shared problems.

Case study 4 is written from the perspective of a practitioner–

researcher employed as an outside consultant to assist senior managers from a social services department to plan the future of residents of a home for people with severe physical disabilities. Like case study 1, it underlines the need for senior managers to be committed to the aims and approach of action research and to be willing to support what those involved at grass roots level are trying to do. It also underlines a point that runs throughout each of the case studies, that in action research even a project that might be deemed on one level to have failed may be successful in terms of realizing underlying values (such as those of collaborative working) and in generating findings which may usefully be generalized to other groups facing similar problems.

The final case study is the smallest in scale and focuses on a classic problem in organizational change: how to overcome resistance on the part of established workgroups, in this case a group of care workers in a residential home for older people. It shows what can be achieved even in situations where no additional resources are available to support such a project, and how it was possible to involve a part-time volunteer as a key change agent and participant observer. Apart from the fact that such projects rely on the commitment of insiders to work in their 'spare time', there is another downside to unfunded projects such as this: in this case, since senior managers from the social services department had not funded the project, they had no stake in its outcome and no interest in extending what had been learned about medication practices to improve the quality of life of older people in similar settings.

Chapter 10 takes the form of a 'toolkit', which has been generated out of the work described in Chapter 4 and in the case studies, and is best read in conjunction with them. It provides a combination of materials which we have found valuable in helping us and others to think through the processes and purposes of undertaking research. The chapter begins with a questionnaire which encourages consideration of the how, why and what of a proposed project, as well as of the power relations and vested interests which may impinge upon it, and includes a mapping exercise which assists in identifying allies and tracing networks that can be utilized in getting started and carrying a project through. Other 'tools', such as resources for groupworking and examples of ethical guidelines, evaluation and diary keeping, are provided. The book concludes with a chapter offering readers a way forward in terms of action research by 'working from a project perspective'.

Taken together, the case studies represent a range of approaches to action research, from organizational to empowering types, and from the different perspectives of managers, academic researchers and practitioners. A synthesis of the issues raised by each of them reveals emergent themes. These include the centrality of our change agent role to each of the accounts. Looking back at our experiences we recognized some of the limitations and risks of our change agent role, particularly as mature women who attempted to work in an action research way in hierarchical organizations. In situations where we became engaged in work with less powerful groups, such as ward nurses whose experience as women and as professionals was of being 'muted' (Ardener 1986; E. Hart 1991), we ran the risk of being marginalized by senior people who perceived change as a threat. But we also realized that the change agent role was invaluable in creating room for manoeuvre, in promoting a climate in which change became possible, and in taking care of the issues of process, thus freeing participants to take change forward. Part of this involved creating alliances and opening up space for others to become change agents, so that the role was not an isolated or individual one.

Another theme is that action research which is initiated by senior people to promote change at grass roots level is fraught with potential difficulties. Our analysis would suggest that this often involves a clash both of values and of methodological approach, such that top-down goals and bottom-up initiatives come into conflict, despite what might appear as a convergence of interests around a particular problem. Such conflicts would seem to confirm the argument Clarke (1972) draws from an analysis of a number of action research projects: that the structure and values of the organization, the sponsors' value system, and the willingness of sponsors to approach the problem in a spirit of enquiry all influence the possibilities for action research as an appropriate and effective approach for change. Here, action research can play an important role in overcoming such conflicts by making different value per-spectives explicit from the very beginning – which might be a central part of the change agent role – and by being clear about the purpose of the project and the type of approach. It also became evident from our case studies that ownership and control are linked, and that as a project moves through its lifetime, ownership by one group might preclude ownership by another, so that in some situations even senior people may feel disempowered.

Timescale is another important theme running through the case studies. Each one of them was conducted under pressures of time, and each was constrained by externally imposed deadlines. Two important issues here are that it is not always possible, or even advisable, to try to 'hurry up' the process of action research, and that part of the change agent role might involve creating time to work in the face of imposed deadlines. Consideration of the impact of timescale upon the process and outcome of action research projects has led us to speculate that time may be a crucial factor in the extent to which a 'top-down' project within the organizational type of action research may move away from a task focus, and towards a more empowering, diffuse and multi-level approach, more commonly associated with community development. This kind of developmental movement raises an important issue for professionals, about what position they might take up as the project moves forward over time, and whether or not they might decide to step back from the project and initiate another one elsewhere, or to stay with it and lay aside their professional 'expert identity' in favour of an insider role.

The way in which a project is funded, and by whom, is another central thread linking the five case studies. It is not only the extent of funding that is (or is not) made available which can make the difference between being able to take a project forward or having to abandon it part way through, but also the nature of the relationships among stakeholders. Case study 1 provides a particularly clear example of a situation in which both researchers and managers were under an obligation to the funding body, and of the implications of this for the perceived independence of the researchers. As Heller (1986: 7–8) argues, the source of funds 'can be a critical influence on the development, objectivity and outcome of the research', and 'there is the delicate question of the extent to which a research analysis can be critical of people or issues closely associated with the piper who pays for the tune.'

A final theme from the case studies is that there is a variety of forms which the researcher–practitioner relationship might take and it would be counterproductive to assert that one form is better than another. The case studies reveal that there are certain problem contexts which are helped by the intervention of an outside researcher, just as there are others which are best tackled by an inside practitioner. This simple dictum is, of course, confounded by the fact that over the life of a project roles and relationships change, so that an outsider might move into an insider role at a certain moment in the project's development, and an insider might find that conditions change so that he or she becomes defined as an outsider (Sparrow and Robinson 1994). The most important lesson seems to be that the process of defining the problem and formulating research questions arising from it needs to be collaborative. The implications of this are that action research is not something that is done to participants by researchers, and that action researchers are not put in positions where they feel coerced and controlled to define the problem according to the goals of the most powerful group.

Each of the case studies, in a different way, illustrates that in action research generalization can take a number of forms, including using the findings from one project to initiate another, and extending what has been learned to a different setting. As may happen with the case studies in this book, a practitioner audience for action research reports might recognize similarities with their own situation, so that comparisons of more general relevance to practice are made (Winter 1989). Such a comparative approach, particularly where it presents the practitioner with detailed descriptive ethnographic data of other people's practice, may be used to evaluate one's own practice, and can prompt further action for improvement (Bloor and McKeganey 1989).

One of the features of the book is that it has a multi-disciplinary, inter-professional and inter-agency focus. This is reflected in each of the case studies, none of which is concerned solely with a single professional group. All of them recognize that problems are not the property of one group and that the process of working across professional boundaries on shared problems can itself lead to improvements in practice. The case studies illustrate such issues as: the tensions that can arise when working across boundaries between accountants, general managers and nurses in a district general hospital; the opportunities for change which come about when social workers, health visitors, district nurses and informal carers work together in a collaborative way; the contributions made by pharmacists and doctors to changes in practice. Throughout the book we identify areas of shared concern between professionals in health and social care, and even where, as for instance in Chapter 4, the focus is on social work practice, the issues highlighted are of more general relevance to nurses and other practitioners working in the community. However, in the concluding chapter we recognize the key position of social workers in being able to work with groups in social care settings, and the numerical and strategic importance of nurses in health care, by concentrating specifically on these two groups in our discussion of the relationship between theory, research and practice. This final chapter considers a problem which seems to be shared by professionals in health and social care, that is the need to encourage research-minded practice in the face of scepticism on the part of practitioners about the uses and purposes of research. After discussion of the obstacles to and opportunities for research in nursing and social work, we conclude by arguing for the need to work from a project perspective, and propose a way of thinking about combining research and practice which practitioners and researchers might wish to take forward.

NOTE

1 Throughout this book we refer to 'users', although we recognize that this term is problematic, that users are not a unitary group and may be more appropriately described as 'recipients', for instance in those situations where they have not exercised choice in the provision of a service. We also recognize that the decision to use certain terms, such as 'user', 'consumer', 'patient', 'client' or 'recipient' (Campbell 1990), is an indication of the position taken up in relation to them and affects the type of methodology that might be selected in working with them. For a discussion of these issues in relation to health services research see Winn (1990) and Ong (1993).

2

Action research in context

We begin by tracing some important threads in the history of action research, focusing in particular on the pioneering work of Kurt Lewin (1890–1947), and moving on to outline related developments in organizational research, community development, education and nursing. Our aim is to show how action research has developed from an Americanized form of rational social management to a more robustly democratic and empowering approach to change. This chapter is not intended as a definitive history of action research, but rather as a selective tracking of points of overlap, linkage and divergence in the emergence of differing action research approaches.

KURT LEWIN AND THE EMERGENCE OF ACTION RESEARCH

It is important to understand clearly that social research concerns itself with two rather different types of questions, namely the study of general laws of group life and the diagnosis of a specific situation.

(Lewin 1946: 204)

Elden and Chisholm (1993: 121) argue that 'Although its exact origins are open to dispute, action research has been a distinctive form of enquiry since the 1940s. Kurt Lewin (1946) generally receives credit for introducing the term "action research" as a way of generating knowledge about a social system while, at the same time, attempting to change it.' Even a cursory glance through the action research literature reveals the continuing influence of Lewin's ideas upon latter-day action researchers, despite the fact that he wrote relatively little about the subject and died before he was able to see the outcome of his planned action research experiments in industrial participation. Yet, as Adelman (1993) points out, Lewin (1951) is probably more popularly known for his contributions to 'field theory' (from which 'force field' analysis is derived) than as the originator of action research. According to Hodgkinson (1957), the beginnings of action research can be found in a 1926 text by Buckingham entitled *Research for Teachers*, and Kemmis *et al.* (1982) cite Corey (1953) to the effect that the origins of the term 'action research' can be traced back at least to the work of Collier in North America between 1933 and 1945 as Commissioner at the Bureau of Indian Affairs.

Nevertheless, in the action research literature Lewin is recognized as the founder of action research, developing the approach very late in his career and using the term from about 1944. Lewin, a Prussian psychologist who emigrated to America in 1933 to escape Nazi persecution, is considered by van Elteren (1992), a historian of social psychology, to be one of the most eminent psychologists of this century. Kemmis *et al.* (1982: 16) observe that Lewin's influence on social psychology has so pervaded the discipline that it is difficult to identify what are his greatest contributions. In Lewin's case it may be that, as Russett (1966: 1) argued in discussing the way ideas gain admission into intellectual circles: 'One key figure may distil the essence of an emerging idea so convincingly that his name becomes inseparable from it, but usually the way has been prepared for him.'

As a young man in Germany Lewin had completed his doctoral research at the University of Berlin, where he also taught, and had studied at the universities of Freiberg and Munich. As a student in Berlin he had held strong left-wing views, which motivated him to make his ideas relevant to the daily life of the working classes, and to find ways of humanizing the factory system (van Elteren 1992: 36–7). However, the political stance of his student days seems not to have withstood his 'Americanization', and his Marxist friends were critical of what in their view was an overidentification with American social and political life.

> They felt that Lewin became 'too good an American', immediately putting his talents at the disposal of the United States government and fully endorsing its policy without any reservations – they themselves thought that there was too little freedom of thought and discussion. From a more distant perspective one is struck by the fact of how soon after his arrival in America, and also how strongly, Lewin committed himself to both the typical American tradition of 'liberalism' and the social movement . . . labelled 'democratic progressive engineering'.
>
> (van Elteren 1992: 52)

Van Elteren disagrees with those writers who see in Lewin's work a continuation from his early days as a socialist and, citing Rose, argues that the development of Lewinian applied psychology was 'frankly manipulationist'. To what extent Lewin's approach to social research was manipulative or democratic thus remains a matter of debate. In the foreword to *Resolving Social Conflicts* (1948) Lewin was described by G. W. Allport, Professor of Psychology at Harvard University, as the 'psychological exponent' of a form of democracy of which John Dewey[1] was described as the 'outstanding philosophical exponent', and moreover that:

> Both agree that democracy must be learned anew in each generation, and that it is a far more difficult form of social structure to attain and maintain than is autocracy. Both see the intimate dependence of democracy upon social science. Without knowledge of, and obedience to, the laws of human nature in group settings, democracy cannot succeed. And without freedom for research and theory as provided in a democratic environment social science will surely fail.
>
> (Allport 1948: xi)

ACTION RESEARCH AS RATIONAL SOCIAL MANAGEMENT

In a seminal paper, 'Action research and minority problems' (1946: 205–6),[2] Lewin described the processes involved in action research, which he also referred to as 'rational social management', that is, a form of research which could marry the experimental approach of social science with social action in response to major social problems of the day (Kemmis *et al*. 1982: 13). Although this paper was criticized for its lack of clear conclusions and as seeming to be 'caught in the maelstrom of "action research" ', this was set against the fact that Lewin had died before his vital work on the action research 'change experiment' had reached a conclusion (Allport 1948: xii–xiii).

For Lewin action research proceeded in a series of steps, initiated by a general idea and a general objective. The first step was to examine the general idea in relation to the means available for reaching the objective, including more fact-finding about it. From this an overall plan was developed about how to reach the objective and a decision was taken about the first action step, which might involve a modification of the original idea. The action step was then evaluated, and on the basis of this, further modification and replanning took place, and a decision was made about the next step.

> The next step is composed of a circle of planning, executing and reconnaissance or fact-finding for the purpose of evaluating the results of the second step, for preparing the rational basis for planning the third step, and for perhaps modifying again the overall plan.
> Rational social management, therefore, proceeds in a spiral of steps each of which is composed of a circle of planning, action, and fact-finding about the result of the action.
>
> (Lewin 1946: 206)

Meyer (1993: 1066), a nurse researcher, has argued that the four-step framework of planning, acting, observing and reflecting, which developed from Lewin's work, forms the basis for more modern definitions of action research.

Evaluation in the form of 'fact-finding about the result of the action' is central to action research and provides the means of establishing whether or not the action has led to an improvement. Lewin argued that: 'If we cannot judge whether an action has led forward or backward, if we have no criteria for evaluating the relation between effort and achievement, there is nothing to prevent us from making the wrong conclusions' (Lewin 1946: 202). Lewin was impatient with community workers who based their actions solely on their own feelings about what had been achieved at a community meeting, without also having regard for objective criteria. He likened their approach to the captain of a ship who, on realizing that the ship has veered too far to the right, turns the steering wheel sharply to the left and happily goes to dinner, leaving the boat to go round in circles (Lewin 1946: 206). For Lewin action research represented the translation of social research into social action and, as van Elteren (1992: 35) has argued, 'In his conception of action research he arrived at the integration of theory and empirical (mainly experimental) research on the one hand and direct application of the findings on the other.'

According to Allport (1948), Lewin pioneered the transfer of the experimental method of the natural sciences to the social sciences, using the 'change experiment' to try to understand some of the most pressing social problems of his day, including the growth of authoritarianism, low morale among the military in the Second World War and anti-semitism. Lewin was not alone in his interest in applied social psychology. As a result of rapid advances during the war in the techniques available to social psychologists it became possible to apply the experimental method to important social problems which had previously been amenable only to descriptive study (Cartwright 1948: 333).

Lewin's main concern was with the nature of group dynamics and with studying group behaviour under controlled conditions (Gill and Johnson 1991: 58), whether this was in the laboratory, the training workshop, the factory or the community. Cartwright (1948: 334), a contemporary of Lewin, argued that by the late 1930s it was becoming clear that social groups could be studied experimentally in the laboratory and observed objectively, and that their behaviour could to some extent be measured. In the Foreword to *Resolving Social Conflicts* (1948), a book which brought together papers written by Lewin at various times between 1935 and 1946, Allport notes that, 'The unifying theme is unmistakable: the group to which an individual belongs is the ground for his perceptions, his feelings, and his actions.' Lewin's early laboratory experiments into group behaviour had shown the importance of the power of the group in promoting changes in attitude and behaviour, and this influenced his later work on action research (Lippitt 1968; Gill and Johnson 1991). As Hodgkinson (1957: 64) observes, 'Science and sociability came together in the work of Kurt Lewin, who began the scientific study of groups, trying to determine when they reached their maximum productivity.'

THE AMERICAN CONTEXT OF THE DEVELOPMENT OF LEWINIAN PSYCHOLOGY

Lewin's background and the American context in which he developed his ideas about leadership and social change help to explain his concern to use social science in a practical way to bring about change in a democratic direction. Cartwright (1948) argues that the pressures created by the Second World War had led to a rapid growth of social psychology on a scale unprecedented in its short history. The rigorous development of experimental techniques and mathematical and technical procedures, combined with the collection of a mass of data, shifted the focus of psychology from pure research to applied research. By the end of 1942 virtually all researchers were orientated towards the application of social psychology to social problems rather than to the theoretical problems of the science.

It was in the early 1940s, towards the end of his career, that Lewin helped to establish the Commission for Community Interrelations, an action research organization, and it was here that he refined the concept of action research as a method of planned social change. Lewin's research had led him to the view that every practical problem required basic conceptual analysis, research and what, as already mentioned, he termed a 'change experiment' (Lippitt 1968: 269). Lewin believed that leaders in government, education, industry and the community were developing an increasing awareness of the need for a scientific understanding of the social problems arising from industrialization and the disruption wrought by the Second World War.

Lewin was a productive research manager who received financial support from, among others, the Rockefeller Foundation (van Elteren 1992). While at the University of Iowa as Professor of Child Psychology, Lewin was invited by the company president to work as a consultant to the Harwood factory in Virginia. It was here that he planned a field experiment into the effect of worker participation on the productivity of work groups. The experiment had been inspired by earlier work by his students on the relationships between autocracy and democracy in the workplace, although the opportunity to conduct the experiment did not arise until after Lewin's death (Adelman 1993: 9). According to Rose (1978: 163) the Harwood experiments illustrate that Lewin's followers were applying the aims of Elton Mayo[3] and the movement known as 'Human Relations in Industry' to an industrial milieu. The views of the Lewinian psychologists converged with the Mayoite credo that effective leaders could use their skills of communication to increase worker participation in industry, thus raising the levels of morale, job satisfaction and output, as well as improving relations within the workgroup.

At the Harwood factory changes in methods and jobs that were a characteristic of the ruthlessly competitive conditions of American industry were expressed in grievances about piece rates, high turnover, low productivity, restriction of output and aggression towards management. Earlier attempts by management to improve the situation had failed. Management wanted to know why it was that change was resisted so strongly by the (mainly female) workforce and what could be done to overcome this resistance (Coch and French 1948: 512). In the words of Coch (the personnel manager) and French, a 'real life action experiment' was devised and conducted in the context of the factory situation. The problem was that workers resented being transferred from one job to another. Transfer was frequently followed by aggressive behaviour towards the supervisor, a drop in output, absenteeism and increased labour turnover. A theory of frustration was developed, based on Lewin's (1951) field theory and his equilibrium theory of change, which hypothesized that frustration arose from a conflict between two opposing forces, the driving force corresponding to the goal of reaching the standard rate for the job, and the resisting force corresponding to the difficulty of the job (Coch and French 1948: 517). The more difficult the job and the faster the work, the greater was the degree of frustration. For the experiment the required changes in jobs were addressed in three ways. In one the first group did not participate in the changes, in another the group participated through appointed representatives, and in the third the group as a whole participated fully in all aspects of the changes and took an active part in discussions with management. The experiment demonstrated that, following transfer from one job to another, the non-participating group underwent a drop in morale and productivity, and a rise in turnover and aggression, while in the two participating groups this was not the case. The fully participating group worked well with supervisors and quickly regained the pre-change level of output, which continued to climb strongly.

The action experiment appeared to demonstrate that there was a relationship between the degree of democratic participation in the workplace and the level of job satisfaction, output and morale. This drove home Lewin's point that democratic participation was far preferable to the type of autocratic coercion associated with scientific management. However, to quote Adelman:

> Lewin's ideas on democratic participation in the workplace did not include any critique of the wider society, particularly the range of economic relations between worker and employer, capital and labour. Indeed a fair observation would be that although Lewin and his co-workers demonstrated the efficacy of action research for improving productivity, they did not develop conceptual structures that took explicit account of the power bases that define social roles and strongly influence the process of change in the modes of production.
>
> (Adelman 1993: 10)

Adelman's criticism alerts us to the fact that the Lewinian vision of democratic participation in industry took no account of the key issue of power relations between managers and workers and assumed that management goals were rational and unquestionable. Adelman quotes Landsberger (1958) to the effect that the followers of Lewin and the group dynamics approach, such as Coch and French, were blatant in accepting management's goal of efficiency and the desirability of manipulating workers to realize this. In the case of the Harwood factory, as Rose (1978: 164) points out, although the findings seem plausible enough, shortly after the experiment had been completed there was a strike over a unionization dispute with management and the 'changed' groups were as pro-union as the others.

A reading of Lewin's writings suggests that he was conscious of the fact that action research was manipulative while also recognizing

its power as a force for change. His own experience of the growth
of fascism in Germany led him to the belief not only that American
democracy was the ideal but that if the horrors of the Second
World War were not to be repeated, effective means of engineering
social change were needed as a matter of urgency, given the social
unrest and growth of racism in post-war America. Lewin viewed
the dropping of the atom bomb on Hiroshima and Nagasaki as the
social consequence of the natural sciences having set free humanity's
destructive capacities. This reinforced his belief that social facts
were no less real than physical facts and could be studied objectively
in the same way and by similar experimental means:

> The bomb has driven home with dramatic intensity the degree
> to which social happenings are both the result of, and the
> conditions for the occurrence of, physical events. Gradually,
> the period is coming to an end when the natural scientist
> thinks of the social scientist as someone interested in dreams
> and words, rather than as an investigator of facts, which are
> not less real than physical facts, and which can be studied no
> less objectively.
>
> (Lewin 1947: 7)

MODERN DAY ACTION RESEARCH

Carr and Kemmis, two current exponents of action research, identify
three main areas in which contemporary action researchers would
take exception to Lewin's approach:

> First, they would regard group decision-making as important
> as a matter of principle, rather than as a matter of technique;
> that is, not merely as an effective means of facilitating and
> maintaining social change, but also as essential for authentic
> commitment to social action. Second, contemporary exponents
> of action research would object to the notion that participants
> should, or could, be 'led' to more democratic forms of life
> through action research. Action research should not be seen
> as a recipe or technique for bringing about democracy, but
> rather as an embodiment of democratic principles in research,
> allowing participants to influence, if not determine, the con-

ditions of their own lives and work, and collaboratively to develop critiques of social conditions which sustain dependence, inequality or exploitation. Third, contemporary action researchers would object to the language in which Lewin describes the theoretical aims and methods of social science ('developing deeper insights into the laws that govern social life through mathematical and conceptual analysis and laboratory and field experiments'). This language would now be described as positivistic and incompatible with the aims and methods of any adequate social or educational science.

(Carr and Kemmis 1986: 164)

Modern day action researchers do not seek to find universal laws of human behaviour through which behaviour can be measured and social change engineered. Neither would they subscribe to the view of action research as a form of re-education for social engineering. It is not for the social scientist to set the agenda in advance. The emphasis is much more upon awareness-raising and empowerment and upon finding ways for researchers and practitioners to work collaboratively and for practitioners to become action researchers in their own rights.

THE SCIENCE OF ACTION RESEARCH

The roots of the revival of interest in action research lie in criticisms of positivist[4] approaches to social science which draw on the natural sciences, and with the impracticality of much organizational theory for problem-solving. In a seminal paper Susman and Evered (1978) put forward a case for the appropriateness of action research to organizational problem-solving and for its status as a science. They argue that as research methods and techniques are becoming more sophisticated, research is becoming relatively less useful for the purposes of organizational problem-solving. So marked is the gap between theory and utility that they refer to the situation as a 'crisis' (Susman and Evered 1978: 582). This crisis is rooted in the inappropriateness of positivist science for the study of human organizations, for which action research is ideally placed to provide a much needed corrective. Furthermore, they argue that action research may be validated as a science. Rather than action research being judged by a set of criteria drawn from positivist science, more appropriate criteria should be used from a different philosophical tradition. Furthermore, they argue that positivist science's approach is ahistorical and ignores the role of the observer in the production of knowledge, yet is itself a product of the human mind.

As a corrective to the limitations of positivism, Susman and Evered (1978: 589–90) argue that the cyclic process of action research has characteristics which make it appropriate to the needs of organizations. It deals with practical concerns of people about the future and their ideals, goals and intentions, and as such is closely linked to the planning process. Actions are jointly planned by researcher and client, and the values which the researcher brings are taken into account rather than being denied. Action research provides a means to enhance the system of problem-solving and communication, thus enabling the organization to adapt to its environment better; it serves both to alleviate the problem and to generate new knowledge about the system. It is the role of the action researcher to act as a catalyst to help members define a problem or think differently about an existing one, and interventions may be made by the researcher which offer the organization a new way to think about an old problem.

Susman and Evered have been influential in the trend to define action research as a non-positivist form of social research, suited to the problem-solving needs of complex organizations and appropriate where quantitative methods are not (Gummesson 1991; Eden and Huxham 1993). Susman and Evered argue that the differences between positivist science and action research are extensive, although whether or not one approach is better than the other depends upon what the researcher wants to study and under what conditions. They suggest that the researcher ought to be sceptical about the usefulness of positivist science when research is for the purposes of problem-solving or when it concerns individuals whose relationships with others are influenced by the way they define the situation.

In the following sections we move on to trace the development of action research from its use in American industry in the 1940s through to its more recent use in health and social welfare.

ORGANIZATIONAL ACTION RESEARCH

Action research was applied to problems in American industry from the early 1940s. Industrial conflict, morale, absenteeism and the relationship of the work group's behaviour to productivity (that is, the classic problem of output restriction) were all matters of interest for action research (Lewin, G. W. 1948). In the 1950s and 1960s in the USA issues of conflict and power relations, which Lewin had been studying in the early 1940s, became of central concern, echoing the growing interest among industrial psychologists in the issues of power and conflict (Kahn and Boulding 1964).

In Britain in the late 1940s the Tavistock Institute of Human Relations developed a research approach to organizational consultancy which, although the term 'action research' was not specifically used to describe it until the 1960s, is acknowledged as pioneering (Gill and Johnson 1991: 59; Rapoport 1970). Payne *et al.* (1981) note that the techniques employed by the Tavistock Institute are now taken to be action research. They further point out that the approach was based on the traditional client–consultant model, which was problem-specific in both perspectives and conclusions. The Tavistock Institute was founded in 1947 with the aim of making available to industry the psychological expertise acquired during the war on personnel and other problems, and had close links with Lewinian psychologists in America (Rose 1978).

Holter and Schwartz-Barcott (1993: 299) point out that unlike Lewin, whose theoretical foundation was based in social and experimental psychology, the Tavistock researchers were rooted in psychoanalysis and social psychology. Gill and Johnson (1991) note that the psychoanalytic approach, in which the client is confronted with the researcher's perception of what is actually happening, is still a feature of much work in the area of organizational change. As in North America, so in Britain the Second World War was a major impetus and source of data for action research (Kemmis *et al.* 1982; Gill and Johnson 1991). At that time industrial research involved a multi-disciplinary approach, with anthropologists, psychologists, physiologists and psychoanalytically-orientated psychiatrists working together on a number of problems. During and just after the war, action research was used in personnel selection and recruitment and in the treatment of returning prisoners of war. The Tavistock Institute's work included a problem-centred approach, a commitment to establishing relationships with clients over time, a focus on client needs and an emphasis upon research as a social process. Tavistock researchers also involved themselves in the implementation and monitoring of change (Gill and Johnson 1991: 59). The consultancy style of the Tavistock Institute was designed to enable an organization to work through conflict by a therapeutic process underpinned by action research. In Jacques's (1951) *The Changing Culture of a Factory*, psychoanalytic theory was combined with Lewin's field theory to try to understand large-scale problems of British industry through a case study of one factory. This combination of approaches was 'a fusion that became deeply embedded in the Tavistock tradition' (Menzies Lyth 1989: 72). A few years later, in a classic paper, Menzies (1960) applied the psychoanalytic approach of the Tavistock to the study of nursing and refined the concept of social systems as a defence against anxiety in analysing the nature of nurses' task-centred work routines. According to Holter and Schwartz-Barcott (1993: 299), 'Lewin and the Tavistock Institute have been the two major forces behind the development of action research throughout the world.'

Researchers from the London School of Economics (LSE) developed a rather different approach from that of the Tavistock consultants (Town 1978; Payne *et al.* 1981). Unlike the Tavistock researchers, those from the LSE were independently funded and this may have given them more room for manoeuvre in deciding upon the extent and nature of their involvement with an organization, including taking on an advocacy role in feeding back findings. As Town's analysis suggests, this may also have allowed them to try to serve the interests of a number of parties – such as a public bureaucracy and its clients – rather than those of one client as in the Tavistock approach.

More recent research in North America is illustrated by an action research programme which used a range of methods and was successful in increasing employee involvement in solving a widespread problem concerning repetitive strain injury, which was badly affecting productivity (Pasmore and Friedlander 1982). The study took place in a large electronics corporation typical of its kind, with 335 employees of whom the majority were women.

About a third of all employees suffered tenosynovitis with varying degrees of intensity. Over a five-year period the situation continued to worsen, despite the involvement of outside technical and medical experts, to the extent that average annual injuries had increased from approximately two to eighty. The problem demanded an urgent solution and the plant manager called in behavioural scientists who decided upon an action research approach. The basis for the researchers' choice was that action research would encourage employees and managers jointly to inquire into the problem, providing them with experience of a new way of working together, and this in turn would increase the researchers' knowledge of the nature of relationships between the two groups (Pasmore and Friedlander 1982). The researchers believed that the problem identified was representative of a broader range of labour–management issues (in particular the separation between managers and workers), which seemed not to be amenable to traditional research, where employees are seen as passive subjects of the research.

At the core of the study was a representative group of five employees with, in addition, two foremen, the researchers and the manager of employee relations. No one in the group anticipated that, as they became more assertive, top managers in the organization would feel increasingly threatened, and early data pointing to the style of management as a factor in the injury problem were vigorously attacked by senior staff. Although relations were never completely repaired, the researchers reported that managers did eventually listen and take steps to alleviate the problem. From the response of senior managers Pasmore and Friedlander (1982: 350) learned that 'researchers engaged in such action research must prepare management for the shock of dealing with the information gathered by a powerful group of employees, if constructive discussions between the two groups are to occur.'

A more radical form of organizational research which draws on the later work at the Tavistock is what Whyte has termed 'participatory action research', which was used successfully in the Xerox Corporation in New York and with the Mondragon cooperative in the Basque region of Spain. As Whyte defines it:

> In participatory action research (PAR), some of the people in the organization or community under study participate actively

with the professional researcher throughout the research process from the initial design to the final presentation of results and discussion of their action implications. PAR thus contrasts sharply with the conventional model of pure research, in which members of organizations and communities are treated as passive subjects, with some of them participating only to the extent of authorizing the project, being its subjects, and receiving the results. PAR is *applied* research, but it also contrasts sharply with the most common type of applied research, in which the researchers serve as professional experts, designing the project, gathering the data, interpreting the findings, and recommending action to the client organization. Like the conventional model of pure research, this is an elitist model of research relationships. In PAR, some of the members of the organization we study are actively engaged in the quest for information and ideas to guide their future actions.

(Whyte 1991: 20)

Although, as in conventional management consultancy, participatory action research focuses on the client's problems, Whyte is in no doubt that it involves a scientific endeavour which has to meet daunting standards of scientific rigour. In Whyte's view, the strengths of the approach are that it contributes both to problem-solving and to theory building. Participatory action research draws on earlier work at the Tavistock Institute and on worker democracy in Norway, and as such is not a new invention (Whyte 1991: 21). In the emphasis it places on the researchers working collaboratively with participants it has more in common with Lewin's early notions of action research than later developments in 'practitioner action research', where roles of researcher and practitioner merge, and the tendency is to individualize the change process.

ACTION RESEARCH AND THE COMMUNITY DEVELOPMENT PROJECTS

The Community Development Projects (CDPs) emerged in the 1960s in the context of the 'rediscovery' of poverty. They were influenced by a range of other developments, which included the American Anti-Poverty Programme and in Britain the Educational Priority

Areas (EPA) initiative led by Halsey from Oxford University (Halsey 1972; Town 1978). Mayo (1975) argues that the CDPs need to be seen as one part of the British poverty programme, designed to ameliorate the worst effects of urban deprivation and the so-called 'cycle of deprivation' through which social problems associated with poverty – failure of marriages, unemployment, poor health – were, it was argued, transmitted from generation to generation. Poverty and deprivation were seen by the government as the problems of marginal groups, who either through their own individual or collective inadequacy or because of the ineffectiveness of the welfare services had 'fallen through the net' of the welfare state. This so-called 'individual pathology' approach, whereby poverty was seen as a disease, was criticized and challenged by the CDPs.

Town (1978) argues that action research suited the goal of applying social science knowledge and research techniques to the solution of social problems. The CDPs were set up in 1969 by the Home Office as an attempt at a social experiment in which resources would be concentrated on areas of greatest need. Project teams were to investigate the causes of social problems in twelve places across the country, experiment with new ways of tackling them and monitor the results. These findings were to be reported back to the government and the local authority sponsors, who would decide together on their implications for policy. The central objective of this and the Educational Priority Areas Project, mentioned above, appears to have been the 'generation of new forms of practice which might become accepted social policy' (Town 1978: 161–2). As one of a series of government initiatives designed to tackle poverty, the CDPs were unique in that community work was built in from the start (Green and Chapman 1991: 56). Using an action research framework, this was an attempt to use research for the benefit of action, with teams of researchers providing information in the form of social surveys on which the action teams could base their work. According to Green and Chapman the action research model on which the projects drew came not from government but from established academic traditions within social policy. This view is reinforced by Payne *et al.* (1981: 163), who have defined action research as a special case of policy research.

By 1972 a range of pressures and difficulties had created the conditions for greater local autonomy of CDP teams as government bureaucrats at the centre made a tactical withdrawal. This left local teams vulnerable to failure since they had little central support and had to 'go it alone', but it also freed up such teams to identify and work around major issues in their communities, such as redevelopment, planning and the clearing of demolition sites. Mayo (1975) concludes that the tactics adopted by the local teams showed the failure of the original reformist approach to poverty and that, as a consequence, the CDPs took on the characteristics of traditional pressure groups. The approach to poverty that emerged from the project teams was critical of the 'victim blaming' which, it was argued, underlay the Home Office view, and focused instead on poverty as a consequence of fundamental inequalities in the present political and economic system (Green and Chapman 1991).

The CDPs and action research were integrally related from the start and the anti-poverty initiative was based on an interdependence between research teams of academics and action teams of community workers. The history of the CDPs spans the late 1960s to the late 1970s, during which time their work created the conditions for poverty to be viewed not as a failure of the individual but rather as arising from the inequalities inherent in a social and economic structure based on differences in class and power. In these years the basis was laid for later community development work on health issues and in health promotion. In particular, the influence of community development as both an approach to working with groups at grass roots level and a value-based practice can be seen in the work of the Health Education Council. In common with the CDPs, the community development approach to health problems questioned the usefulness and validity of the medical model and in particular of the 'individual pathology' approach, which sees ill health as the fault of the individual. This view threatened those in authority and contributed to the disbanding of the Health Education Council and the establishment of the Health Education Authority (HEA), with its more medically oriented approach. Community development workers are still active in the HEA and at management level but, from what their accounts suggest, there are limits to the extent to which community development is to be allowed an influence within the system (Smithies 1991). Beattie (1991) has reviewed current approaches to the evaluation of community development initiatives in health promotion, and notes at least forty reports since the late 1970s, with no systematic study of the evaluation methods or strategies used.

A number of related matters of relevance to action research as a problem-focused approach to change are raised by a consideration of the CDPs. A major issue is to what extent it is possible through local initiatives to promote the kind of fundamental socio-economic change at national level that might be necessary to overcome such problems. Related to this is the point raised by Payne *et al.* (1981) about what level of intervention may be appropriate given the analysis of the nature and extent of a problem, and to what degree it might be counterproductive to locate the change initiatives at the local level rather than centrally. These themes are not exclusive to the CDPs but arise in a similar way in organizational action research, where marginalized or low status groups within an organization may face problems that require a restructuring of power relations, which may so challenge the status quo that initiatives are blocked and/or incorporated by the institution.

ACTION RESEARCH IN EDUCATION

According to Kemmis *et al.* (1982: 17) action research was absorbed into education from the earliest beginnings of the development of Lewin's ideas, with the latter working alongside teachers in action research programmes. In 1946 the Horace Mann-Lincoln Institute, Teachers' College, Columbia University, was using action research for social reconstruction and collaborative research with teachers and schools. During the late 1940s and early 1950s (after Lewin's death) action research became associated with Stephen Corey, who became one of its strongest advocates in American education. Corey's book *Action Research to Improve School Practice* (1953) was the first systematic attempt to define action research in education (McNiff 1988: 19). But the popularity of action research and the way it became a rallying cry for pioneering teacher training colleges was met with a backlash of criticism and a decline in interest in action research in the mid-1950s. Among other things action research was criticized for being 'all things to all men' and for a lack of rigour in defining what it was (Kemmis *et al.* 1982: 17).

In Britain and the USA in the late 1950s and early 1960s the political climate favoured large-scale, centrally funded research rather than small-scale (action research) projects but dissatisfaction with top-down approaches to research and shrinkage of funds reawakened an interest in action research (McNiff 1988). Kemmis *et al.* (1982) argue that action research in education has been 'rediscovered' in the context of the development of widespread interest in curriculum research and development in Britain, the USA and Australia.

In the USA the publication in 1969 of an influential paper by Schwab, 'The practical: a language for curriculum', and in Britain the publication in 1975 of Stenhouse's *Introduction to Curriculum Research and Development*, are generally recognized as major turning points, each challenging the orthodox research approach. Carr and Kemmis (1986: 18) argue that Schwab and Stenhouse were both 'spokesmen for the practical: both recognised the need for teachers to be central to the curriculum exercise as doers, making judgements based on their knowledge and experience and the demands of practical situations.' These two texts heralded the arrival of the 'teacher-as-researcher movement'. These and Stenhouse's personal influence brought about a redefinition of the role and function of research in education. New forms of evaluation also emerged, which were concerned more with process than outcome as measured in terms of performance. These related developments provided a supportive framework for more qualitative and reflective practices to develop. Collaborative research between academic researchers and practitioners was of particular concern to Stenhouse, as was the growth of critical communities of teacher researchers. Critical reflection, grounded in everyday practice, and a problem-focused approach laid the basis for a rediscovery of action research.

Carr (1989: 85) argues that Elliott's article 'What is action research in schools?' (1978) 'marked the arrival of a British research paradigm which had been developed in the USA as a radical alternative to orthodox approaches to social and educational research'. Carr contends that the dominance of positivist theory supported an institutionalized division between teachers and an academic elite of educational researchers. Dissatisfaction on the part of teachers with the 'expert' role of outside academic researchers has prompted the development of educational action research in which the teacher and researcher become one and the same, and where action research becomes a vehicle for professionalization (Winter 1989; Elliott 1991; McKernan 1991). As Kemmis *et al.* (1982: 6) argue:

> The major aim of action research is the establishment of conditions under which self-reflection is genuinely possible: conditions under which aims and claims can be tested, under which practice can be regarded strategically and 'experimentally', and under which practitioners can organise as a critical community committed to the improvement of their work and their understanding of it.

As in nursing, action research in education is seen as a means of closing the so-called 'theory–practice gap'. For influential educationalists such as Kemmis it represents a counter to the positivism of earlier educational research, and a challenge to the idea of the researcher as a neutral observer. Its power for change lies in the use of action research to develop a critically reflexive practice, in which theory and practice are integrated, and in which theory emerges from practice. Elliott (1991) views action research as a form of reflexive practice and argues that it can become a 'cultural innovation'. By this Elliott means that the deskilling of teachers, which he likens to the shift from artisan to machine minder during the process of industrialization, has created the conditions in which the culture of the traditionalists can be transformed. However, to be effective action research has to be part of a collective movement rather than an individual endeavour. In a recent article Adelman (1993) argues that action research, or 'participatory research' as he prefers to refer to it, could provide a way of bringing together two different trends, that of individual reflexion (following Schön 1983), and that of organizational and group development in the tradition of Lewin. In essence Adelman argues that if improvements are to be made in educational practice, the strands of democratic practice, organizational change, group process and reflexive practice need to be brought together in a methodological framework of participatory research.[5]

ACTION RESEARCH IN NURSING

Although the use of action research in nursing has lagged behind its use in education, their lines of development seem to have converged in the past decade. Meyer (1993: 1066) argues that 'the development of action research in education is of particular interest to nurses owing to the parallels that can be drawn with nursing research.' By 1984 action research was well established in education but, according to Lathlean and Farnish (1984: 34), had as yet played little part in nursing or nursing research, apart from action research in hospitals which affected the organization of nursing services (Revans 1964; Cope 1981). Nevertheless, Lewin's classic change theory (1958) informed influential work by Wright (1985) when implementing change strategies in one district general hospital. Smith (1986), who undertook an action research project in a hospital for the elderly, points out that over twenty years ago Hockey (1974) advocated the need for more attention to action research in nursing. Sparrow and Robinson (1994) speculate that nurse re-searchers may have initially been reluctant to use an action research approach because of their concern to establish nursing as an academic discipline in a context dominated by the medical profession, which values the positivist paradigm and is preoccupied with the generation of quantitative data from experimental designs.

Webb (1989: 404) summarizes the variety of ways in which action research has been used in nursing and refers to Towell and Harries's (1979) adoption of action research to facilitate change in a psychiatric hospital, which involved them giving advice and emotional support to participants. They saw action research as a way of enabling staff to reclaim the authority to clarify their own roles, and establishing conditions under which they could organize their work most effectively. Lathlean and Farnish (1984) used an action research approach to evaluate a developmental project for ward sisters, and Webb also cites Hunt (1987), who used action research to promote change and innovation in nursing practice but met with resistance from ward staff. Webb (1989) points out that nurses are increasingly seeing action research as an approach which has much to offer them in analysing and solving problems, devising action plans to improve standards of care and evaluating such plans. Moreover, she observes that by engaging with action research in this way, nurses are also learning more about research. Owen (1993) used an action research approach to explore the role of tutors in clinical areas and worked with trained nurses on a psychiatric ward. Although she encountered resistance there was also evidence that some ideas were being put into practice and that during the project many staff had become self-directed in their learning.

An action research framework was also used to introduce changes related to a 'new ideology of nursing' at Burford, a small community hospital in Oxfordshire (Pearson 1992). The Institute of Nursing in Oxford has been undertaking a four-year action research study of the development of patient-centred nursing at the John Radcliffe Hospital, Oxford, which aims to unravel the complex processes involved in change, to identify strategies that are likely to be effective and to make the findings available in an accessible form for nurse professionals throughout the UK (Titchen and Binnie 1993: 858).

The main attractions of action research for nurse researchers seem to be that it offers the possibility of working with people in a way which is non-hierarchical and non-exploitative, that it may be used to make changes, and that it closes the theory–practice gap (Webb 1990). Greenwood (1994: 13) welcomes the growing interest in action research in nursing and nurse education as it 'reflects a recognition . . . that nursing is a social practice the central purpose of which is to bring about positive change in the health status of individuals and communities'. Nevertheless, a note of caution is sounded about the possible implications of the use of emancipatory change strategies by nurses whose autonomy to act may be limited. Sparrow and Robinson (1994) conclude both from their experience as action researchers and from a review of the literature that action research may be appropriate for small-scale projects on wards or small units, but that its use with larger populations becomes problematic. As their experience was that the two participating wards were closed down while their project was in progress, they suggest that the rapidly changing NHS may be too unstable an environment either to enable an action researcher to complete a project, or to allow for the continuity and commitment of staff over time. They empathize with Meyer (1993) who, during her year of fieldwork, saw eighty-nine members of staff leave and eighty-five new members arrive.

Nevertheless, among nurse researchers and educationalists there is a growing interest in collaborative or 'new paradigm' research (Reason and Rowan 1981; Reason 1988) which echoes trends in education a decade earlier. The term 'new paradigm' research refers to a form of cooperative enquiry which:

> is a way of doing research in which all those involved contribute both to the creative thinking that goes into the enterprise – deciding on what is to be looked at, the methods of the inquiry, and making sense of what is found out – and *also* contribute to the action which is the subject of the research. Thus in its fullest form the distinction between researcher and subject disappears, and all who participate are both co-researchers and co-subjects. Co-operative enquiry is therefore also a form of education, personal development, and social action.
>
> (Reason 1988: 1)

In common with critical theory and feminist research, new paradigm research has emerged as a result of criticisms of positivist social science. New paradigm research does not treat those who are the focus of the research as passive subjects but seeks to empower them to act on their own behalf as active participants in change. As Meyer (1993) argues, new paradigm research is also popular because of disenchantment with qualitative approaches such as ethnography and participant observation which, despite claims to 'tell it like it is', do little to address the unequal power relationship between researcher and research subject. However, within the new paradigm the collaborative approach has also been criticized by Meyer as a far more subtle form of exploitation of research subjects by researcher, and one which may use friendship to mask the true nature of the relationship and oblige those being researched to participate.

CONCLUSION

In the preceding pages we have traced some important threads in the development of action research, highlighting themes and issues such as the shift from action research as a form of rational social management to that of an anti-positivist approach to social change.

Continuity and change can be seen in the way that Lewin's ideas of action research as a form of collaboration between social scientists and practitioners sowed the seeds of modern day empowering approaches. In Lewin's insistence that academic research was not the fount of all knowledge, and in his concern to use social psychology as a way of combating racial intolerance, we can see the emergence of action research as 'an expression of an essentially democratic spirit in social research' (Kemmis *et al.* 1982: 14). Drawing on the social and natural sciences, and being applied to a range of different problem situations, action research has a hybrid genealogy, and this is expressed in the variety of approaches which it has generated.

NOTES

1 For an evaluation of the contributions of Lewin and Dewey to the development of 'action science' see an influential text by Argyris *et al.* (1985). For a more recent discussion see Adelman (1993).
2 First published in 1946 in the *Journal of Social Issues*, vol. 2, pp. 34–46 and in 1948, after Lewin's death, with twelve other papers in *Resolving Social Conflicts: Selected Papers on Group Dynamics by Kurt Lewin* (Lewin, G. W. 1948).
3 See especially Mayo (1960) and, for a critical view of the ideas of Mayo and Lewin, Landsberger (1958).
4 Positivism is a nineteenth-century doctrine which holds that social science can be scientific in a similar way to physics or any other of the natural sciences, and can produce general laws about human behaviour with predictive power on a par with laws which govern the movement of the planets or heat through iron. Positivism assumes that phenomena exist independently of the observer, can be comprehended through the senses and as such can be measured and quantified (see Russett 1966; Abercombie *et al.* 1984: 163–4; von Wright 1993).
5 See McNiff (1988) for a summary of the lines of development of action research as an educational tradition and of the differences between its main exponents in Britain.

3

Action research in process

INTRODUCTION

In Chapter 2 we outlined the history of action research from the time of Kurt Lewin through to the Community Development Projects and initiatives in education and nursing. Although the histories were not intended to be exhaustive, it has been possible to show that action research has a research pedigree dating back at least half a century. Its origins lie in social psychology, the natural sciences, organizational science and social planning. It is a hybrid which has generated differing action research approaches. As Holter and Schwartz-Barcott (1993: 299) rightly point out:

> The variety of approaches, definitions and uses that have emerged since Lewin's original work have created much debate within the social and behavioural sciences (Whyte 1991). Kalleberg (1990) has called the resulting confusion 'terminological anarchism'.

They argue that this confusion has been carried over into the nursing literature without any attempt to identify the core characteristics of action research, or debate the multitude of definitions. We agree, and recognize the need to clarify what is meant by 'action research', including taking account of different approaches within it. It seems to us that there are practical benefits in identifying criteria by which action research might be distinguished from other methodologies and used as a part of an action research vocabulary. We are not alone in this. Holter and Schwartz-Barcott (1993: 299) identify four core characteristics of action research: collaboration between researcher(s) and practitioner(s), solution of practical problems; change in practice; and development of theory. Lathlean (1994) restricts herself to three distinctive features: action research always involves an intervention and is context specific, and generalization of findings is theoretical rather than statistical (as in experiments and surveys). Eden and Huxham (1993: 5), in the context of management consultancy, identify six criteria, including that 'action research demands a concern with theory as well as a practical orientation.'

With the aim of clarifying what is meant by 'action research' we present an action research typology (Table 3.1), which builds on the four broad traditions outlined above (Lewin's experimental approach, organizational change, community development, education/nursing) and we distinguish, as a framework for the typology, seven criteria. The criteria have been generated from our reading of the action research literature, and from our experiences as action researchers. The aim is to make sense of what otherwise might appear as diverse and disconnected ways of applying action research to a range of different problems and settings. After presenting the typology we discuss issues raised by the distinguishing criteria, underlining the need for a way of classifying action research which is able to penetrate the appearance of 'anarchism' and reveal underlying consistencies and patterns.

We have selected seven criteria to distinguish different types of action research, and would argue that these seven, in dynamic interaction, distinguish action research from other methodologies. Each of the seven criteria is listed in summary form in the left hand column of Table 3.1. Action research:

1 is educative;
2 deals with individuals as members of social groups;
3 is problem-focused, context-specific and future-orientated;
4 involves a change intervention;

5 aims at improvement and involvement;
6 involves a cyclic process in which research, action and evaluation are interlinked;
7 is founded on a research relationship in which those involved are participants in the change process.

The typology illustrates that within the broad parameters of action research four types may be distinguished, which we term 'experimental', 'organizational', 'professionalizing' and 'empowering'. As we move across the typology, from the 'experimental type' at the far left to the 'empowering type' at the far right, each criterion varies according to the particular type in which it is located. Take, for instance, the criterion of the educative base of action research: in the experimental type 're-education' tends to be defined in behaviourist terms as bringing about a measurable change in what the individual can do and/or a measurable change in individual perception. In the organizational type the social-psychological approach to behaviour and perception is still evident in the emphasis on education and training as a means of bringing about a change in behaviour, and this may encompass a strong social-psychological dimension in which re-education is aimed at overcoming resistance in situations where individuals or workgroups feel threatened. In the professionalizing type the concept of education takes the form of reflective practice in which the practitioner develops by grounding knowledge and action in the everyday experience of professional practice. In the empowering type education has shifted radically from the strongly behaviourist concept of re-education in the experimental type, and takes the form of consciousness-raising (Robottom and Colquhoun 1993; Mies 1993) or 'conscientization' (Freire 1972a), in which education is rooted in the everyday experience of vulnerable groups, rather than being validated by abstract theoretical knowledge. Table 3.1 indicates in what ways each of the other criteria vary within different action research types.

ACTION RESEARCH TYPOLOGY

A typology has been designed to illustrate that action research is able to retain a distinct identity while spanning the spectrum of research approaches from experimental to social constructionist.

The apparently contradictory ways in which it is defined by different writers obscures an underlying pattern and gives the impression of action research as being amorphous. For instance, management theorists Gill and Johnson (1991: 57) define it as a valuable variant of the 'quasi-experiment'. Similarly, Sapsford and Abbott (1992: 101–3), writing for the caring professions, describe it as an experiment of the simplest kind and as a 'change experiment' for the purposes of measurement. In contrast Cohen and Manion (1984: 47), writing on the use of action research in educational settings, see it as the very antithesis of experimental research, and both Susman and Evered (1978) and Eden and Huxham (1993) argue that action research is fundamentally qualitative, and appropriate in organizational settings where the experiment is not.

The need for a typology such as the one presented in this chapter arises from the lack of precision in the use of terms, which is an enduring feature of social research and is not a problem exclusive to action research. The tendency to apply the label to almost any research which involves elements of collaboration or feedback serves to reinforce the criticism that the label is meaningless and that action research is not 'real research'. Writing in the late 1970s when action research was enjoying a revival in Britain, Town (1978) argued that action programmes which employed a researcher used the label to enhance scientific and academic credibility, while research programmes used it to give their activities an appearance of practical relevance. Lathlean (1994) has commented that when she first undertook action research in nursing in the early 1980s, she shared the commonly held view that the label was applied to research which involved any combination of research and action. Eden and Huxham (1993: 1) have argued that one 'way of excusing sloppy research is by labelling it "action research".'

So Table 3.1 distinguishes four types of action research, roughly corresponding to the four broad approaches outlined in Chapter 1. The experimental type is most closely associated with the early days of action research and the scientific approach to social problems, which characterized Lewin's change experiments and his concern to discover general laws of social life to inform policy-making. The organizational type represents the application of action research to organizational problem-solving, including such problems as restriction of output and absenteeism, and has at its core a concern

Table 3.1   Action research typology

Action research type	Consensus model of society → Rational social management		Conflict model of society → Structural change	
Distinguishing criteria	Experimental	Organizational	Professionalizing	Empowering
1 Educative base	Re-education	Re-education/training	Reflective practice	Consciousness-raising
	Enhancing social science/administrative control and social change towards consensus	Enhancing managerial control and organizational change towards consensus	Enhancing professional control and individual's ability to control work situation	Enhancing user-control and shifting balance of power; structural change towards pluralism
	Inferring relationship between behaviour and output; identifying causal factors in group dynamics	Overcoming resistance to change/restructuring balance of power between managers and workers	Empowering professional groups; advocacy on behalf of patients/clients	Empowering oppressed groups
	Social scientific bias/researcher focused	Managerial bias/client focused	Practitioner focused	User/practitioner focused

2 Individuals in groups	Closed group, controlled, selection made by researcher for purposes of measurement/ inferring relationship between cause and effect	Work groups and/or mixed groups of managers and workers	Professional(s) and/or (interdisciplinary) professional group/negotiated team boundaries	Fluid groupings, self selecting or natural boundary or open/closed by negotiation
	Fixed membership	Selected membership	Shifting membership	Fluid membership
3 Problem focus	Problem emerges from the interaction of social science theory and social problems	Problem defined by most powerful group; some negotiation with workers	Problem defined by professional group; some negotiation with users	Emerging and negotiated definition of problem by less powerful group(s)
	Problem relevant for social science/ management interests	Problem relevant for management/social science interests	Problem emerges from professional practice/experience	Problem emerges from members' practice/experience
	Success defined in terms of social science	Success defined by sponsors	Contested, professionally determined definitions of success	Competing definitions of success accepted and expected

Table 3.1 Continued

	Consensus model of society → Rational social management			Conflict model of society → Structural change
Action research type Distinguishing criteria	Experimental	Organizational	Professionalizing	Empowering
4 Change intervention	Social science, experimental intervention to test theory and/or generate theory	Top-down, directed change towards predetermined aims	Professionally led, predefined, process-led	Bottom-up, undetermined, process-led
	Problem to be solved in terms of research aims	Problem to be solved in terms of management aims	Problem to be resolved in the interests of research-based practice and professionalization	Problem to be explored as part of process of change, developing an understanding of meanings of issues in terms of problem and solution
5 Improvement and involvement	Towards controlled outcome and consensual definition of improvement	Towards tangible outcome and consensual definition of improvement	Towards improvement in practice defined by professionals and on behalf of users	Towards negotiated outcomes and pluralist definitions of improvement: account taken of vested interests

	Research components dominant	Action and research components in tension; action dominated	Research and action components in tension; research dominated	Action components dominant
6 Cyclic processes	Identifies causal processes that can be generalized	Identifies causal processes that are specific to problem context and/or can be generalized	Identifies causal processes that are specific to problem and/or can be generalized	Change course of events; recognition of multiple influences upon change
	Time limited, task focused	Discrete cycle, rationalist, sequential	Spiral of cycles, opportunistic, dynamic	Open-ended, process driven
7 Research relationship, degree of collaboration	Experimenter/ respondents	Consultant/researcher, respondent/ participants	Practitioner or researcher/ collaborators	Practitioner researcher/ co-researchers/ co-change agents
	Outside researcher as expert/research funding	Client pays an outside consultant – 'they who pay the piper call the tune'	Outside resources and/or internally generated	Outside resources and/or internally generated
	Differentiated roles	Differentiated roles	Merged roles	Shared roles

to overcome resistance to change and create more productive working relationships. The professionalizing type is informed by an agenda grounded in practice which also reflects the aspirations of the new professions, such as nursing, teaching and social work, to enhance their status on a par with the established professions, such as law and medicine, and to develop research-based practice. The empowering type is most closely associated with community development approaches and is characterized by an explicit anti-oppressive stance to working with vulnerable groups in society. The typology can be read from left to right as representing a developmental process over time as action research has shifted from a scientific approach to social change to a more qualitative and social constructionist methodology. The framework is based on a binary opposition between rational social management, assuming a consensus view of society on the left, and a structural change and conflict model of society on the right.

In constructing the typology we employ Weber's (1946, 1947) concept of 'ideal types', using it as a methodological device for capturing a particular form of action research within a particular context. As Morgan (1986) argues, the ideal types Weber developed were abstractions intended to serve as clear-cut concepts against which to compare empirical reality and were not intended to describe an actual empirical reality or prescribe which type was best.

We have used the typology to help to clarify the complex processes of action research by simplifying them. To do this in the form of a typology we have had to sacrifice something of the fluidity and dynamism of action research. But as the typology is a guide to practice rather than a prescriptive device, we feel justified in distinguishing between different types of action research in this way if, in doing so, it becomes possible to begin to make sense of what is going on.

Although our typology is original we are not the first to distinguish between different types and models of action research, as we mentioned earlier, nor the first to identify distinguishing criteria. As Adelman (1993) has argued, drawing on Marrow's (1969) biography, Lewin and his co-workers distinguished between four types. 'Experimental' action research entailed a controlled study of the effectiveness of various interventions in similar social situations. 'Empirical' action research involved the accumulation of data from research with a succession of similar groups, such as boys' clubs, leading to the gradual development of generally valid principles of group behaviour. 'Diagnostic' action research was designed to recommend remedial measures for a problem and to propose a plan of action. 'Participative' action research involved residents of a community as participants in the remedial action, including making decisions about the action plan. Halsey (1972) distinguished action research from other forms of social planning, and included such types as political action research aimed at responding to a recognized social problem, and social science action research designed to test theory in the field. Heller (1986) listed a variety of problem-solving approaches, and included action research as one subtype. More recently Chisholm and Elden (1993) have identified five dimensions, including the goals and purpose of the research effort and role of the researcher(s), that may be used to compare and contrast different action research approaches.

Within nursing Holter and Schwartz-Barcott (1993: 301–2) identify three approaches. The 'technical collaborative approach' aims to 'test a particular intervention based on a pre-specified theoretical framework'. The approach is deductive and predictive and would be encompassed within what we term 'experimental action research'. The 'mutual collaboration approach' brings researcher and practitioner together to identify problems and seek out possible causes and ways of intervening to change them. The approach is deductive and descriptive and can be encompassed within what we term the 'organizational type' of action research. The 'enhancement approach' has two goals: one is to align, as far as possible, theory and practice in the interests of resolving problems; the second is to 'assist practitioners in identifying and making explicit fundamental problems by first raising their collective consciousness'. In this it 'goes beyond the other two approaches'. At first reading, the 'enhancement approach' would seem to be encompassed within what we term the 'empowering type' of action research. However, a closer examination reveals that although the former is influenced by Freire (1972a, b), essentially it is what we have termed a 'professionalizing type' of action research, which strongly overlaps with the 'organizational type'. The main aim is the improvement of professional practice at the level of organizational and cultural change, rather than in terms of a challenge to existing power relationships or the involvement of users. It is instructive to note that Holter and Schwartz-Barcott's survey of the nursing literature reveals that, 'While the majority of studies reported in nursing using action research can be placed under the technical collaborative approach to action research and a few studies can be placed as inquiries within the mutual collaborative approach, no studies have been found which convey the enhancement approach to action research (Holter and Schwartz-Barcott 1993: 302).

As with our own typology, each of the above models recognizes more or less explicitly that, as Lathlean noted, 'the relative weights attached to the two elements of "action" and "research" have tended to provide quite contrasting types of study' (Lathlean 1994: 34). In our case, an action research type is defined by a particular configuration of distinguishing criteria, of which the relationship between research and action is just one. Generally speaking, an action research type to the left of the continuum will be more strongly research focused, while an action research type to the right of the continuum will be more strongly action focused. In particular cases, such as, for instance, in the organizational type, there may be a tension between research and action, arising from a dual aim on the part of the consultant–researcher to meet the requirements of both managerial problem-solving and social science research (Rapoport 1970; Eden and Huxham 1993). Halsey (1972) referred to the 'complex interplay' between research and action, making a political point that strong research control could be an obstacle both to generalization and to the evaluation of unintended outcomes of action programmes.

During the life of an action research project it may shift from one type to another as it moves through the spiral of cycles. For instance, the research phase might use a more traditional research design, such as a survey or a randomized control trial and this would locate it in the experimental type. This might then be followed by a professionalizing phase during which practitioners evaluated the findings of the experimental phase in practice. From here, the findings of this phase could be disseminated by professionals to the users of the service, expressing a move towards a more empowering type of action research. During the course of such a project the action research would have shifted from being outcome-led to process-led, and from being weighted towards research to being weighted towards action. It would have moved along the rational social management–structural change framework, towards a focus on change and engagement with participants, and away from research and control of research subjects.

The shift from one type to another may come about as part of a planned series of discrete cycles or phases of action research, especially when the project is located towards the experimental side of the typology. Shifts may also occur in response to the context in which the action research is situated and as part of the political nature of action research. The means by which change is generated, and the position the action researcher takes up, say something about the thinking behind how change is brought about. In the experimental type, where research informs practice, change is seen as a rational activity which can be planned and controlled. To some extent this view is shared by the organizational and professionalizing types, but as one moves away from the experimental type there is a much greater recognition of the political nature of social life. Research becomes just one of a range of influences upon change, and change comes about by people being active players in the process. The longer an action research initiative lasts, the greater the scope for movement. In our experience a project of less than six months' duration allows less scope for outside influences to force a shift in orientation. Moreover, since any shift towards a more empowering approach requires that others are engaged in the process as participants, this means that activities cannot be speeded up simply by the imposition of a time limit.

In presenting this typology we are aware that, since it is not prescriptive, it is open to different interpretations. One possible interpretation might be to take up a position to the far left of the typology and treat action research as a technique. As such it could be used to extend the range of influence of a traditional research design in order to improve dissemination and applicability of research findings. This way of looking at action research envisages it in terms of discrete phases, each mainly under the control of the action researcher. Although the purpose would be to realize predetermined outcomes, some attention would be given to the involvement of respondents. Even where the aim in using action research is to overcome some of the limitations of traditional approaches in respect of the participation of users, the approach to action research as technique tends to be mechanistic. Despite its good intentions it may remain caught in the notion of action research as something which is done 'on' people. Another interpretation might be to take up a position towards the far right of the typology. This would involve a more conscious and integrated process-led approach, rooted in a holistic philosophy which would underpin every aspect of the project, including especially the notion of action research as being highly participative and undertaken 'with' people. There is also a third position which may be taken up in interpreting the typology. Advocates of the type of 'participatory action research' (PAR) associated with Cornell University recognize that during the life of a project it may encompass both quantitative and qualitative approaches for which participatory action research forms a framework (Centre for Action Research in Professional Practice 1993). Thus a 'PAR' approach may be one component of a larger project, such as a comparative study, that may incorporate components that are, for instance, less responsive to purely local context as the project moves towards national policy formulation. Although there are, of course, other ways of interpreting the typology, these three seem to us to capture three different approaches to action research. These three ways of conceptualizing action research reflect wider distinctions within the social sciences, which as Robottom and Colquhoun (1993: 50) have argued, represent traditional positivist research (*on* other people), interpretative and enlightening research (*for* other people), and collaborative (action) research (*with* other people).

ISSUES IN ACTION RESEARCH

In this section we focus on issues raised in relation to the distinguishing criteria set out in the typology, including the alternative models of society on which it is framed. The reader might find it helpful to refer to Table 3.1 while reading the remaining sections. Although we discuss each of the criteria separately, they are in fact interlinked facets of the action research process, so that in practice they overlap and interweave.

Consensus and rational social management versus conflict and structural change

The typology is organized around alternative models of society: to the left of the typology a consensus/rational social management model, and to the right a conflict/structural change model. An analysis from a Community Development Project report (Coventry CDP 1975) of the relationship between different theoretical models and approaches to poverty shows that where the problem is conceptualized in terms of consensus values and a cultural model of poverty it will be located in the internal dynamics of deviant groups, and the method of change will be social education and social work treatment of groups. In contrast, where the values are informed by a structural class conflict model the problem will be located in the relationship between the working class and the political and economic structure, and the method of change will be towards changes in political consciousness and organization. In a similar way our typology indicates that such factors as research relationships, problem definition and ownership, notions of improvement and the degree to which the focus is on process and/or outcome tend to vary depending upon the extent to which they are informed by a consensus or conflict model of society.

Educative base

As described in Chapter 1, action research emerged in the early 1940s in the USA as a form of rational social management, and re-education and a concern to increase the self esteem of participants have been its cornerstones from the beginning (Lewin 1946). As the typology illustrates, changes in the meaning of the term 're-education' have come about as it has been redefined to encompass the idea that valid knowledge is rooted in experience, reflecting a shift in value base away from a consensus model of society towards a more radical and empowering approach to experiential learning and social change within a conflict model of society. A shift in value base over time is also evident in much contemporary action research in social care and education, in which 'awareness-raising' and 'consciousness-raising' have displaced 're-education', with its overtones of social management and manipulation. The way in which education is conceptualized in each of the types will depend upon the value base by which it is informed. For instance, in case study 2, of groupwork with ward sisters, we show that the different value bases of action researchers and sponsors affected the way each approached the developmental work, and gave rise to potentially conflicting views of what each meant by empowerment.

Individuals in groups

The empowering type of action research embodies similar notions of human action to 'groupwork', a field of study to which Lewin made a major theoretical contribution through his research on group dynamics (Lippitt 1968). Both accept that groups attempt to achieve their goals through the interaction of their members. In discussing community development Graham (1991) pointed out that, in traditional research, individuals are defined as respondents who are selected because they happen to meet the criteria for the problem under study, such as depression, poverty or unemployment, rather than because they are all members of the same neighbourhood (Graham 1991: 239). In action research there is likely to be a combination of means by which groups are selected and, as the typology shows, boundaries, membership and accessibility are defined. As the 'research relationship' criterion shifts from left to right of the typology, selection changes from being under the direction of the researcher to self-selection by participants.

As with all research enterprises, gaining access to groups is a key issue, but it has particular implications within an action research approach. Especially in the case of outsider researchers in the context of the organizational type, it is likely that, in order to gain the approval of powerful gatekeepers and access to an organization such as a hospital, it will be necessary to incorporate aspects of the managerial agenda into the action research brief. As in the case of Meyer (1993), a nurse researcher using an action research framework to work with ward nurses, this can introduce elements of a 'top-down' approach into what might have started out as a genuine attempt at a 'bottom-up' approach. The dilemma is that the action researcher may find herself or himself dependent upon the patronage of the most powerful group to continue the project and this may undermine the collaborative relationship established with a less powerful group, as seemed to be the case with Meyer. Meyer's experience confirms our view that difficulties arise which may put participants at risk of scapegoating or dismissal when academic researchers use an empowering approach to realize a professional agenda within an organizational 'management of change' context. In these circumstances action researchers may be vulnerable to a range of competing academic, professional and managerial pressures. As in Meyer's case this may restrict their ability to act in a way which protects the group boundaries and they may find that their position shifts uncomfortably away from an empowering type towards an organizational type, as they unwittingly take on the role of management consultant. This can be a disturbing experience in which action researchers may feel, as Meyer did, that they have in some way betrayed the trust of the collaborating group. In identifying conditions under which action research in nursing may or may not be successful, Sparrow and Robinson (1994) draw attention to Meyer's point that action research which is directed towards an academic qualification runs the risk of becoming manipulative in order to allow the researcher to achieve his or her academic goal. This underlines our view that in action research it is important to focus on process, and not become task-orientated.

High status insiders who may wish to use action research to ensure that top-down initiatives are owned at grass roots level may encounter particular difficulties in gaining access to certain groups. They may find that although their status assists them in gaining access to senior staff groups, it either carries no weight lower down the hierarchy or acts as an obstacle to access. The advantages of conducting action research from a position of influence in the organization may be offset by the perception by groups lower in the hierarchy that the research is too closely associated with senior managers. As Ong found out when working as Research and Development Officer for South Sefton (Merseyside) Health Authority;

> As the postholder is directly accountable to the UGM [Unit General Manager] she is structurally tied-in with management and therefore has a high degree of credibility because the implementation of research results can be initiated from the

highest level. On the other hand, the relationship with grass roots staff can be distorted precisely because of the link with management.

(Ong 1989: 507)

The action researcher needs to develop skills of a kind similar to those required by what Hunter (1990) has termed 'interface managers', who are individuals such as a senior ward nurse or a social worker who occupy a position at the interface of a number of interconnected individuals, groups and agencies and who deal on an everyday basis with a range of different occupational and user groups. Such individuals need to establish networks on the basis of shared interests rather than in terms of an organizational hierarchy, and to negotiate across occupational and social boundaries and with individuals and groups at different levels within an organization or community.

Problem focus

One of the distinguishing features of action research is that it is concerned to solve problems in an immediate situation and within a particular setting (Bell *et al.* 1984: 43–6; Robson 1993: 60). Cunningham has argued that the word 'problem' implies there is something wrong, when what is meant in action research terms is that 'a problem is a definition of a need for change and describes how certain issues can be addressed' (Cunningham 1993: 75). Action research is problem-sensing and problem-focused, and the researcher is involved in an immediate and direct way with the problem situation. The combination of these factors makes action research attractive to participants as it is geared to their problem and promotes their active participation in its resolution. In action research the intentions which underlie action are directed to a future state in which the 'real' comes closer to the 'ideal'. As Greer (1990: 49) has observed, it is from the gap between the ideal and the actual that policy problems emerge. Moreover, those involved in the change are more likely to be committed to it through their own involvement in planning for their future (Susman and Evered 1978, Eden and Huxham 1993). A recognized dilemma in action research is that of who takes the initiative to bring forth and identify the problem (Rapoport 1970; Elden and Levin 1991). As we have indicated in the typology (Table 3.1), towards the experimental side the 'problem' is defined in relation to social science and/or management interests, while towards the empowering side of Table 3.1 the 'problem' emerges from the everyday practices and experiences of group members. The extent of negotiation about the nature of the problem differs in the four types, so that for instance in the professionalizing type there is some negotiation with users. A further dilemma related to the identification of problems is that in the experimental and organizational types, where the approach is 'top-down', it may be difficult to generate a sense of ownership of the problem at grass-roots level, while in the empowering type, the sense of ownership at grass-roots level may not be matched by any commitment from powerful people to the problem.

Change intervention

A fundamental belief of Lewin (1946), which resulted from his early experiments in group dynamics, was that the individual will not change on his or her own without an outside intervention, such as a 'change experiment'. More recently, Gill and Johnson (1991) defined action research as a research design which involves a planned intervention by the researcher or an outside consultant into an everyday event. They argue that this is similar to an experimental design, where the intervention is analogous to the independent variable and its consequences analogous to the dependent variables. As in an experiment proper the intervention may involve the use of control groups to screen out extraneous variables and allow inferences to be made about the relation between cause and effect. Lathlean (1994: 35) has argued that a distinguishing feature of action research is that it 'is about taking action in the real world and a close examination of the effects of the action taken, thus it always involves intervention'. In the empowering type the intervention may not be so discrete or identifiable as in the experimental type, and may take a variety of forms, including building alliances, opening up lines of communication and reframing issues. It may be that the intervention is about changing the ways in which problems are discussed, which has the effect of initiating other changes. The first may not be the sole, direct cause of the second, although it may be a contributory factor.

Improvement and involvement

Of the seven criteria, those of 'improvement and involvement' and of 'cyclic processes' which follow are linked particularly closely. Within health and social care the aim is to improve professional practice for the benefit of users of a service and to involve those concerned in the processes of change. This aim has to take account of the fact that there may be competing definitions of what counts as improvement and success, and this may include differences between professionals and users of the service and/or between different professional groups (Smith and Cantley 1985). In the empowering type the direction of the action research is towards agreed improvements, although these may be renegotiated in the light of increased understanding and evaluation of action. Outcomes are negotiated and this involves working with pluralist definitions of improvement and taking account of the fact that among the stakeholders there are likely to be different views about what counts as success, depending on the 'social context of its use' (Smith and Cantley 1985: 12). This pluralist approach may introduce tensions and conflicts into the process of 'improvement', including the potential for competition between individuals and groups as they seek access to scarce resources. Towards the experimental side of the typology, the tendency is to assume that the change process is rational and controllable, and that its direction is towards consensual definition of improvement. These assumptions are supported by the research-led and social scientific aspects of the experimental type of action research.

Cyclic processes

Carr and Kemmis (1986: 162) describe action research as a 'spiral of cycles', underlining the notion that the process is not linear and does not follow a series of stages. It is a dynamic process in which the three strands of research, action and evaluation interact in a way which we picture as like a Russian wedding ring. We agree with Elliott (1991) that action, research and enquiry are not separate. Our experiences suggested that at each phase only one of these three strands may be dominant, although it still touches upon and interacts with the other two. This is similar to reflective practice, where research, action and evaluation may be so tightly linked as to be at times indistinguishable. As a project develops over time there may be a shift so that action components dominate the research components or vice versa.

'Action research' and 'evaluation research' are closely related (Lathlean and Farnish 1984; Patton 1990). Within any single action research project, evaluation may take a more or less important role. But evaluation of some kind is nevertheless essential, since without it, it is not possible to assess progress or redefine the problem. The interplay of research, action and evaluation is thus a fundamental feature of action research (Lewin 1946). Action research may involve sophisticated types of quantitative evaluation designed to infer the relationship between cause and effect (research intervention and outcome), or may use qualitative and/or much more informal means of evaluating processes, such as asking the participants directly for their comments on progress so far. Hopkins's (1989) work on the use of evaluation in school development is an exemplar of the best in recent developments which are readily transferable to health and social care settings. *Does it Work?* (Aggleton *et al.* 1992) presents perspectives on evaluation in the context of HIV/AIDS health promotion, within which Prout's (1992) discussion of the MESMAC[1] Project reinforces the importance of collaboration and negotiation as an ongoing process.

Research relationship and degree of collaboration

The nature and extent of collaboration between what in traditional research would be defined as 'researcher' and 'research subjects' are issues of major importance in action research, as is the degree of participation achieved by a particular project. Drawing heavily on Lewin (1946), Holter and Schwartz-Barcott (1993: 300) have argued:

> In action research the principle focus of collaboration involves interaction between a practitioner or a group of practitioners and a researcher or a research team. The term 'practitioner' refers to an individual(s) who knows the field or workplace 'from the inside'. This individual is seen as the expert for the given situation and setting under study...In past studies, the practitioners involved have ranged from executive directors, staff nurses, military personnel, policemen and coal miners in England.

As action research has developed, there have, however, been a number of variations on this 'outsider/insider', 'researcher/practitioner' theme. As Table 3.1 shows, the degree of collaboration, the nature of participation and the way in which research roles are defined alter as you move across the typology, from the more conventional 'experimenter and respondent' relationship in the experimental type, to the more progressive 'co-researcher/co-change agent' relationship in the empowering type.

In the context of mental health, Morgan (1993) cites Chamberlain (1988), who argues that the concept of user empowerment requires changes in attitude and behaviour on the part of both users and workers. Chamberlain proposes three models: the partnership model in which there is collaboration between professionals and non-professionals, although the traditional distinction is upheld between those who give and those who receive help; the supportive model in which non-professionals and users have equal rights, and professionals are only permitted external roles, such as writing letters of support; and the separatist model, which excludes all professionals, so that users and ex-users of mental health services provide support exclusively for each other. In any one project an action researcher might take on a variety of positions in relation to participants, which may encompass similar 'partnerships' to those proposed by Chamberlain above. The point is that towards the empowering side of the typology the decision about the degree and type of involvement does not rest with the action researcher, as it does in the experimental type. Part of the process of empowerment involves shifting ownership to participants, even if this means that the action researcher may eventually be marginalized or even excluded from the group. This is one of the risks the action researcher takes when working in a participatory way.

The participation of those directly involved in a change situation is at the heart of action research, irrespective of which type, although what is meant by participation differs markedly across the typology. In the Lewinian type of experimental action research described in Chapter 2, participation was a variable to be measured in order to identify its effect upon such things as productivity and worker–manager relations. It was Lewin's guiding belief that participation was an essential component of democracy, and that change which was brought about with the voluntary participation of the individuals concerned was more effective than change imposed autocratically from above. Nevertheless, at the experimental/organizational side of the typology, the relationship between experimenter or consultant and respondents or participants may in practice retain traces of the unequal power relationships of more orthodox approaches. The participation of respondents may be an instrumental technique rather than central to an underlying collaborative philosophy. Particularly in the organizational and experimental types the roles of researcher and participant are differentiated and, as in the quasi-experiment, it is the researcher who controls and manipulates the situation. In contrast, in the empowering type the lines between researcher and participant become blurred to the extent that they become co-researchers and co-change agents.

The participation of groups is not only an issue towards the empowering side of the typology, and does not only concern vulnerable or low-status groups in society. Indeed, one of the challenges for the action researcher, particularly when working within a dominant organizational type, is how to involve a range of groups with different degrees of formal and informal power within an organization as participants in the process. Moreover, the involvement of senior people in a project may make it more likely that the findings are extended to other settings, the project is properly resourced and change is carried forward. However, as Greenwood et al. (1993: 175) have argued, it is not possible to mandate in advance that the action research process will become fully participatory, since that is the 'joint result of the character of the problems and environmental conditions under study, the aims and capacities of the research team, and the skills of the professional researcher.' Moreover, they argue, 'Participation is a process that must be generated. It begins with participatory intent and continues by building participatory processes into the activity within the limits set by the participants and the conditions. To view participation as something that can be imposed is both naive and morally suspect'.

CONCLUSION

The four types within the typology are 'ideal types'. In practice they are not distinct: they overlap and, as we have suggested, in the course of one project the style of working and the strategies adopted may spiral from one type to another. Nevertheless, there is much to be gained by using the typology to select a style of working according to the type which seems most appropriate to a particular policy context and particular phase of development. Action research, as we have seen, offers the possibility of a range of strategies and methods. The way in which problems are formulated and solutions are sought will depend upon the particular configurations of power and vested interests within a particular policy context. The typology indicates the capacity of different types of action research to bring about change in relation to different ways of defining improvement and success. Above all it shows the primacy of context in selecting an appropriate strategy, and this includes taking account of power relationships. In this book we apply the label 'action research' to each of the five case studies in Part II, even though they range in scope from a large-scale project, involving an academic research team working with senior National Health Service personnel, to a small-scale study by a social care worker engaging with staff and older people in a residential home. Our justification for this is that each of the case studies can be located within a recognized action research approach, which is encompassed within the action research typology. Thus we would reject the charge that the label 'action research' is meaningless, although we do accept that the label covers a wide range of research activities.

NOTE

1 'Men Who Have Sex with Men: Action in the Community', funded by the Health Education Authority.

4

Action research in practice

INTRODUCTION

We build on the discussion of the seven distinguishing criteria of action research given in Chapter 3 by exploring them in the context of an action research proposal. This was prepared in response to a research brief from sponsors who had obtained local authority funding to study the provision of services for women with known abuse histories. This chapter focuses specifically on the process of thinking through and preparing an action research proposal, and in doing so raises a number of issues that are at the heart of the participatory endeavour, especially when working with vulnerable groups in society. Although the emphasis is on an empowering type of action research, the issues raised are of more general relevance to the whole range of types within the typology presented in Chapter 3 (Table 3.1), since they extend to action research both as research activity and as action for improvement.

We present a reflexive account of the way decisions were made about such things as the interpretation of the sponsors' brief and the theoretical position from which the task was approached. The exploration of a thinking process which we present here illustrates how difficult it is to locate the boundaries between research, theory and practice, and to separate them. The process involves making decisions about a range of issues, such as whether or not action research is an appropriate methodology given such things as the nature of the problem, funding and timescale. Lathlean (1994) has observed that many different aspects have to be taken into account when choosing a methodology. As this account shows, selection involves a subtle interplay between live practice issues, the practitioner's intuitive knowledge and a range of literatures, including in this case feminism, sociology and policy research. Moreover, the task of responding to a call from sponsors for a research bid involves looking critically at the assumptions underlying the research brief and, in turn, those underlying the researcher's own choice of methodology. This includes paying attention to power relationships between sponsors, funders, researchers and research participants (Burgess 1991). The thinking processes uncovered here are not abstract and academic, since they reveal that the issues and questions emerging from and in practice are not pre-given and fixed, but constructed by a complex interweaving of concrete experience and abstract theorizing. Thus the discussion highlights the essentially political nature of the research enterprise, whether or not it is action research.

THE DILEMMAS OF IMPROVEMENT AND INVOLVEMENT IN PRACTICE

Carr and Kemmis (1986: 165) consider that the two basic aims of action research are to improve and to involve, which we included within our seven distinguishing criteria in Chapter 3. In using the term 'improve' these authors are not talking merely about a commitment to dissemination of research findings. Rather they point to the engagement by action researchers in a process of change for the better in terms of professional practice and service delivery to users of education, health and welfare services. As Cohen and Manion (1984: 41) put it, 'Action research investigates problems identified by practitioners, and is essentially directed towards greater understanding and improvement of practice over a period of time.' But within the notion of improvement lie important questions about how the direction of change and the meaning of improvement are determined, and by whom. These in turn focus attention upon the existence of stakeholders in any action research initiative. It is their involvement in negotiation on these issues and their participation in the processes of action research which are recognized as definitive.

In order to explore in more detail the related concepts of improvement and involvement we discuss a recently submitted research proposal. We begin by setting it in context and provide relevant information as sent out by the research sponsors, but modified to exclude identifying features. We spell out the rationale underpinning the decision to opt for an action research strategy rather than some other approach, and then draw out some central issues about action research as a methodology, using extracts from the document. This proposal was written from a position within the empowering type of action research, and as such was informed by both community development approaches and feminist perspectives.

THE CONTEXT AND THE SPONSORS' WORKING BRIEF

A group of policy-makers and practitioners, working across departmental and agency boundaries, had obtained some local authority funding in connection with a proposed study into the services received by women who were known to have been abused and who lived in ethnically mixed areas of an inner city. As can be seen from the condensed brief below, which was sent out inviting tenders for the research, the sponsors did not make any reference to an action research approach, although we would argue that an action research framework was implied by the nature of the brief.

The sponsor's brief

It is proposed to conduct an eight month study into services to women with known histories of child abuse and/or sexual abuse in childhood/adolescence. The research will focus on particular geographical areas and will be managed by a steering group. The budget for the project is £21,000 to cover day to day supervision, translation, transport and administrative costs. The aims of the research are:

- to provide a breakdown of the numbers of women with known histories of abuse who have come into contact with statutory and voluntary agencies;
- to identify the cost of interventions/services provided by statutory and voluntary agencies to meet client needs;
- to identify points of intervention;
- to assess the appropriateness and effectiveness of services provided;
- to consult with service users regarding assessment of services and recommendations for improvements;
- to produce a comprehensive report on the above, outlining recommendations for improved service provision and better targeting of resources.

The methodology will include the following: interviews with and research covering a representative cross section of service users, including women of differing ages, sexual orientation, ethnic origin, and socio-economic and health status; identification of reason for intervention/seeking help; liaison with a wide range of health, social welfare, education and employment agencies in both statutory and voluntary sectors. Prior to submission of a final report, the researcher will be expected to produce progress reports at agreed intervals together with a timetable for the next stages.

When this document was received a preliminary phone call was made to the contact person managing the tendering process. From this it emerged that an alliance of interested people from the statutory and voluntary/self-help sectors were mounting an initiative intended to benefit abused women across the city, but focused on the needs of poor women. Staff coming into contact with women in formal and informal settings had begun to question the extent to which those who had been abused at some earlier point in their lives were subsequently seeking or being referred to, for instance, mental health and family welfare services, which compounded their problems by labelling them as mad, or as bad mothers. As a result workers were wondering whether scope existed to establish some sort of women's centre which would respond more appropriately and holistically to their needs.

THE THINKING BEHIND THE CHOICE OF AN ACTION RESEARCH BID

From the information contained in the written brief and that gleaned through the exploratory conversation with the sponsors, it was concluded that those commissioning the study were asking radical questions about service provision which potentially had consider-able change implications in terms of professional practices and organizational structures. Moreover, the research was apparently being seen as both 'a weapon', and 'a flashlight' (Shipman 1988: 92). Drawing on Weiss's (1979) analysis of the use of policy research, this suggested that the sponsors were adopting a predominantly political model of policy research aiming to produce evidence in support of a case. But they seemed also to be employing a problem-solving model of research 'whereby a problem is identified and research contracted to guide requisite formation of policies' (Shipman 1988: 166). As such the methodological assumptions from which the sponsors were working were implicit. In terms of our typology, the brief contained elements of a range of types, from research-led/experimental to action-led/empowering, and was underpinned by a strong professionally led agenda. Although its aims seemed most consistent with the empowering type of action research, the research brief was something of a 'mish mash' in that the sponsors seemed to be wanting one thing and yet asked another.

Such situations, in our experience, are by no means unusual. Writing about a ward sister training project, Lathlean and Farnish (1984: 38) say that the original aims of their study were 'to define a model for ward sister training and define the effect on the ward environment and patient care'. In the event the researchers were expected to evaluate a particular and given model of training in practice. Research commissioned from the top of welfare bureau-cracies or generated by workers 'on the ground' about a service problem or practice dilemma may well be couched in terms which hint at ways forward or, indeed, specify possible solutions. There may be a risk in this for a researcher whose horizons become prematurely narrowed. The risk for outside researchers coming into such a situation is that at the points of negotiating engagement and entry, their capacity to understand and make manageable the research topic is limited by their dependence on the sponsors, whose views cannot be taken as necessarily representing those of all other interested parties.

It seemed that one way of dealing with these difficulties was actively to take on board the political and problem-solving nature of the study while also adopting an interactive approach to carrying it out. This would acknowledge from the outset that improvements – indeed potentially major changes – in service provision were on the agenda and that the role of the commissioned research was actively to contribute towards this. It would also recognize that the nature of the problem(s) and the solution(s) could not be taken as given or shared by all parties: rather they were contestable and probably contested. A contribution of the research could be to enable interested parties to reach some common understanding about the nature of their shared initiative in order to implement any findings and thus maximize their investment in their commissioned research.

Everitt *et al.* discuss the essentially contentious nature of social research problems in a way that relates directly to the aims and objectives identified above:

> Different interest groups represented in practice may all favour different forms of data. Funding agencies may prefer to see formalised statistics being gathered; managers may be seeking to find out what forms of intervention are effective; service users may want to expose an unacceptable philosophy underlying current service delivery.
>
> (Everitt *et al.* 1992: 91–2)

The brief for this study showed evidence of the existence of different interest groups and served initially to highlight the potential for the outcome of the project to be disputed, since it would be unlikely to meet the expectations of all of them. Indeed it is only now, as we have subjected the paperwork associated with it to close re-examination, that the significance of this insight is fully recognized. Making an exploratory telephone call to the nominated person in the sponsoring organization to discuss the outline seemed, at the time, no more than routine good practice. This was indeed the case. But such practice, which may have become so second-nature as to seem natural rather than considered and purposeful, stemmed from a recognition that, as Carr and Kemmis (1986: 180) observe, social research takes place 'in social situations which typically involve competing values and complex interactions between different people who are acting on different understandings of their common situation and on the basis of different values about how the interactions should be conducted.'

Since this applies as much to researchers as to anyone else, the researcher must inevitably engage in this process of negotiating meanings, ideas and proposals for change, especially if recommendations for action are to stand any chance of being meaningful, realistic and acceptable. Moreover to be effective, such negotiation cannot be left to the point when study findings are presented and implementation is under discussion. Current thinking about the promotion and implementation of organizational change suggests that involvement by participants needs to underpin the whole process of research in these sorts of situation, so that there is a widely shared sense of ownership in its outcome and a commitment to its products including any reports. As Walton and Gaffney (1991: 101) say:

> Innovative change efforts by practitioners that incorporate the spirit and techniques of inquiry, discovery, and invention produce more significant and lasting innovations and greater understanding of why they do and do not work. We also propose that fact finding and theorising that tap the wisdom and knowledge of those who work in the system under consideration produce knowledge that is more relevant to practice and, therefore, in certain respects, of greater validity. Finally we emphasise the advantages of broader rather than narrower participation in both the action and the research aspects of change.

Subjecting the research brief to this kind of analysis and interpretation, it was concluded that action research offered the most appropriate methodological approach and the proposal was developed along these lines. It did not adopt the model of the professional researcher being invited in to act as expert:

> to study a situation and a set of problems, to determine what the facts are, and to recommend a course of action ... Those aiming to help organizations carry through major

processes of socio-technical change have come to recognize the limitations of the professional expert model. In such situations, we need to develop a process of change, resulting in organizational learning, over a considerable period of time. To be useful in stimulating and guiding this process, the researcher cannot simply stand aside and just report research findings to the decision makers. For major organizational change processes, we need a hands-on set of relationships with the social researcher.

(Whyte 1991: 9)

Action research was not, of course, the only possible approach. Another researcher, especially someone working within a positivist and quantitative tradition, when faced with similar circumstances would probably have come up with different interpretations and/or suggested a different research strategy as the most appropriate. In some respects, as Bell (1993: 6) points out, 'The approach adopted and the methods of data collection selected will depend upon the nature of the inquiry and the type of information required.' But it is also the case, as Bryman (1984) says, that the use of a particular research technique is determined not so much by the nature of the problem, but by the researcher's prior orientation to a particular philosophical approach. Indeed Gill and Johnson (1991: 145) suggest that researchers 'largely choose the research strategy with which they are most familiar, giving little attention to alternatives.' They go on to point out that the acceptance by the sponsors of one proposal rather than another will depend on the practical utility of the outcomes for the interests it serves, rather than on notions that there is an optimal way of undertaking research.

THE ACTION RESEARCH PROPOSAL

In terms of our action research typology in Chapter 3, the proposal which was drawn up was located within an empowering type. It argued that the nature of the topic and the 'subjects' of the research – women who had been sexually abused – when set within the context of a plurality of interest groups and an initiative for change, pointed in the direction of such a methodological approach. As the following extract from the proposal indicates:

Underpinning this tender is an acknowledgement that women, and particularly those of minority groups, routinely experience oppression in the course of living their daily lives (Ahmad 1990; Begum 1990). Women who have been abused as children or young women, and who perhaps continue to suffer abuse, are additionally oppressed, and their experiences are frequently compounded by the discriminatory and insensitive practices of many so-called 'helping' agencies who negate their accounts and render their needs invisible (Rouf 1989). Such women, whose needs are the focus of this study, are therefore potentially vulnerable to further abuse by any research practices which objectify or devalue them and/or which further disempower them by falsely raising their hopes about speedy personal and structural changes. It is therefore considered essential that those engaged in the research processes of this study conduct their affairs in such a way as to empower women.

Such a commitment to empowerment demands policies and practices which actively seek to shift the balance of power towards those who are oppressed by, for example, sharing information, encouraging partnership in decision making, and enabling active participation (Frost and Stein 1989: 142) from those contributing to the research.

IMPROVEMENT: VALUES AND PURPOSES

Problems of social welfare are not simply technical problems, for instance about the distribution of resources among individuals and groups. They are also problems about the realization of far from universally agreed values about issues such as justice and equity. Practitioners, policy-makers and researchers are not only faced with working out what services should be provided for whom, but must also determine how services are to be provided and why. Everitt *et al.* put it thus:

The first question in undertaking participatory or indeed any research should always be 'What is the purpose of the research?' . . . Clear reasons for practising must underpin decisions as to what kind of data is needed and how best to obtain it . . . in practice as in research, where values are to the fore, the question 'why?' must assume equal importance with the questions 'what?' and 'how?' In research we cannot jump from deciding what is to be studied to the technical how questions. We cannot select the tools for the job without first considering why we are asking the questions in the first place and what we hope to find out. Neither can we decide on what services are to be delivered, in what ways and by whom, without considering – why these services?

(Everitt *et al.* 1992: 91)

Carr and Kemmis (1986: 180) address a similar point and highlight what they consider to be the overarching purpose of education and therefore of research in and for education. They state that the 'problems of education are not simply problems of achieving known ends; they are problems of acting *educationally*' (their emphasis). In the research proposal it was decided to make explicit the importance of acting caringly, and specifically to empower users of services – to leave them 'stronger than before', as Everitt *et al.* (1992: 92) put it. This implied a changing, an improving, of the status quo, which itself is a key tenet of action research, and a rejection of the position held by traditional positivist researchers, who, to quote Graham (1991: 240), 'do not expect to alter the way their respondents see and live their lives. Their aim is not to disturb the world they are studying: their aim instead, is to trawl their data collecting net quietly through the social world.' Thus the following statements were included:

The primary purpose of the study will be to give voice to the experiences and views of women who have suffered/survived abuse. The range of people contacted and the depth of contact with them will be determined in large measure by a recognition of the painful, damaging, secretive, hidden and denied nature of abuse and of the issues at stake in its discussion, all of which have implications for the form and pacing of the data collection activities. The preferred methodological approach will be one of exploratory action research undertaken from a feminist perspective, the implications of which are that such a study will be concerned to make a beginning in a difficult area, and that women taking part will be seen as contributors and participants who have a vested interest in its outcomes and will need information for example about what is to be done about emergent issues . . .

In order to obtain accounts from fifteen to twenty women, guidance will be sought initially from members of the sponsoring group as to how contacts should be made and with whom. But it is anticipated that the process of identifying a range of women who are willing to be interviewed, setting up these interviews and conducting them will be time consuming and difficult. Much is at stake for a woman in talking to a stranger – and particularly to one whose race, class, educational opportunities, sexual orientation, life chances and so on have differentially advantaged her – and in talking about the impact of her abusive experiences on her subsequent life and help-seeking history. The fact that such a discussion may in addition include accounts of oppressive practices and failures on the part of supposedly helping agencies is likely to make being interviewed and doing the interviewing particularly taxing. In addition, some interviews may have to be conducted by, or through, a third party (a specially recruited interviewer with particular linguistic and interpersonal skills or an interpreter) if appropriate contact is to be established with a range of women service users.

Unless such women feel that they can trust the interviewer(s) they will not help with the research and the building of a trusting relationship cannot be speeded up. It is for this reason, combined with a belief in the value of in-depth rather than superficial interviewing strategies, that it is intended to build up fifteen to twenty case studies and to conduct the research on an average of three days a week over a period of ten months. The draft budget allows for the payment of a small fee to each woman interviewed in recognition of the importance of her contribution to this research. If time and finances permit and women are willing to participate, it may additionally be possible to conduct some discussions using focus group techniques.

The adoption and spelling out of such a perspective was more than a statement about a personal value system. In its references to promoting change it incorporated some of the sponsors' stated aims and drew upon theorizing about, as well as established professional practices in, work with women who have been abused, who were identified in the research brief as the 'sample population' or 'subjects' of this study. Such work has been concerned with therapeutic interventions with women about their abuse *per se* (Rouf 1989; Modi and Pal 1992), while other feminist work has been concerned with the related issue of doing research more generally about women (Oakley 1981; Woodward and Chisholm 1981). These influences came together in the proposal and forced on to the agenda from the outset questions about the nature of the relationship to be established between those being researched and the researchers.

WORKING RELATIONSHIPS WITHIN PROCESSES OF RESEARCH

Research of any kind about aspects of social life raises issues about the nature of the relationship between the person doing the research and those being researched. Rapoport (1970: 499) defines action research as taking place 'within a mutually acceptable ethical framework' and this serves as a reminder that researchers who fail to address the ethics of their involvement with participants risk behaving in an exploitative way towards them. Research into sensitive areas such as the abuse of women, as Lee says, raises a number of wider issues in relation to the legal, political and ethical dimensions of research:

> Those researching sensitive topics may need to be more acutely aware of their ethical responsibilities to research participants than would be the case with the study of a more innocuous topic . . . In many cases neither the problems raised by studying sensitive topics, nor the wider issues involved, can be dealt with in any simple way. The relationship between method-ological or technical decisions in research and ethical, legal or political considerations is often complex and reciprocal.
>
> (Lee 1993: 2)

As we have said, this proposal made the case that in these circumstances it is necessary to take an anti-oppressive and collab-orative stance because without such an approach the overriding purpose of the research (and of policy and practice), that of empowerment of service users, cannot be achieved. A neutral stance is not tenable, and oppression and exploitation of women as research 'subjects', particularly those who have already suffered abuse, is clearly unethical. Furthermore, it was argued that in the absence of an empowering stance on the part of the researcher towards them, women with experiences of being abused would be unlikely to agree to take part in the study which, according to the sponsors' brief, explicitly sought consultation with such service users.

Oakley (1981: 58) considers that social science in general requires the replacement 'of "hygienic" research with its accompanying mystification of the researcher and the researched as objective instruments of data production . . . by the recognition that personal involvement is more than dangerous bias – it is the condition under which people come to know each other and to admit others into their lives.' Qualitative researchers in general would not necessarily translate into a relationship of empowerment their recognition of the significance of the social relationships which exist and are built up between researchers and those being re-searched. And it would be misleading to suggest that the espousal of 'a feminist perspective' inevitably leads to a proactive attitude towards empowerment on the part of researchers in their relation-ships with interviewees. For one thing, as Woodward and Chisholm (1981: 183) point out, there is, 'no single unitary "feminist per-spective" [which] can be (a) identified and then (b) applied in the research situation.' This is a point which is increasingly being made by black women and women with disabilities, for instance, whose experiences in the past have been subsumed, made invisible and misinterpreted in work with and writings about women in general. In focusing on women as opposed to men, white middle class feminists have been criticized for their failure to acknowledge the differences between women in terms of such factors as health status, ethnic origin and class.

However, it is the case that feminist researchers, in recognizing women's subordinated position within male-dominated society, have emphasized the value of establishing non-hierarchical rela-tionships between researcher and researched. Those engaged in participatory action research similarly seek to narrow the differentials and to establish collaborative working relationships with research 'subjects' – in this case service users and providers – and with research sponsors and funders. Strategies for operationalizing this stance may include working collectively through focus groups, the drawing up of agreements about the way in which interviews are to be conducted, and the payment of fees to participants. In Part III we provide examples of ethical agreements, including the one used by Fogg (1988) in his nurse education study.

GENERATING DATA AND NEGOTIATING UNDERSTANDINGS

Central to all research is the generation and analysis of data, but within an action research project these activities are entwined with gaining access, reading relevant literature, analysing emergent findings, evaluating progress and planning subsequent phases. The cyclical and problem-solving nature of the enterprise as a whole results in a blurring of lines between 'finding out more' and 'doing something about' the issue or situation selected for investigation and improvement.

It is recognized by workers using such an approach that, from the outset, intervention of any kind has within it the potential for changing people and settings, and that those who in the early stages act as contributors may subsequently have a crucial contribution to make as collaborators in initiatives for change. Moreover, action researchers, and particularly those working within an empowering type, deal with the complexities of social life by building into their enquiries a recognition of the 'constructed' nature of phenomena; that is, they proceed on the basis that what are often seen as facts are more often understandings formalized through interactions between people. This means that investigative activities encompass the development of an understanding not just of how many people are, for example, listed on hospital waiting lists, recorded as having committed offences or registered as 'in need', but also of the processes by which they achieve such a status and are labelled as offenders, patients, disabled people, abused women and so on. Such thinking underpinned the preparation of the research proposal. Reference was made early on to the need to 'negotiate' the parameters of the study, including the definitions of 'abuse', 'known histories of abuse' and 'representative cross sections of service users', and to develop shared understandings of these key terms in use.

Commonly, researchers begin a study by clarifying definitions and setting the boundaries of the territory under investigation, because they must make manageable the task before them and have mechanisms for determining what is relevant for exploration or experimentation. But few problems are as simple as they initially appear, and the richness of the human condition combined with the innate curiosity of the researcher can lead to wide-ranging journeys of discovery. Without a clear focus for enquiry the researcher can easily lose all sense of direction and become overwhelmed with material which becomes increasingly difficult to manage.

Within an action research strategy, the researcher treats the need to set a course not as an occasion for imposing definitions and limitations but rather as an opportunity for discussion about understandings and for the establishment of collaborative working relationships. This was recognized in the research proposal by posing the question 'What is this research about?', and by entry into a debate about the perceptions underpinning the proposal and the issues at stake. In recognition of the essentially process-led nature of empowering action research, an approach was suggested by which shared understandings could be developed, parameters agreed and data generated. The involvement of women who had been abused as children and of service providers, individually and collectively, was central to this, as were the sponsors of the research.

It is suggested that essentially this research brief may be seen as posing questions from two broad perspectives – from the perspectives of women who have been abused as children and from the perspectives of helping agencies . . . At the heart of the study will be a series of in-depth interviews with women who were abused as children/adolescents, in order to identify their involvement as adults with welfare agencies and organizations/self-help groups and to elicit their views of the help they received. Interviews will also be conducted with key workers in these organizations in order to build up a picture of their awareness of the existence among their users of women who were abused as young people and of both their helping and recording practices . . . The tendering process for this study and the tight lead-in to its commencement pose particular difficulties for researchers committed to qualitative approaches, action research and collaborative styles of working. We would like this paper therefore to be seen as a starting point for further discussion rather than as a definitive statement of what independently and in isolation we have decided should be done.

Generation of material was seen as inextricably linked with action for change. It was emphasized in the proposal that 'women taking part will be seen as contributors and participants who have a vested interest in [the study's] outcomes and will need information, for example, about what is to be done about emergent issues.' 'Emergent issues' were seen in terms of both public and personal matters. It was expected that women who agreed to be interviewed and therefore to 'opening doors on their private lives' (Graham 1984: 108) would expose examples of less than adequate service provision, and perhaps unmet needs and unresolved difficulties. On occasion it might be necessary and appropriate to adopt an advocacy stance to protect and promote their interests. This would be part of behaving caringly and reciprocally towards them, and additionally recognized that intervening with and on behalf of individuals would in turn test the scope which was present for bringing about improvements. Moreover, the adoption of such an ethical position also suggested that it would be equally important at least to let participants know about, and at best to involve them in, developing initiatives to respond to the common components of their individual problems. As Freire (1972a, b) so powerfully argues, engagement of this kind individually and collectively has the potential to raise the awareness – consciousness – of those who are oppressed and thereby to create the conditions for change and improvement.

COMBINING TECHNIQUES

In the course of preparing this proposal, consideration was given to the use of methodological approaches other than action research. The brief presented by those commissioning the study suggested that they might have been thinking along predominantly quantitative lines in expecting the researcher(s) to determine the numbers of women recorded at or over a given period of time in the files of a range of agencies as having histories of abuse. This could have involved designing forms, perhaps to be sent out by post, to key record keepers, asking them to draw on their internal systems to provide relevant statistics of women falling within predefined categories. In addition, or as an alternative, the sponsors might have assumed that the researcher(s) would work more qualitatively by setting up some (semi-)structured interviews with abused women and representatives of appropriate agencies to find out about help-seeking behaviours and service provision in response to them. Partly because of the perceived difficulties in relation to such approaches as these, and partly as a result of the initial 'reading' of the situation, an action research strategy was opted for which contained within it qualitative and quantitative 'tools'.

> In the light of an analysis of the findings of some of the early interviews, and resources permitting, consideration will be given to the potential usefulness of seeking permission to trawl through selected record keeping systems and/or of gaining the cooperation of agencies in data collection exercises tailored specifically to meet the needs of this study. It is anticipated that this will provide the basis for looking at the costs of services provided.

Combining techniques in an informed manner offers the action researcher the opportunity to compensate for the limitations of one with the contributions from another, and to take bearings on the problem under investigation in different ways and from a number of perspectives. In this, action research draws upon ideas about triangulation in research which, as Bromley says in his text on case study method, is:

> a metaphor derived from surveying and navigation. The survey metaphor suggests that particular facts, e.g. about persons,

incidents, or institutional arrangements, can be placed systematically in relation to other facts. The navigational metaphor
suggests that if several independent sources of evidence point
to a common conclusion, then one's confidence in that conclusion is strengthened.

(Bromley 1986: 10)

Smith and Cantley adopt a similar line of argument in their exploration of the issues at stake in evaluating the performance of a day
hospital for elderly people with mental disorders. They argue that:

Evaluative research must pay much more attention to evaluating the ways in which policy is formulated and implemented.
An understanding of these processes is part and parcel of
policy evaluation. The policy as subjectively perceived by
the participants to the policy process is also critical. Moreover
the plurality of perspectives and operating tactics at work
within these processes calls for attention to detail and the
collection of varied data sources as a key feature of evaluative
research.

(Smith and Cantley 1985: 12)

In that the brief for this study specified assessment of 'the
appropriateness and effectiveness of services provided', it necessarily
included activities of evaluation. As we observed in discussion of
the seven distinguishing criteria in Chapter 3, action research
strategies incorporate evaluation alongside enquiry and action as
integral parts of a cyclic process in a context of participatory
problem-solving. It is hardly surprising therefore that the proposal,
couched in terms of action research, recommended a multi-method
approach to data generation and proposed combining 'surveying
through stories' (Graham 1984: 104) with more structured interviewing, collecting statistics, trawling through files and negotiating
understandings in focus groups. It was not, of course, appropriate
for the exact combination or sequence of deployment of such tools
to be specified in advance by researchers reaching independent
conclusions away from the problem site and in isolation from the
research sponsors and participants. To do so would have denied
them the opportunity to collaborate from the outset in key decision-
making about the nature and direction of the research and it would

have placed barriers in the way of creating a shared sense of ownership of the initiative. For action researchers it is essential to facilitate the engagement and cooperation of others, individually and collectively, in the research enterprise and pave the way for the implementation of improvements.

CONCLUSION

In this chapter we have placed a discussion of a research proposal, and the research brief which prompted it, within the context of our action research typology. In discussing some of the key features of the proposed action research strategy, we have highlighted the importance of the underlying value base and of collaborative relationships within a cyclic process aimed at improvement. We have made clear that intervention for change on the part of the researchers began at the point of submitting the proposal and incorporated a recognition of the need to negotiate meanings and to work with groups as well as individuals. In relation to the typology's seven criteria, the proposal is clearly and consistently positioned within the empowering type of action research, and as such it was informed by a conflict model of society and a commitment to work towards change at both the individual and structural levels. In Part II we move beyond the proposal stage to look further at the practice of action research through an examination of five case studies.

Part II

Action research case studies

5

Case study 1
Micro-politics of action
research at a district
general hospital

INTRODUCTION

This is the first of two case studies which consider issues raised by a two-year action research project into the management of change in respect of improving standards of care at a district general hospital. It was a relatively large-scale project, adequately funded by a regional health authority, which I (Elizabeth Hart) discuss from my perspective as project leader, including lessons learned from my mistakes. Over the two years of the project six people were involved in the team: a social anthropologist (myself), an experienced groupworker, a research adviser, a financial consultant, a research assistant (a graduate nurse) and a research secretary. An outside consultant assisted with a two-day workshop for ward sisters and the analysis of questionnaire data. Although I refer throughout to a project 'team', it would be misleading to give the impression that the individuals concerned were organized according to a team model of some formal kind.

As in other insider accounts of research projects of this kind (Shipman 1974; Hickson 1988), I present this as a personal interpretation of events which may have looked very different from the viewpoints of others involved in the project. To paraphrase Hickson, although this is one person's truth, it is not even for me the whole truth, not least because the truth of the project keeps changing as time moves on. Although officially the project came to an end some time ago, the change process it generated has continued beyond the formal deadline and completion of the final research reports. Moreover, whereas half way through the project senior people viewed it as a failure, since then it has been publicly recognized as a success by both the regional health authority which funded it and key figures within the organization.

The project was commissioned by the then regional nursing officer, for whom I had conducted research before, in response to an independent report which had commented unfavourably on standards of nursing care at the district general hospital, specifically in one directorate. The aim of the project was to seek ways of improving standards of care within this directorate by the use of a problem-solving approach, and to extend the outcomes elsewhere to other directorates and other hospitals. More generally, the regional health authority wanted to shift this 'backwater' hospital out of the organizational inertia for which it was apparently well known.

One point about my role as an action researcher is that my training as a social anthropologist meant that it went against the grain to intervene directly in a situation to change it. However, over the course of different research projects I found myself moving towards something akin to an action research approach. I became increasingly uncomfortable with the researcher–research subject relationship, and more concerned to feed back and disseminate findings in order that they might be used by those who were the subjects of the research. Thus the opportunity to undertake action research proper seemed part of an almost natural development towards a more participative way of working.

There follows a seven-phase summary of the two-year project as a reference point for the discussion of issues raised, and the project is then analysed in terms of the action research typology presented in Chapter 3 (Table 3.1). The following sections cover the establishment of the project, relationships with sponsors and problems in engaging senior managers as participants in the process. The final section explores issues around project leadership and researcher roles more generally and concludes with suggestions about how to avoid such problems when setting up similar projects.

THE SEVEN PHASES OF THE ACTION RESEARCH

The action research timetable (Figure 5.1) illustrates that the project unfolded as seven overlapping phases. This was not planned in advance. It became apparent as the project progressed that the change process had its own momentum, which lent itself to the notion of interconnecting phases.

Phase 1: getting the ball rolling

During phase 1, which lasted from early March to mid May, I was involved with my head of department in preliminary discussions with the regional health authority about the possibility of such a project, including drafting a research proposal and negotiating a budget to cover a two-year project and a multi-disciplinary research team. Once the sponsors had agreed to the proposal a meeting was arranged with senior managers at the district general hospital to obtain formal permission and negotiate access. Managers expressed concern that the project would subject them to scrutiny by the regional health authority at a time when they were under great pressure to implement the White Paper reforms (DoH 1989) within a limited timescale, and were also preparing an application to become an NHS trust for approval by the regional health authority. There was also some scepticism about the usefulness of the project, particularly from the clinical director of the directorate where it was hoped to conduct a case study (and who was later to become one of its strongest advocates). Nevertheless, the overall feeling was one of interest in the project.

Phase 2: getting managers on board

The second phase involved exploratory interviews with general managers, clinical directors and senior nurses. During this time I was also seeking openings for the action research within the clinical directorate which was to be the focus of a case study and attending meetings with senior nurses and others to inform them of the action research and gain their cooperation. Thus I was engaged on a number of overlapping tasks which, although they fell within the exploratory research phase, spanned the range between research

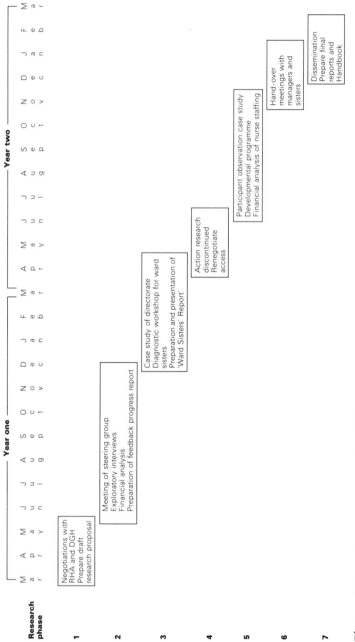

Figure 5.1 Action research timetable

and action. In addition, a parallel project was being conducted by the project's finance consultant into the financial history of the district general hospital. This served as a preliminary to further financial analysis and was intended to add to both the researchers' and the managers' understanding of the organizational context.

There were three setbacks during this time, involving the sudden resignation of the nurse manager with whom I had negotiated collaborative working on problems within the case study directorate, an unanticipated intervention by the sponsors which forced me to abandon a plan of work negotiated with the clinical director of the same directorate, and the death of a close relative. The intervention by the sponsors took the form of initiating the appointment of a nurse as assistant to the clinical director, before the planned research to define the role collaboratively with him, the nursing staff and others had been conducted. Despite these setbacks, over the course of time the exploratory phase was successful in identifying common ground between senior managers, directorate managers and senior ward nurses about what the problems were and in negotiating a plan of action with the action research steering group.[1] The central problem was identified in terms of how to bring about a change in the role of the ward sister to that of ward manager, in line with the requirements of the Resource Management Initiative and in a way which would empower ward sisters to take on the full responsibilities of a G grade post.

Phase 2 began as problem-sensing and research-focused, developing into a more action-focused phase by the time of the presentation of the second progress report to the steering group in December, that is seven months into the project. Not only were a number of issues now on the agenda for discussion but some deeply embedded assumptions on the part of senior managers about the traditional and change-resistant nature of the ward sisters were being challenged by the research findings. During this time good working relations had been established with directorate managers and ward sisters in the case study directorate, including agreement on a collaborative plan of work with the business manager and senior nurse (who unfortunately both left before the work was completed). Collaborative working relationships with managers at unit level were more difficult to establish. Although polite and helpful, unit managers seemed to be keeping the project at arm's length, and did not seem to want to engage with it in any positive way. Nevertheless, by the time of the arrival of the research assistant in early December, which marked the start of the developmental work within the directorate, the groundwork had already been laid for the action phase to unfold.

Phase 3: from celebration to despondency

In phase 3, as a research problem had now been formulated with which all parties seemed willing to identify, the case study of the directorate began. This phase covered a period of four and a half months from December until April. It involved interviews with general managers, senior nurses and ward sisters within the directorate, the administration of an Occupational Stress Indicator (Cooper *et al.* 1988), a two day problem-focused workshop for the fifteen ward sisters and the preparation of a report based on the outcomes of the workshop. This report (known as the 'Ward Sisters' Report') was presented by me on behalf of the ward sisters to a well attended meeting of ward sisters and consultants, including the clinical director. The report was favourably received at directorate level. The meeting evaluated very well and was heralded as a 'new beginning' for the directorate. Consultants and ward sisters reported that following the meeting working relations were much improved. One successful outcome of the meeting was to initiate a dialogue between ward sisters and clinical consultants around issues of common concern in the delivery of care, which continued in the form of regular directorate meetings.

However, the success of this phase, which had been hard won given the setbacks at the beginning, was not to last. In April, after a wait of nearly four and a half months, the 'Ward Sisters' Report' was again presented this time by me and the ward sisters to an invited group of senior managers and directorate managers. The presentation of the report created a crisis similar to that which Robinson (1994) encountered when she presented the findings of research into perinatal mortality, which raised questions about the way some pregnancies were managed. In both her case and mine the validity of the respective findings was denied by senior people. In my case, in not accepting what the sisters were saying, senior managers reacted very differently from those at directorate, level, who endorsed the findings of the 'Ward Sisters' Report'. Among other things, general managers and the senior nurse took exception to the ward sisters' view that the shortage of nursing staff was a long-standing and serious problem. Despite the fact that directorate managers had endorsed this view, there was a reaction of denial from senior managers to the claim that the directorate was working with nurse staffing levels which were bordering on the unsafe, in the professional judgement of the nurse manager and ward sisters. In comparison with the earlier directorate meeting with clinical consultants, which had ended with feelings of goodwill and celebration, this second meeting with senior managers ended in gloom and despondency. When I returned to the hospital to begin the next phase of the project I was asked to cancel future plans. When I departed that day I did not expect to see the hospital again.

Phase 4: getting our breath back

Phase 4 covered a period of just over two months, during which the future of the project was uncertain. Eventually the unit general manager agreed that the project could continue subject to my preparing a new research proposal for the second year of the project, to be approved by the regional health authority and the steering group. After a 'cooling off' period the project resumed, although on a different basis from before since senior managers no longer wished to be directly involved and restricted the case study to one directorate. Permission to extend the case study to another directorate, as had been agreed and prepared for, was withdrawn.

Phase 5: steady progress and recovery

Phase 5 lasted from June until the end of November and proved to be one of the most fruitful phases of the project. The project's momentum had not been dissipated by the negative response of senior managers to the 'Ward Sisters' Report'. The steering group had given permission for the ward sisters' developmental programme to continue, for a participant observation study of two wards by the research assistant and for research by the finance consultant into the way the nurse staffing budget was managed.

Phase 6: handing over and letting go

Phase 6 followed the completion of the ward sisters' developmental programme. It was marked by the sisters' increased participation in meetings with managers and senior nurses about the ward manager role, including at directorate and unit level. The aim of this phase was to enable ward sisters to discuss these issues about the ward manager role with managers in a positive and helpful way, without the direct involvement of the action researchers. The response of managers at senior and directorate level was that the ward sisters seemed to have undergone a radical change in attitude, such that the sisters were now enthusiastic and confident about the changes which were taking place.

Phase 7: withdrawing and moving on

Phase 7 involved a process of withdrawing from the hospital to prepare the final research reports and a handbook for ward sisters. At the final meeting of the steering group (which was not attended by the unit general manager), despite the difficulties half way through the project, the reports were well received by sponsors and managers. The success of the developmental work with ward sisters could not be denied. In addition to a range of initiatives, including some at ward level, that had spun off from the project, the final reports provided managers with insights into how the problems looked from the perspectives of directorate and ward, to which they responded in a positive way. It was noticeable that senior managers seemed to feel a sense of ownership of the outcomes of the project. The project nurse from the regional health authority said publicly that the project had been a success and it was agreed that the findings should be put in the public domain (subject to an agreement not to name the district general hospital).

THREE TYPES OF ACTION RESEARCH

This case study provides a particularly clear illustration of a project which vacillated between three types of action research: the organizational, professionalizing and empowering. As an umbrella term 'action research' masked the existence of different agendas, and obscured recognition of what Ball (1987) has termed the micro-politics of vested interest, self-interest and ideological interest. Here the typology has been helpful retrospectively in recognizing the three different types the project had to contain. The sponsors and senior managers cast the action researchers in a role akin to that of outside management consultants. As in the organizational type, the researchers were expected to work to a managerial change agenda in the interests of enhancing managerial control and engineering behavioural change towards predetermined outcomes and consensus. Senior people did not like the research findings they had requested and blamed me personally for the report. This negative response enhanced the capacity of the action researchers to work in an empowering way with staff at grass roots level, and contributed to the shift to an empowering type of action research in the second year.

The project also contained a professionalizing agenda on the part of senior nurses in terms of reforms such as primary nursing and the change from ward sister to clinical manager. These professional reforms became a point of convergence for the interests of general managers and senior nurses, particularly at times when the momentum of the project was perceived by both groups as shifting the balance of power to staff at ward level. Robinson (1992: 36) has argued that although historically there has been a battle of interests between the professionalizers and employers with respect to the organization of the nursing workforce, with the implementation of primary nursing and the separation of elite nurses at the core of the workforce from other nurses, including part-time at the periphery, the interests of elite nurses and employers appear to be coinciding. However, within the professionalizing type there were also empowering elements, informed by recent arguments about nursing as a gendered occupation and of nurses as an oppressed (female) group (Robinson 1989). This introduced yet another dynamic into the project, since senior nurses also vacillated between the language of professionalization and the rhetoric of an anti-oppressive, empowering approach.

The interplay between the organizational, professionalizing and empowering types was a feature of the project which seemed at times to block progress. Had these different approaches been recognized more clearly at the time and made an explicit part of the change process, it might have been possible to use the tension between them in more creative ways.

SETTING UP THE PROJECT

A feature of this case study was that action research was the choice of the regional health authority which sponsored the project. Why was it that those involved in commissioning the research selected action research as a strategy to manage change, and what did it offer that other approaches did not? Conversations with key people from among the sponsors suggested that long experience of the National Health Service had convinced them that change imposed from above would be subverted by staff at grass roots level. Action research, with its 'bottom-up' philosophy, seemed to promise a means of overcoming such resistance by promoting a sense of ownership and involvement in those most directly affected by the change. Thus the regional health authority took an enlightened position with regard to the choice of approach, including putting high on the agenda that it should be empowering of staff lower down the hierarchy at strategic points in the delivery of care.

The political context may also have influenced the choice of action research. Senior people within the regional health authority were anxious about whether or not the Conservative Party would win the next election and, although there was great pressure from above to rush in the White Paper reforms, the politically sensitive situation made it unwise for them to be seen to use a heavy hand. 'Soft landings' was the popular catch-phrase and the regional health authority did not want the approach to be prescriptive or 'top-down'.

Action research may also have been attractive because the sponsors were not prepared to spend money for which they were publicly accountable on research that would simply produce a research report to languish on a shelf at the regional health authority. In this the sponsors implicitly voiced the concern to improve the dissemination and use of research findings expressed in a Department of Health report entitled *Taking Research Seriously* (Richardson *et al.* 1990).

The sponsors stipulated that they wanted the action research to be generalized to other hospitals as part of the drive for 'value for money', and this was an important consideration throughout the research. The generalizability of research findings was also part of the regional health authority's broader change strategy. If action research could facilitate change in the direction of restructuring the skill mix, empowering staff and generating interdisciplinary cooperation across professional boundaries in a 'backwater' hospital, then the outcomes could be used to pressure the more powerful teaching hospitals to fall into line on the basis that 'if it works there, it will work here'.

The university researchers accepted the action research brief, and indeed I welcomed it as an opportunity to engage participants in such a project, and it was on this basis that the draft research proposal was written. At the time I put to the back of my mind unease about the sponsors seeming to want the researchers to have a free hand in defining the problem while at the same time talking about the problem in terms of needing to dilute the nursing skill mix and break down professional boundaries. To quote Bell and Encel:

> It is not just whether those that pay for the research get what they pay for, but . . . it is not always clear they know what they want. Social scientists all too frequently find themselves in the situation of having to define the objectives of those who hire them and then find themselves blamed for distorting the original objectives of the organisation.
>
> (Bell and Encel 1978: 5)

The impact of the above situation on the drafting of the research proposal was to make it intentionally general with reference to a 'problem of an as yet indeterminate nature'. I phrased it thus to allow the project team room for manoeuvre in defining the problem and wrote specifically for the regional nursing officer and the project nurse. The draft proposal acknowledged the unpredictable nature of action research and the need for a flexible rather than a rigid research design. At this stage the focus was on obtaining permission and funding from the regional health authority. In applying for research funding action researchers face a dilemma: on the one hand the research proposal has to follow certain conventions, including specifying research methods, timescale and structure; on the other hand, action research is not a linear progression towards a predetermined goal, so that an 'action research proposal' is almost a contradiction in terms. In this case, as the change process gathered momentum, the sponsors seemed to use the research proposal to focus the researchers' activities on certain tasks and the production of outcomes, perhaps as a way of constraining change.

I did not assume that the unit general manager's permission to undertake the project at the district general hospital would be automatic, but it was first necessary to gain the approval of the sponsors and this tended to focus all attention on them. However, it was a mistake to assume that the action research proper could start as soon as the formalities of obtaining funding were completed. To my knowledge, no one from the district general hospital was involved in the preparation of the draft proposal, either in terms of contributing to the writing of it or through participation in early discussions with the university researchers and the regional health authority. Yet, as Cohen and Manion point out, the stage of preliminary discussions and negotiations among the interested parties is vital to success:

> This is often the crucial stage [i.e. drawing up a draft proposal] for the venture as it is at this point that the seeds of success or failure are planted, for unless the objectives, purposes and assumptions are made perfectly clear, and unless the role of key concepts is stressed (e.g. feedback), the enterprise can easily miscarry.
>
> (Cohen and Manion 1984: 52)

Although, as mentioned, the regional health authority was acting from an enlightened position in commissioning action research in the first place, it too behaved as if it was a method the researchers would employ once the project had officially started. Even though senior managers at the district general hospital gave their formal permission for the project, it was a mistake for the university researchers to have entered discussions with them about access and the objectives of the research only after the regional health authority had in effect negotiated entry to the organization on our behalf. The extent to which senior managers had felt obliged to agree to the project only became apparent once the exploratory interviews had begun. Over the course of time, as senior managers came to know me better, it became clear that the early meetings I had attended to gain permission and negotiate access with senior managers had been something of a formality, since they had felt under an obligation to cooperate. This helped to explain why it was that senior managers seemed to be holding the project at arm's length. The interview phase then revealed some of the tensions which underlay the setting up of the project and alerted me to their longer-term implications for relationships between managers, sponsors and the research team. The tensions around ownership and control were hard to reconcile and increased as the project gained momentum.

Although the project could not avoid becoming caught up in the subterranean forces that underlay power relations between region and district, it might have been possible to minimize some of the more counterproductive aspects of the hierarchical relationship between region and district by paying attention to its implications from the beginning. This might also have involved more open discussion about the personal interests of the researchers and others in terms of the politics of career (Ball 1987), including recognition that any conflicts between the university researchers and sponsors might have implications for relations between the university department and the regional health authority. Burgess's (1991) experience of projects led him to argue that at the start it is essential to think critically about research sponsorship. He found himself in a similar situation to the one I have described, in that his sponsors opened up some doors (to headteachers), but in doing so closed off others because participants became suspicious of the sponsors' motives. This in turn raised questions about Burgess's independence from the sponsors and, as in my case, fuelled uncertainties about the implications of the project for the work situation of participants.

The tensions outlined above illustrate how important it is to pay attention to the way in which a project is set up and to the political context in which relationships between sponsors, participants and researchers are situated. An action research way of thinking needs to inform the project from the very beginning. Although situations of this kind are not exclusive to action research, they have particular implications where the intention is not simply to understand a problem but to work in a participatory way to bring about improvements.

ENGAGING MANAGERS AS PARTICIPANTS

One of the consequences of the way the project had been established was that it became essential to find a means of engaging managers as participants in it as soon as possible. During the first weeks I sought to identify a problem for the action research which emerged from their concerns, which could be used as a basis for an action plan and as a focus for cooperation between participants, sponsors and researchers. The action plan had to satisfy all parties and form a basis for gaining the cooperation of nursing staff. I thought it vital to the success of the project that a problem focus for the research should be identified which had meaning for both managers and nursing staff, even though they might see the problem differently, and which they would want to own. To do this it was first necessary to engage senior managers in a dialogue about their issues of concern and how they saw the research assisting them with these. The approach I took to problem-solving finds support in the organizational literature. Management researchers Eden *et al.* (1983: x) argue that 'a process of assisting the defining and formulation of a problem is a crucial and often neglected precursor to any attempts to solve it.' Cunningham (1993: 74) has emphasized that the successful identification of problems is at the heart of the action research effort.

My response as an anthropologist to the fraught situation described above was to retreat to the safety of research and to focus on method. This was also a way of asserting my independence as an academic researcher from the sponsors. The research focus expressed itself in the way I went about undertaking in-depth interviews with managers at all levels within the organization as if I was an ethnographer. By the end of phase 2 a substantial amount of data about the history and present situation of the health authority and hospital had been generated, in addition to access being gained to a wide range of individual views about what the problems were.

However, the concentration of my research efforts on the exploration of the problem led to what Robottom and Colquhoun (1993: 57) have referred to as a 'politics of diversion'. Concern with the credibility of the activity as research resulted in the marginalization of major issues, such as the sponsors' underlying political agenda and the potential use of the action researchers as managerial change agents by proxy. Gender issues were never discussed openly, despite the fact that all but one of the action research team were female and the organizational changes were directed mainly at a predominantly female profession. The focus on method also led to the neglect of what, in retrospect, seems obvious: that the uninvited intervention of the action researchers was itself a problem for senior managers. They had to deal not only with the problem of how to implement the government reforms within an almost impossible deadline, but also with the problem of having to negotiate with researchers who wanted to help them (Eden *et al.* 1983). As Robottom and Colquhoun (1993) argue in relation to their own experience as action researchers, 'political issues concerning the methodology were marginalized and/or neglected'. They underline their point by citing Kemmis and DiChiro (1987: 57), who state that action researchers may work in ways which 'treat others as objects of their action' by 'trying to "get" others to "feel ownership" of problems', rather than starting from the point of view of the concerns and problems others already own.

Moreover, in order to have an overview of the research process as a whole I needed to be involved directly in the action research throughout the two years of the project, so I needed to undertake fieldwork rather than relying on what Porter (1994) has termed 'second-hand ethnography'. Without this overview it would have been very difficult to define tasks for the two research consultants, to integrate the research assistant's individual agenda into the goals of the action research and to relate appropriately to the university-based research adviser. The tension between the goals of the client and of the academic community, between action and research, is a familiar theme in the literature. In a classic paper Rapoport (1970: 505) referred to the tensions between the goals of social science and those of action as a 'goal dilemma' and as one of the three dilemmas of action research (the other two being ethical dilemmas and the dilemmas of initiative). However, in this case the 'goal dilemma' was compounded by the conflict of interests between sponsors and senior managers. Despite their espoused preference for 'action', the sponsors were as concerned with the research as quality research and with the academic credibility of the project as were the university researchers.

During the early phases the project was contained within the limits of the organizational type, with some overlap with the professionalizing type. When it became apparent that this research strategy was not working in the way I had envisaged, my position shifted from one of negotiation to one of challenge. I used my increasing knowledge of what was happening at directorate and ward level to question senior managers' view of their organizational reality and to try to get them to respond to what the project was trying to do. Out of sheer frustration with their apparent lack of interest I shifted from doing research *for* them to researching *on* them. Had this shift been part of a more conscious move to an empowering way of working it might have been possible to highlight problems of shared concern to the different groups involved, while also taking account of differences between them in the way the problems were perceived.

Although I have referred to the early phases of the project as a 'retreat into research', in action research it is not possible to keep research and action phases apart. As Halsey (1972: 175) observed over twenty years ago, whether intentionally or not, research creates 'action situations'. In this case the process of conducting the interviews established alliances between individuals and groups at a range of points throughout the organization, including at senior management level. The exploratory phase, which culminated in the presentation of a progress report to senior managers and others who had participated in interviews, put issues on the agenda for discussion and raised awareness of what the problems were. In particular it identified a difference of viewpoint between managers at unit and directorate level about the problem of nurse staffing levels, such that it became a live issue.

In the next section I move on to consider briefly problems of how my role and that of others in the team were defined, and conclude by suggesting ways in which such problems might be minimized in future projects.

DEFINING TEAM ROLES AND WORKING TOGETHER

Although as project leader I was accountable to the regional nursing officer and project nurse for the project's success I was not the most senior person in the team, and neither was I a nurse, nor indeed a health care professional of any kind. My position was non-aligned. As a lecturer in an academic department, I occupied a position on the margins of the nursing profession, while leading a project which aimed to bring about improvements in the quality of health care. 'Above' me there were the project nurse from the regional health authority, the regional nursing officer who commissioned the action research and became involved in it from time to time and, as research adviser, my head of department. The reality of the situation was that it was my head of department who was ultimately accountable for the expenditure of grant money and the way I spent my time. My role was ambiguous. In many respects it was akin to what Hunter (1990) terms an 'interface manager', positioned at the intersection of a range of competing interests and professional boundaries with all of the tensions that implies.

Cox *et al.* (1978) discuss the issue of role definition from their experience as research consultants on a project exploring Australian attitudes to sexuality and sex roles for a Royal Commission on Human Relations. They argue that had their roles been more clearly defined and the Commission clearer about whether they were employed as consultants with subject expertise or as experts in research techniques (or both), this would have removed the cause of many of the difficulties they were to encounter, as well as easing the problems they presented to the Commission and to others in the research team. Cox *et al* also observe that the higher the status of the researcher within his or her profession the less of a problem does role definition become for him or her personally, since 'professors and readers are eminent enough for them to define their own role in relation to projects without being questioned' (Cox *et al*. 1978: 140). This suggests that, as in my case, the issue of role definition may be far more of a problem for lower status individuals in a research team who are less able to do anything to change the situation. So it may be especially important, when working with vulnerable groups and/or in project teams which encompass inequalities in class, gender, status and race, that particular attention is paid to the issue of role definition for all team members.

LEARNING FROM EXPERIENCE

Were I to take on a similar role in an action research project again, what kinds of changes would be desirable? It is essential to discuss and agree with sponsors beforehand the responsibilities and decision-making capacities of the project leader role and the degree of direction and influence it might involve both on a day-to-day basis and, strategically, in the longer term. This needs to take place in relation to discussion about the purpose(s) of the project and the reasons underlying the choice of methodology, and in terms of identifying stakeholders and making their interests as explicit as possible. The project leader role needs to be defined in relation to clients, sponsors and other team members, including identifying named individuals from among the sponsors to whom the project leader would be accountable. The scope of that accountability would need to be agreed, including recognition that the researchers cannot easily work from a position of independence if they feel reliant on the funders and/or sponsors for their professional reputations or careers.

It is also important to agree contingency plans to cover situations where key figures move on during the life of the project. This might involve an agreement that a departing manager hands over his or her part of the project to a successor, perhaps in the form of a progress report, and ensures as far as possible that commitments are carried forward. (This project was bedevilled by the rapid turnover of middle managers and other key individuals who were involved in the project, including two business managers and four nurse managers).

In such projects it is also essential to define group boundaries, including those of the project team, and to be prepared to renegotiate them as the project moves forward. Relative roles and responsibilities need to be clearly defined, including who is in overall charge of the project. It also needs to be recognized that the roles of other team members might change over the life of the project and cannot be fixed for all time. A process needs to be agreed about how these fluid roles are to be coordinated and links established between the project leader, the core team and other teams or groups which might spiral from it as the project goes forward. In respect of senior people operating on the periphery of the team it is important for them to recognise that they are not free agents, pursuing their own individual change agendas under the umbrella of action research. Such individuals need to respect the goals and aims of the project and, in common with others, work within negotiated, and re-negotiable, ground rules.

These requirements would seem to suggest that all members of the team, and especially the project leader, need to be skilled at interface management, including working across professional boundaries. A key task is the integration of different initiatives (Geddes *et al.* 1993). Experience suggests that a feature of action research, or indeed any projects in the complex settings of health and social care, is that they require multi-disciplinary cooperation. This includes such groups as accountants, managers, nurses and social workers, 'creating a web of links and contacts between individuals in order to get things done' (Geddes *et al.* 1993: 32). It is to be expected that professionals may operate from different positions which will include different values, interests, occupational histories and ways of working with users. Thus it is important that individuals work from an awareness of position, and attempt as far as possible to maintain a consistency of approach. As discussion of this case study has shown, it contained at least three different action research types, each with a different approach. Had these been more clearly recognized at the time it might have been possible to find a means of integrating them and identifying a point of convergence for the different interests and agendas. Integration and coordination are the essential craft skills of project leadership.

Oja and Smulyan (1989) have suggested that within an action research team contributions may usefully be differentiated into being primarily task or maintenance related. While some team members may initiate important elements of the project, some may perform maintenance functions by supporting others and facilitating communication within the team and between the team and other groups. They further argue: 'Although most people on an action research team will take on a combination of task and maintenance roles, at certain points in the process we may see individuals fulfilling specific functions in the group. Individual roles will change during the project as the team faces the different interpersonal and tasks demands' (Oja and Smulyan 1989: 146). The action research team of which Oja and Smulyan were members moved through a five-phase process, which they argue paralleled the process undergone by problem-solving groups, from negotiating research and group boundaries in phase 1, to evaluating the process and project in phase 5.

The organizational literature relating to project management and the management of change more generally reinforces some of the above points, and in particular the need to manage projects through a series of episodes and cycles of shift and development, and to see change as a process rather than a single event (Easton 1982; Haynes 1989; Pettigrew and Whipp 1991; Geddes *et al.* 1993); to expend time and effort in problem definition and the setting of goals (Eden *et al.* 1983; Cunningham 1993); and to seek practical ways of minimizing competition and maximizing cooperation within project teams, such as agreeing beforehand ground rules about shared authorship of reports and publications (Hickson 1988).

A number of factors identified as influential within this account have been found to affect the outcomes of social research, whether or not it is action research (Halsey 1972; Haas and Shaffir 1973; Platt 1976; Cox *et al.* 1978; Hickson 1988; Porter 1994). Role definition and boundary management seem to be important factors in influencing the success or otherwise of projects. Cox *et al.* found that in their experience conflicts and problems can arise when different members of the research team have different definitions of their roles and those of others.

In action research it would seem that, although the problems of role definition are similar to those in other research enterprises, they may be rendered more problematic by the need to redefine roles and relationships throughout the life of the project as it shifts through different phases and types. However, these problems are not exclusive to action research. Reflecting on their experiences of traditional fieldwork Haas and Shaffir (1973: 244) argue that: 'The interactional, situational, and ever-changing character of fieldwork roles and relationships militates against the development of exact procedures.' They argue that working as a team and establishing relationships with other researchers and gatekeepers involves continuous processes of establishing and maintaining relationships by negotiating and renegotiating. In relation to an action research approach this argument would be supported by Prout's (1992) more recent work, in which he too underlines the need for renegotiation of roles, group boundaries and relationships throughout the life of a project.

Attention to process may involve ensuring that hierarchical structures from one context – such as, in this case, that of a university department – are not carried over inappropriately to the action research context. The problem might be similar for insider researchers working within a multi-professional team, who might find that there is a need to redefine their roles and relationships as action researchers, breaking free of embedded hierarchies, before being able to move a project forward. This needs to be done in the early stages, and account should be taken throughout the project of the importance of rethinking and renegotiating roles and relationships.

CONCLUSION

To others in a similar situation to the one in which I found myself, whether working from a university base or from within the health and social care services, I suggest that the pressure to obtain funding and/or approval for a project should not mean that potentially difficult preliminary negotiations with sponsors, clients, gatekeepers and other researchers are deferred, or avoided, until the project is formally set up. Establishing such agreements is to the advantage of all parties concerned. Moreover, if sponsors and others are not prepared to enter into this kind of discussion at the opening of a project, then what chance is there to realize an action research approach of any kind during its life? Setting up agreements and keeping them under review is part of the process of action research but it would be misleading to suggest that it is ever easy or straightforward. Nevertheless, there is a political life about working in projects which the action researcher ignores at his or her peril. What such opening negotiations do is to recognize and deal with the politics of projects in a creative and constructive way, rather than leaving them to fester and become counterproductive. This way of working with people recognizes that change is not something that action researchers do to participants, but that the members of the project team are themselves participants in the change process, and subject to change and development over the life of the project.

NOTE

1 The steering group consisted of representatives from senior management and from the regional health authority, the clinical director and senior nurse from the case study directorate and the action researchers. In effect the steering group was an extension of the management board, the role of which was to consider and approve progress reports and action plans. It is usual in research projects funded from government sources to have a steering group of a similar kind.

6

Case study 2
From sister to manager – empowerment through a staff development programme

INTRODUCTION

This is the second of two case studies into the management of change in respect of standards of care at a district general hospital, funded by a regional health authority and conducted by a team of six university-based researchers. The first case study, in Chapter 5, presented an overview of central issues over the two years of the project. It described the way the project was established and discussed issues of engaging managers in the action research, and roles and relationships within the team, and suggested ways in which certain problems might be avoided in future projects. This second case study focuses on a smaller project within the larger one, which was interdependent and yet had a life of its own. As such it illustrates the notion of cyclic process and of the spiralling off of one project from another which action researchers explicitly recognize as part of the change process (Kemmis *et al.* 1982; Carr and Kemmis 1986) . It is written from the perspective of the two facilitators, one the project leader and the other an experienced groupworker, who worked in partnership during this phase (Elizabeth Hart and Meg Bond).

The material included in this case study is not written as an all-embracing definitive text for 'doing' this kind of staff development. There are, for example, substantial literatures on developing management skills and on groupwork practices, for therapeutic and educational purposes, which have informed this work and for which this chapter serves as an introduction. References for further reading are provided at the end of the 'Groupwork guidelines' in Chapter 10.

The staff development programme that is the focus of this case study grew out of earlier exploratory work, which had identified an unmet need among a key group of thirteen sisters and two charge nurses within the directorate that was the subject of the change initiative. The project leader was able to deploy the project's resources to support the programme, both financially and by bringing in a specialist groupworker as a co-researcher. The developmental programme was not separate from what had gone before, or from other action research initiatives running in parallel within the directorate, which included an analysis of the management of the nurse staffing budget by the project's finance consultant, and an ethnographic study by the research assistant of the perceptions of change at ward level.

One of the practical aims of this case study is to offer an introduction to, and a demystification of, a process of staff development which builds on the skills and resources of professional groups and enables them to take control of meeting their learning needs, with appropriate support from their organization. A related aim is to look critically at such a process of staff development by raising questions about the extent to which it may be counterproductive to embark on such collective projects, to establish arenas of empowerment among groups lower down the hierarchy, when these may come into conflict with an individualistic and autocratic organizational culture. This is a crucial issue for any change agent about to embark on such a project and, as Pasmore and Friedlander's (1982) account illustrates, can be a classic dilemma faced by any action researcher who attempts to work in a participatory way with less powerful groups to solve organizational problems. In turn the dilemma for corporate managers can be, as this project showed, that on the one hand collective ways of working on problems may be successful where top-down approaches have failed, and yet on the other hand their very success threatens the established pattern of power relationships between managers and workers. Our experience suggests that one organizational response to the success of such projects in empowering staff groups is to institutionalize them, so that they become incorporated into the status quo. Nevertheless, we conclude that despite these limitations such projects open up the possibility of managers and staff groups working together on problems, and this includes working through conflicts that arise as part of the process. We would also argue that the success of the work described in this case study reinforces the view that an instrumental focus on outcome may not be the best way of bringing about change, and may even be counterproductive in cutting off lines of development and limiting the range of possible solutions.

The outcome of the programme was that the different groups involved – sisters,[1] managers, sponsors and researchers – defined it as a success. For the sisters it enabled them to influence the future direction of events and experience the empowerment that comes through collective working. For senior managers it overcame what they saw as the immediate problem of the sisters' resistance to becoming ward managers and, in the longer term, led to an improvement in working relationships between the two groups. For the sponsors it vindicated their belief that action research could be effective in bringing about change through the empowerment of staff groups, and in unblocking organizational inertia more generally. For us as action researchers the programme represented all that is best in groupwork as a vehicle for change and development. Although at the beginning the majority of the sisters had been against the ward manager idea, by the end of the eight-week programme all were so positive about it and confident in their approach to change that their managers admitted to being pleasantly surprised. In situations where before they would have been daunted, the newly confident sisters were able to discuss the ward manager job description in a critical yet positive way even with senior managers. Using their considerable management experience and their understanding of the local context they identified problematic aspects of their new role and generated realistic suggestions for improvement.

BACKGROUND

The action researchers started work with the ward sisters during the early part of phase 3 (Figure 5.1), at which time the group was composed of nine ward sisters, three night sisters, one sister from a department, one from a day hospital and one staff nurse 'acting up'; that is, fifteen sisters in all. The inclusion in the programme of sisters from one directorate only was intentional on the researchers' part and was welcomed by the sisters. One of the aims was to redefine the group's boundary as a first step in breaking down the 'us' and 'them' divisions between day and night sisters, which the directorate's nurse manager and the ward sisters had identified as having negative effects on patient care.

However, by the time of the developmental programme in phase 5, such was the state of flux among the group that the number of ward sisters had been reduced from nine to five (all women) and out of the original group of fifteen, four had moved to different posts within the organization, including a demotion, and three to temporary posts in research, training and management respectively. We now worked with a group of fourteen, only five of whom were ward sisters. Action researchers typically find, especially in nursing, that they are working with changing groups of participants, which can create difficulties in terms of commitment and continuity over time (Meyer 1993; Sparrow and Robinson 1994). In this case there was no lessening of commitment to the project on the sisters' part, but they were conscious that these changes, which disrupted long-standing relationships, were breaking up the original peer group as key individuals were 'picked off'.

The purpose of the programme was to explore problems and issues around the proposed change to the ward manager role, including the implications for night sisters of those on days taking twenty-four hour responsibility for their wards. During this time we both worked in close collaboration with the sisters. A problem-solving approach was taken, centred on the sisters' concerns, which took account of them as members of the local community, as individuals with financial responsibilities for their families and as nursing professionals with commitments to their patients and their organization. We did not draw a rigid distinction between 'home' and 'work', and theoretically our approach was informed by recent work by labour historians and feminist sociologists on women, work and family (Hareven 1982; Grieco and Whipp 1984; Pollert 1981; Westwood 1984; L. Hart 1991).

As mentioned in case study 1, the impact (albeit unplanned) of these events was to shift the project from an organizational type to an empowering type. The general problem of the changing role of the ward sister remained the same, but the ward sisters' perspective became increasingly influential as the project moved away from an organizational type. After all, the problem was of immediate concern to the ward sisters and the developmental programme encouraged sisters to own it. This changing focus towards the empowering type was reflected in the changing role of the researchers, who worked with the ward sisters as co-researchers. We did not present ourselves as outside experts but as facilitators wishing to work collaboratively with the group of sisters on their common interests. The approach drew on community development in the way it worked collaboratively with sisters to define the problems and in its perception of them as a bonded group sharing interests in common as members of the same profession, community, hospital and directorate (Graham 1991). Throughout the programme their professional experience and status were recognized and the process also validated their growing awareness of themselves as a marginalized group within the organization.

THE ORGANIZATIONAL CONTEXT

A feature of the managerial culture in this setting was that it was individualistic and competitive. The organization seemed to be dominated by rival interest groups in competition for territory and professional control. Cross-cutting these was rivalry between general managers and nurse managers over which professional group was to control the nursing workforce, and overlaid on to this was the division into clinical directorates and the split between purchasers and providers. One of the early project progress reports had identified individualism as a problem, and highlighted the need for managers to consider how it might be possible to integrate a range of different endeavours, including the action research. Later on, a progress report towards the end of the first year had concluded that one of the main generators of change, as far as the action researchers could see, was the individual career ambitions of managers, including in particular business managers and those at middle management level. A senior manager described the corporate management style as 'managed conflict', with the stated intention of managers at the centre being to introduce assertive change agents, such as young business managers, into directorates to challenge what they perceived as the inertia of the nursing profession, especially at middle management and sister level.

General managers were almost evangelical in their desire to change what they described as the 'traditional culture' among nurses and other professional groups by breaking down professional boundaries, and yet paradoxically were protective of their own professional territory and status. Senior nurses too were critical of the traditionalist and culture-bound practices of the nursing staff, particularly of ward sisters. Despite the tensions between general and nurse managers, and particularly between senior nurses and young business managers, there was a convergence of interests around the need to reorganize the nursing workforce and to move towards 'team nursing' (Robinson 1992).

The situation seemed characteristic of what has been termed the 'new managerialism' in the NHS, which as Spurgeon and Barwell (1991) argue involves an increase in control at the centre and individual accountability reinforced by performance appraisals. These three in combination tend to create an environment in which organizational relationships are vertical rather than horizontal, and where: 'The general manager's dilemma lies in balancing the desire to achieve organizational results using tighter organizational controls whilst recognizing the danger that these control strategies themselves are likely to stifle the dynamic flow of formal and informal information which is vital for ensuring responsiveness of the organization to new change initiatives' (Spurgeon and Barwell 1991: 83).

Understandably, in this context the action researchers were perceived as another rival interest group. As project leader Elizabeth Hart had felt constrained to conform to these cultural norms by acting at times in a more individualistic way than she believed appropriate for an action researcher, because she was under constant pressure to prove to senior managers and those funding the research that the programme was being effective and giving 'value for money'. In this context it was important for her and the project nurse from the regional health authority that particular changes could be shown to be attributable to intervention by the action researchers. This situation put the emphasis on outcome rather than process, and created a tension between the empowering and process-led style of the ward sisters' developmental programme and the hierarchical and outcome-driven style of the organization. This may be a dilemma for anyone in the role of change agent who works in an organizational context which rewards individual performance and yet which professes to espouse 'bottom-up' change and empowerment.

The developmental programme emerged from earlier problem-solving work with the group of sisters during phase 3, which culminated in the presentation of a report to senior managers. Among other issues, including high stress levels within the group of ward sisters and poor communication between senior managers and the 'shop floor', the sisters had identified short staffing and an inappropriate skill mix with a reliance on bank and agency nurses as a major and long-standing problem within their directorate. In contrast to the response from managers (including clinical consultants) at directorate level, the report was not well received by senior managers and created something of a furore, following which the action research was discontinued subject to renegotiation of access to the hospital and agreement on a new research proposal with senior managers and the regional health authority. Although this situation was particularly stressful for the sisters, it served to strengthen their resolve to work together as a group with the researchers to take things forward. In this they had the support of their nurse manager, who protected the sisters' study days by arranging cover, which was essential to the success of the programme. As action researchers our intention was to work in a participatory way with the sisters, but as Greenwood *et al.* (1993: 176) have argued, it is impossible to impose participation on research processes. In their experience participation increases over the life of a project 'as a dynamic response to emergent possibilities', and may be enhanced even under seemingly hostile conditions.

PAYING ATTENTION TO PROCESS AND WORKING IN A PARTICIPATORY WAY

Although the developmental programme was organized around the problem of how to bring about the change from ward sister to ward manager, this did not mean that the outcome was prescribed in advance. As action researchers working within a participatory framework, we saw the process rather than the outcome as important. The process needed to be led by what the sisters wanted and not by what the researchers or managers decreed. This is not to say that outcomes were to be ignored. We knew, as did the sisters, that there was an interest in replacing the ward sister role with that of ward manager. We suspected, as they did, that once the district general hospital became a hospital trust they might find themselves in the position of having to apply for their own jobs but under the new title of 'ward manager'. We also knew that managers held the view that, with two exceptions, these sisters were not 'ward manager animals'.

We did not accept that the only successful outcome would be a group conversion to the ward manager role. At the end of the eight weeks the sisters might feel that, after exploring the issues, they were even less inclined to take it on than before. In our terms this would have been as successful an outcome as any other. We did not see it as appropriate to act as surrogate personnel managers or to 'do a public relations job' for the ward manager role. Looking critically at the issue from different perspectives, we recognized some of the inherent opportunities and problems in the proposed change, including an increase in responsibility and workload for these sisters, and a lack of training and support generally within the organization.

One of our major concerns was that the change from sister to manager would be rushed through by managers eager to make their mark (three weeks was one timetable proposed to us by the previous business manager). Experience had taught us that what was needed was a course of training linked to a realistic action plan for change. An important part of our role was to negotiate with senior nurses and the business manager to buy time for the ward sisters' developmental programme, and to arrive at an understanding that there were long-standing problems which needed to be tackled if the sisters were to have the opportunity of moving forward. This process would take time. This was also part of the educative role of the change agent. We wanted to explore with the sisters what they felt they needed from a training programme. However, without an understanding of what was involved in being a ward manager the sisters were unable to say what kind of training they might need. One of the underlying aims of the developmental programme was to help them to think this through.

Our approach to the developmental work was an outcome of the earlier phases of the project. It had been observed that the sisters' new nurse manager, who genuinely wanted to support and empower them, became frustrated and disillusioned when they seemed unable to respond to her requests to tell her what they wanted in the ward manager job description and what training they would like. In turn the sisters felt that they were being asked to make important decisions about their future role without having the information or understanding on which to base those decisions. How could they know what was involved? We learnt from this that even with the best of intentions, nurses and managers had become locked into a cycle of disappointment and distrust. This reinforced stereotypes, on the one side that of the manager with hidden agendas, and on the other of the ward sister resistant to change. One of the invisible benefits of the action research was to intervene in this impasse in a way which unblocked it. It enabled the sisters to identify what they had to give to the ward manager role, what it was realistic for them to expect in return, and what they needed from a training programme to meet their own requirements and those of the organization. Given the high cost of such a training programme, and the even higher costs for patient care of failure, developmental work of the kind we describe here is an essential first step in setting up such a programme as part of the change process.

THE SISTERS AS CO-RESEARCHERS AND CO-CHANGE AGENTS

In the event the sisters were fully committed to the programme to the extent of collecting data and undertaking small-scale projects to bring back to the weekly sessions. Far from using the time as a 'moaning session' they grasped the opportunity and put all their efforts into it. Our guiding belief was in the sisters' ability to find their own route through the impending changes rather as Australian Aborigines find their way through the desert (Key 1986). This meant that there was no need to impose a route on them or be anxious if the group appeared to be heading off in the wrong direction or even seemed to be going backwards. The sisters' knowledge of their local context, of the hospital in which they worked and of their patients and staff far exceeded anything we could offer. But we could act as fellow travellers encouraging them to pool their knowledge and experience and to think critically and creatively about their situation and the proposals for change. On occasion we also acted as honest brokers between the group and their managers to promote the sharing of information.

As the developmental work continued outside the one day a week formally set aside for study days, a great deal of ground was covered during the eight weeks and what happened in the time between was as important as what happened during the sessions. The sisters generated a substantial amount of data through their activities as researchers while on their wards, and as critical thinkers during the study days. For example, they used simple work study techniques to analyse their current workloads, noting down the time taken for activities like 'carrying the bleep' that would normally escape quantification, recording everyday events in a more systematic way than usual.

Though the work was small in scale, taking only eight working days over the two-month period, the pace of change during this time was nevertheless rapid. The eight weeks were intense and dynamic, and the experience represented for all of us, researchers and sisters alike, all that is best in groupwork. Several factors contributed to the success of the project. The programme was based upon a commitment to group processes as a vehicle for learning and change. Staff in similar situations were brought together to share their knowledge and resources. The aim was both to enhance their understanding and to develop some ways to move forward in relation to the proposed changes in staff roles. Such a process aimed to validate members' perceptions of their problems and generate confidence in their own abilities to identify and implement solutions. At a time of change and uncertainty, the developmental programme was designed to enhance their self-esteem in a setting which was safe and unthreatening. By working with a peer group of sisters, it was possible for us to capitalize on existing relationships between colleagues to form a reference point and support system which could continue beyond the last formal session.

THE DEVELOPMENTAL PROGRAMME: EMBARKING

Clearly there are costs in running such a programme, chief among which is the release of, and provision of cover for, staff throughout the life of the group. Staff needed to give a commitment to attend all sessions and to be enabled to do so by their managers. We took on a facilitative and helping role in relation to the sisters, which freed them from having to spend time on the practicalities. Many staff groups embarking on such a programme would probably benefit from such outside support, as well as from the sense of security associated with having appropriately skilled persons available to help them through the process. Suitable candidates for such a role may be a nursing colleague from a different unit or another health care professional. Clinical psychologists, health promotion staff and social workers are often experienced group workers, as are nurses with experience in counselling, although it is unlikely that someone in a line management relationship with any or all of the participants would be able to fulfil this role appropriately. Staff might wish to make a bid to their training department for the services of facilitators. Participating in such an exercise could enable some group members subsequently to become facilitators for others embarking on a similar journey.

MAKING THE JOURNEY

The short extracts which follow are from the material that emerged during the eight one day sessions. The extracts included here give a flavour of the sessions, which may be helpful to anyone planning to undertake a similar programme in his or her own organization.

As mentioned, the developmental work was to focus on the

sisters' changing role. With the agreement of the participants an outside facilitator, skilled in groupwork, was introduced to the group. The two facilitators (who were also co-researchers) took on tasks such as arranging the study days, taking and writing up notes and promoting the discussion. As part of the process of negotiating ground rules it was agreed that anything said within the group would be confidential. In practice, this did not mean that the sisters were silenced when they went to work the next day. As professionals, they were able to distinguish between what was private to the group and what could be discussed in a general way.

THE SETTING

As part of the strategy of giving group members time out to take stock and develop their thinking, arrangements were made to meet over a period of eight Thursdays from 9.30 a.m. to 4.30 p.m. in a room in a pub. Tea and a midday meal were provided, the latter in the dining room used by the public. We wanted the group to feel that they were being looked after in a safe environment, that they were valued for themselves, able to 'recharge their batteries', and were free of incoming demands from their work bases. The conversations which passing members of the public struck up with different ward sisters in the course of eating their midday meals acted as reminders that these staff were well known, highly respected and much valued members of the local community.

THE SESSIONS

Day 1

Since all the members of the group, except the second facilitator, had taken part in an earlier programme, introductions were kept to a minimum and the new researcher was welcomed to the group. The first half of the day was spent in exploring plans for the forthcoming sessions, and reviewing developments on the hospital nurse management front since members had last met. This part of the session allowed sisters to pool their knowledge, to fill information gaps and to check on their individual interpretations of events as the first stage in developing a shared understanding of their situation.

This exchange of ideas quite rapidly led members to focus on a particular aspect of their present roles, namely the way in which as first line managers they frequently found themselves 'acting up' for senior colleagues. The assumption of this onerous and often poorly recognized responsibility was symbolized by 'carrying the bleep'. Members felt that a more detailed look at what this meant for the future in terms of time and interruptions would be helpful. It would allow them to consider an aspect of the more senior managerial role for which as ward sisters they already assumed considerable responsibility. They therefore set themselves some 'homework' (as the group jokingly referred to it) and decided to keep a 'bleep diary' in the course of one shift in the forthcoming week. The sisters worked out how between them they would cover a range of shifts and how they would record their material. The intention was to pool their accounts the next time they met in order to build up a picture of what this aspect of their work entailed.

Before leaving they asked the two facilitators to take on chairing and scribing roles (writing up notes etc). One sister confided that she had said to herself at the start of the day that if it turned into a 'moaning session' she wouldn't come again. But now she felt that they had 'gone through' that stage and looked forward to the next time.

Day 2

As on the first day, group members began with some updating of each other on the week's news. Everyone enjoyed this and found it helpful; thus it became the way of starting each day's work. The sisters shared their experiences of 'acting up' during the week, which they had recorded in their 'bleep diaries'. This included a detailed account which showed that coping with these additional senior management tasks accounted for two hours eleven minutes out of a seven hour period. The group then turned its attention to a discussion of the change from sister to ward manager and laid out an agenda for the next few sessions, agreeing to:

- keep some diaries to form the basis for a discussion of the essential elements of a sister's role to be retained within that of a ward manager;
- find out more about how others fulfil these new roles and what their job descriptions said;
- think about the role of night sisters if day sisters were to become ward managers;
- find out more about budgets.

For their 'homework' the sisters decided to think carefully about those elements of their role which they thought essential to good patient care and good ward management.

Day 3

The first part of the day included a discussion of a meeting to be held some weeks hence to discuss the ward manager role with senior managers, for which the sisters wanted to be prepared. They then considered the implications of 'carrying the bleep', leading them to recognize how frequently work associated with this impinged on them and how often they had to make fast managerial decisions with little room for manoeuvre and few staff to delegate to. Each then went through her list of current ward activities and the new ward manager job description was analysed and discussed in detail. Towards the end of the day group members identified the task for the following week, moving on to the topic of 'ward sisters as budget holders'.

Day 4

Sisters arrived at this session with much news to exchange and discuss. The announcement of major job losses combined with reports from a national political party conference caused them to consider the interrelationships between unemployment and ill-health, and between the state of the economy and the level of health care provision. Well aware that their own health authority was awaiting news of its bid for trust status, the sisters articulated a wide-ranging grasp of the political and economic realities which influence both the demand for health care and the supply of nursing and other services.

In the previous week, at the request of their nurse manager, the sisters had been given a draft job description for a ward manager. This led the group temporarily to set to one side their planned work on budget holding in order to continue the previous week's more broadly based discussion of the role of sisters as ward managers. They paid particular attention to the interface between their tier of the hierarchy and that of senior managers. Looking forward to a directorate meeting to discuss the ward manager role, the group, after a break for lunch, decided that they would spend the afternoon working on communication skills. They wanted to be able to put in a positive way their case for preserving aspects of the ward sister's role, which they valued, so that their views might be included in any senior management proposals for a ward manager's job description.

Days 5 and 6

Two subjects dominated the early exchanges: the government's decision to grant the health authority trust status as from the beginning of the next financial year, and a series of acute staffing shortages during the previous days, causing the levels of 'senior cover' and 'pairs of hands' to drop below levels the sisters considered acceptable. But the group quickly became task-focused and began to go through the material which members had collected.

Allowing plenty of time for discussion, especially of areas where views differed, the group made slow but steady progress in reaching a consensus on the first few items of the proposed job description before agreeing that the discussion should be extended into the following week's session. In addition, members were given copies to read of some articles on different models of ward management. It was decided that the write-up of sessions 5 and 6 should be combined into a paper entitled 'Some questions and answers', which one of the facilitators was asked to prepare for discussion at the seventh session. The paper was drafted accordingly and included items such as the following;

Item 6: The ward manager will continually review staffing levels and make recommendations to the senior nurse manager to ensure that service provision reflects the needs of the patient and available resources.

In order to take this on:

- staffing levels must be increased;
- the ward manager must be satisfied that staffing levels are satisfactory;
- she or he must have more control over staff deployment in order to respond flexibly but not exploitatively;
- she or he must understand the ways in which the budget can be used;
- she or he should be provided with a breakdown of staffing costs per hour;
- she or he should fully understand the terms and conditions under which staff are employed.

Day 7

Beginning this session by reading through the drafted paper, members confirmed that it accurately reflected their thinking. They also recognized that such documentation enabled one or two colleagues who had been absent through illness to remain in touch with the group's thinking and progress. They had found the articles previously distributed by the facilitators helpful in making links between their situation and initiatives being developed elsewhere in the country.

The session finished with a discussion of what it feels like to be caught up in the widespread changes which were currently going ahead. The sisters recognized that their earlier apprehension was beginning to give way to an acknowledgement that in many respects they were already functioning as accomplished ward managers. To have more freedom to do this even better was perhaps not so much a threat as an opportunity and a challenge.

Day 8

The first half of the day was given over to a presentation by the invited G grade sister, who had been a new-style ward manager for three years. The group drew upon their earlier work to raise many issues ranging from lines of accountability and budgetary responsibilities to the availability of training and support. Staffing matters were discussed in some detail, including the role of F grade night sisters and the use of bank and agency staff.

Winding down, members looked back over the achievements of the group and committed themselves to finding ways of continuing to work together. They had valued highly the trust and mutual support which they had experienced at the sessions and this had spilled over into their other working hours. They had discovered skills and resources among themselves which they could make good use of in the future. The sisters planned an informal follow-up and a briefing session prior to their forthcoming meeting with senior managers. They had identified some good practices to help them in handling their changing role, and as they said their goodbyes there was a sense of optimism in the air.

ISSUES RAISED

The above account of the programme raises a number of issues of general relevance to this kind of collaborative change initiative. Within this supportive context the sisters came to realize that there was a possibility of them influencing events, which in itself made them less distrustful of senior managers and more confident about the proposed change to their role. Robottom and Colquhoun (1993: 59) argue that there may come a time when participants seek to take control of the research and direct it towards their own agenda, recognizing it as a means for their empowerment. It was certainly true in our case that empowerment emerged from collective work and was not something that the researchers did to the ward sisters. It was only when the sisters realized that they were in a position to influence the direction of the programme and focus on issues of immediate concern to them that they were able to shift from entrenched positions, move forward and take ownership of the problem. Our role was not to have separate and independent views, nor to shore up the sisters' views of their situation, but to challenge assumptions, encourage critical thinking and provide the sisters with such things as articles, contacts and outside speakers. This included offering them alternative ways of viewing their situation rather than imposing our view of what the problems were. We thought in terms of a 'research' problem not as something separate from and outside the group we were working with, but as something generated by them in reflecting on their own experiences.

In any project which involves the establishment of a research relationship between researcher and participants, it is important to avoid the possibility that the friendship which may have developed is not used unwittingly to oblige participants to collaborate, as Meyer (1993) suggests may have been the case in her action research project with ward nurses. Facilitators too need to take account of the fact that they may be co-opted on to the side of the participants, and that their ability to work as a helper from a stance of independence may thus be undermined. In our case a great deal of the first session was spent discussing with the sisters what the project might involve for them, weighing up the pros and cons of their involvement with it, and making it clear that there was no onus on them to opt in. We also made it clear that the outcome was not predetermined and that we had no prior expectations that, whatever we did, senior managers would show any interest. In effect we worked out what each side had to offer the other, balanced possible gains and losses, and struck what Haas and Shaffir (1973) termed a 'research bargain'.

As facilitators we were in a position to offer the sisters support and encouragement over the eight weeks, to listen to what they had to say and to work with them to explore what the change to ward manager might involve, including assisting them in conveying these ideas to senior managers. In turn they were in a position to offer us their commitment to the project and their willingness to work as co-researchers. The realization that both sides had something to gain by making the best of what was offered and being professional in the way we used the time provided the basis for an understanding of what each had to do to help the other.

At the start of any such programme it is essential for both sides to be clear about what they want from the project, and to negotiate and agree ground rules, including that individuals may withdraw from the programme at any time without incurring bad feeling. In addition to minimizing the possibility of participants feeling obliged to take part in such a project, these preliminary negotiations also assist in setting group goals and objectives.

One of the most important lessons learnt from this project was the importance of paying attention to the way boundaries are drawn around the group, including the position of potentially influential people on the periphery, who may occupy the important middle ground between groups such as ward sisters lower down the hierarchy and senior managers. In this case, one of the ward sisters, who had taken a central part in the earlier work during phase 3 (Figure 5.1), was promoted, albeit on a 'temporary' basis, to a nurse manager post within the directorate's management team. This happened shortly before the start of the developmental programme, and at a time when the peer group was in a state of uncertainty following the departure of the nurse manager who had supported them. The implications for the group of the shift of a key member to the position of their line manager was never discussed explicitly by them; neither was a new role in relation to the group negotiated with her. The effect of this neglect was to leave her isolated in a half-way position between sister and manager. While the sisters were working together to see how best to make this transition as a group, one of them was making the change from sister to manager alone as an isolated individual. This middle management position is a difficult one to occupy, especially when, as in this case, the post was a temporary one on a trial basis. The nurse manager is drawn away from a peer group of ward sisters by the wider demands of the unit and the need to forge a new identity as part of the directorate management team, and to prove herself as 'management material' in order to be accepted by senior managers at the centre, which may include the development of a controlling and inflexible style of management (Roberts 1983; Farmer 1993). In the directorate structure this shift to a position in nurse management may also involve dual lines of accountability, one to the clinical director, the other to the senior nurse, which may create divided loyalties.

CONCLUSION

The developmental programme described here illustrates that attention to process helps to generate participation and to create the conditions for change. It is possible to negotiate a process of modification of expectations through collaborative relationships.

The weight that is paid to process in this empowering type of action research avoids the possibility of setting up independently defined outcomes and unrealistic expectations. In the specific case of the sisters they had experienced massive change and upheaval in their working lives, and had come to the developmental programme only after the report arising from earlier collaborative work had been rejected by senior managers. Their response to this was that it was much better to have voiced the problems and brought them out in the open, however difficult this was, than to continue to live with the frustration and stress of being mute, and this further piece of work strengthened them in this position and enabled them to build upon it.

NOTE

1 We use the term 'sisters' to include the two charge nurses involved.

7

Case study 3
'Sitting in the circle' –
working across
professional boundaries
and with older people
in the community

INTRODUCTION

As a narrative account of a practitioner-generated project, this case study of action research with older people about aspects of care in the community illustrates how a project might shift back and forth across the boundary between professionalizing and empowering types in a way which nevertheless retains a consistency of purpose over time. As such it shows how fruitful can be the dialogue between professionals and service users, particularly in terms of enabling marginalized groups to find their voices and in opening up the possibility of change and improvement. Considered in terms of the policy process, this case study shows how it is possible to create arenas for collaboration between concerned local people and health and social care professionals. Such collaboration may promote public action on problems of immediate relevance to, in this case, older people, in a way which finds parallels in development policy in developing countries (Wuyts *et al.* 1992), and in earlier traditions of community development in Britain (Coventry CDP 1975).

ISSUES IN THE INTERPLAY OF RESEARCH, ACTION AND EVALUATION

In Chapter 3 the interdependence of research, action and evaluation was identified as one of the seven distinguishing criteria of action research. Of particular interest in this case study is the issue of how it might be possible to evaluate the outcomes of a project situated towards the empowering side of the typology (Table 3.1), particularly now that the issue of effectiveness is much higher on the public sector's agenda. Outcome evaluation is especially problematic in practitioner-generated action research, where the nature of the problem and the particular setting may require that action strands dominate those of research and evaluation. The project began with a prolonged investigative phase which drew in colleagues from other disciplines and was the forerunner of engagement with local people. It was developed one step at a time from a base in practice and recording of progress was primarily designed to meet professional and functional community work requirements rather than those of research. It is an illustration of a portfolio approach to evaluation, strongly geared to action rather than research, within a professionalizing type which shifted towards an empowering type in the later stages of the project. The portfolio approach reflected the process-led nature of the project, but did not ignore outcomes. Unlike case study 1, which used the Occupational Stress Indicator (Cooper *et al.* 1988), a recognized research instrument, as a 'snapshot' baseline measure, this action research with older people used a more 'archaeological' approach in which a range of material was generated without knowing whether or not it was going to be useful in the future. Nevertheless, the effort was not wasted since merely asking the questions helped to deepen an understanding of problems and to generate ideas about how the situation might be improved. Even simple ways of recording and measuring, such as retaining attendance lists of people coming to events, proved immensely valuable when it came to assessing progress and planning the next stage.

Reinforcing the points made in the two previous case studies about the importance of defining roles and negotiating boundaries, and in this about the need to take account of process, Prout has argued that:

> If collaboration is to take place then a priority task for the evaluation is the negotiation of guidelines on the respective roles, duties, obligations and work practices of the evaluator and other project participants. Such agreement cannot be laid down in advance but must be negotiated according to the wishes and preferences of the parties concerned. It is clear, however, that a process for this negotiation must be established as a routine part of the evaluation. Experience of this so far suggests that the negotiation of boundaries is central to this process – boundaries around confidentiality, gaining permission to collect data, and securing the release of information and interpretation. Such negotiated boundaries are essential to developing trust and respect, but they too may involve trade-offs. Some aspects of the project, for example, may be negotiated out of the documentation.
>
> (Prout 1992: 86)

BACKGROUND

Some of the better known accounts of action research in Britain are to be found in the reports stemming from the 1970s Community Development Projects (discussed in Chapter 2), including those by Lees and Smith (1975) and the Coventry CDP team (1975). The Coventry Project, one of the first of twelve such Home Office sponsored programmes, generated considerable research on the needs of older people living in the Hillfields area of Coventry, including an action survey (Coventry Social Services 1973) which exposed deprivation and considerable levels of unmet need. This led to the establishment of a neighbourhood visiting scheme based in the local social services office, of which I (Meg Bond) was the organizer.

I became involved in community action with local people to extend the provision of domiciliary services, and in self-help training programmes mounted by home care managers, sheltered flatlet wardens and district nurses to improve their caring practices. I later carried out an ethnographic study of the home help/care service (Bond 1982) in order to explore its latent potential to generate change in the community care of older people, and also a small-scale action research project to reduce the numbers of inappropriate hospital discharges of elderly people into unsupported situations in their own homes.

The case study reported here describes a further stage in this programme of action research following my appointment to a newly created post as a social worker attached to a doctors' practice. With roots in CDP thinking and research, and action informed and stimulated by previous community development work, the initiatives described sought to transfer to a wider population of elderly people and their carers some of the ideas and good practices identified earlier.

It is impossible to do more than concentrate here on a small part of the programmes for change. The account which follows highlights an action-dominated middle phase situated in a defined geographical area and bounded by a timescale of approximately two years. It is written in narrative form to convey a sense of the process of the work, which was practitioner-generated and positioned at the interfaces of a number of professional and service user networks.

While the adoption of such a style may be seen to carry an implicit message to 'go and do likewise', it has risks when used in connection with a methodological approach which is essentially adaptable, dynamic and opportunistic. As Hopkins rightly comments in his discussion of action research in the classroom:

> The line between specifying principles of procedure that encourage informed action, and prescribing activities that determine behaviour and limit outcomes, is a very fine one indeed. There is a real danger that teacher research will assume the character of the objectives model . . . 'which is like a site-plan simplified so that people know exactly where to dig their trenches without having to know why' (Stenhouse 1980).
> (Hopkins 1993: 55)

The model of practice adopted here is not without flaws and is not necessarily an appropriate form of intervention in all settings. Action research is after all inherently problem focused and policy context specific. But as Eden and Huxham (1993: 6–7) point out, a key criterion by which to judge action research is whether it has practical utility:

> If the practicality criterion is taken seriously, this suggests that the output of action research should be prescriptive, in the sense that it should give advice on how to do something (though to satisfy our generality criterion it is important that the prescription be general enough to apply in circumstances beyond that in which it was created). *Descriptive theory*, however, can also be appropriate providing it is presented in such a way that it can inform. Descriptive theory from action research must thus also be knowingly, but implicitly, prescriptive in form and style by recognising that the language used will, and is, designed to seriously influence the future thinking and actions of the reader. Thus . . . *what is important for action research is not a (false) dichotomy between prescription and description, but a prescriptive, even if implicit, form and style for the presentation of the research outcomes.*

From the beginning, the work reported here was informed by community work principles (Calouste Gulbenkian Foundation 1968; Bailie 1975), developments in the women's and community health movements (Open University/Health Education Authority 1991; Mies 1993), and an empowerment model of practice (Glendenning 1982, 1985; Morgan 1993) in which older people and professional staff were seen as co-action researchers rather than as subjects or informants. This, therefore, is the story of the steps taken by older people, carers and workers in what may be described as a demonstration project to improve local institutional and community care. It is an attempt to:' "reconstruct the case" . . . The rationality and scientific rigour of such stories is assured not by their predictive capacity but by their capacity for explaining what has already happened. Stories cannot be extrapolated "tout court" to other situations or other contexts, they can only give an "example" of how it is possible to construct an explanation' (Mayer 1993: 318).

My authorship of this study has posed a dilemma which may be more common than is generally acknowledged in reports of action research. It concerns the question of ownership of the emergent account. Many of those involved with the project have moved away, become frail and died, and no mechanism has remained in place for producing a widely agreed story. My decision to write up this work has therefore been taken independently although my assumption of this task of dissemination is in large measure an extension of the roles of facilitator, scribe and evaluator which participants at the time allowed and encouraged me to fulfil. I have done my utmost to recognize fully the essentially collective nature of the enterprise by the use of the noun 'we' and to draw throughout on negotiated accounts written contemporaneously. But the fact still remains that ultimately this version – this 'storyline' (Shakespeare et al. 1993: 10) – is only one of many different but overlapping ones which might have been told by other participants. However, its presentation is intended to 'ring true' in content, and remain true to the style of the work with these older people and their carers, some of whom have read and authenticated this.

THE CONTEXT

As a social worker attached to a doctors' practice I occupied a new post funded jointly by a social services department and a district health authority. I was responsible for establishing a service which aimed to reach those people with health- and illness-related problems who would be unlikely to turn for help to the social services department or, if they did, would rank low on the priority list for allocation of a social worker because no statutory work was involved. This aspect of the service to patients and staff at the practice was firmly in the tradition of medical social work in that it anticipated cooperative inter-professional working in the interests of individual patients though it was community rather than hospital based. Because the surgery was the only one within a deprived inner city housing estate and roughly half of the patients registered there lived within the catchment area of the district social services office where I was based, it was decided that I should also identify and work upon health and social issues affecting local people.

I received numerous requests to see elderly people because, as heavy users of the health services, they had unmet social and psychological needs that were related to their ill-health and were a source of concern to my colleagues at the surgery. Inevitably my work with individuals threw up similar problems and it was not difficult to identify recurring patterns of inappropriate hospital discharge practices, lack of access to domiciliary services and poor take-up of welfare benefits (Bond 1982). I and colleagues in the home care and social work offices began to work more systematically and collectively in our assessments of the needs of vulnerable older people who sought our help and, in putting together case studies of good and poor practices, we began to increase our understandings of people's experiences of growing old in the locality. This work drew explicitly upon the findings of the CDP action research and foreshadowed approaches subsequently to be encouraged among local health workers (Mares *et al*. 1985) and written up as health, school health and poverty profiling (respectively Twinn *et al*. 1990; Health Visitors' Association School Nurse Subcommittee 1991; Blackburn 1992; Hawtin *et al*. 1994). It served the dual purposes of establishing some starting points and sensitizing workers to a number of key issues.

Our move into issues-based work led us into group work with professionals and then community work with elderly people. Eventually it resulted in the setting up of a Special Interest Group for the Elderly (SPIGE) described at the time in one of the group's handouts as 'a mixed group of residents and professionals who had come together to promote a better understanding of the needs of the elderly in the area and to work towards improving the quality of life and the services available after retirement age.' The case study which follows charts key moments in the establishment and life of this group.

CASE STUDY: BEGINNINGS

At a December meeting of our Community Forum, members were bemoaning the fact that some housebound elderly people turned up at all the locally organized Christmas events while many others were never even invited. The workers present – district-based social workers, home help and nursery staff, police officers, teachers, church representatives, wardens of the sheltered flatlets and the community centre, and staff from the local clinic and doctors' surgery – agreed that since many of us were involved in organizing these outings and distributing the invitations, we should look more closely at the situation to see what could be done about it. I offered to lead a discussion at the next meeting.

For some months previously I had been looking for an opportunity to open up for inter-disciplinary discussion the work going on in the social services office about the needs and problems of local older people and shortfalls in services available to them. Individual casework had on numerous occasions taken us into situations where elderly peoples' needs were defined only in terms of existing services, and while staff were often very concerned about the gaps exposed, they had been unable to introduce improvements. For example, most workers in the area knew of frail elderly people who received the practical services of home helps and community nurses but whose emotional needs for companionship and stimulation remained unmet. It had become clear that while we could sometimes do something to help in individual cases, by, for instance, introducing a volunteer visitor, resources were not available to meet the emotional needs of all those referred to us, let alone those of the even greater number whose needs remained hidden. We were beginning to recognize that it was important to identify the common components of individuals' problems and to take action to address them collectively. This required a shift in thinking and working: one-to-one therapeutic interventions and one-off mobilizations of resources unrelated to the perceptions of local people or to the activities of other helping services and networks were inadequate responses. The Community Forum was an obvious arena in which to develop a multi-disciplinary community-based approach which examined the relationship between needs and services, and between elderly people's experiences of ill-health/well-being and the delivery of care. The topic of 'Christmas treats for the elderly – who gets what, how and why, and are they what they want?' encapsulated the issues and presented the opportunity we were seeking.

It was not difficult to enable colleagues to widen the discussion at the next Community Forum meeting. We had many patients and clients in common and inevitably we referred to particular people to illustrate our concerns. Examples of lonely people who were never invited on trips led to discussion about which organizations provided them. Consequently some members found out that there was a local Age Concern group and that the latter's 'Know your rights' booklet was well-used by some workers but unknown to others. More questions arose, for instance about the differences between a community nurse and a home help, and about the sources of information on financial benefits available to older people. People frequently expressed surprise that their perception of a problem was echoed by others from different disciplines and were taken aback by their lack of knowledge of each other's roles and services.

Although it was agreed that a single meeting could not do justice to these concerns, it was also acknowledged that some workers present, like the nursery and school staff, only occasionally came into contact with elderly people. For these people the discussion had put the needs of older people upon the agenda and had promoted some linkages in thinking. For instance, one of the junior school teachers had said that he was engaged in an oral history project. He said that, if only he had realized the extent of its contacts, he could have approached the home care service for the names of people over seventy who would be willing to be interviewed by ten-year-olds, an idea which may well have found favour with some elderly people who were confined to their homes and experiencing loneliness. Later we were to draw upon such ideas, but at the time we agreed simply that two further meetings should be convened to enable interested workers to pursue their discussions further.

FIRST PHASE: MEETING

In the event a splinter group met as the Community Forum Special Interest Group on the Elderly throughout the following year. Initially time was spent describing our different roles and our agencies' contributions to the care of older people in the community. Up to twenty-five people attended these sessions in the community centre and we made notes of useful facts as well as issues requiring attention. The earliest minutes were entitled 'The care of the elderly – what are we doing?' and recorded the concern voiced about, for example, transport problems facing the elderly in getting about, whether it was to clinic appointments or social events. One of the sheltered flatlet wardens described how she had arranged for some residents to be taken out regularly each week in a minibus to do their own shopping, thereby avoiding dependence upon others. This prompted questions about whether other local people could be included; or the vehicle could be used by other pensioners' groups; or a minibus with a tail-lift could be obtained for the sole use of the local community; or dependency in other aspects of elderly people's lives could be reduced by changes in service delivery, for instance by promoting the development of mobile shops or arranging home delivery of grocery orders. We reported back to the Community Forum that our meetings needed to continue.

SECOND PHASE: LEARNING

The second phase covered a series of meetings spread over several months in which we selected from our previous sessions six topics that, with the help of some outside 'experts', we considered in some detail. Damp housing was discussed with reference to research findings from a district nearby with similar poor housing stock occupied by elderly people. A lawyer and a welfare rights worker described legal remedies and financial benefits available to residents in such properties and challenged the view that nothing could be done about 'the problem'. Examination of the relationship between paid workers and volunteers at the next meeting caused some heated debates as we exposed our personal and our agencies' philosophies and tried to develop some agreed pointers towards good practice. A session on 'the invisible elderly' brought to the group's attention findings from local and national surveys and projects about the extent of unmet need particularly in relation to the health of elderly people. From this we went on to look at how assessments of need were undertaken by different group members. The fifth session had as its theme new resources available locally, and was divided into three parts. The leader of a movement therapy group demonstrated the potential of this form of activity and two social work students described a current piece of groupwork in which they were using a tape–slide show to stimulate discussion about health issues among residents of a block of sheltered flatlets. Finally, the primary school teacher talked about the oral history project and brought along a display of materials which had been developed about people and places in the immediate neighbourhood. After a sixth meeting spent looking at the potential of street warden schemes for relieving isolation and improving the quality of life for the elderly in the community, the group concluded this phase of the work with a review of progress. Document 7.1 summarizes the options available at this stage.

Document 7.1: Letter sent at the review stage

Community forum special interest group on the elderly
A series of eight meetings has been held in the community centre during the past six months to enable professionals working locally in the community care of the elderly to look together at issues of common concern. These meetings have been well attended by between ten and twenty people, including members of the local nursing services and social services team, wardens of sheltered flatlets in the area, and staff involved in schools, churches and the Community Enterprise Scheme. The group membership therefore has been multi-disciplinary and a substantial level of commitment and interest has emerged.

A meeting is now planned to review the progress we have made and to consider the direction we should pursue in the future. Three options seem possible. The first is to discontinue the meetings but to recognize the value of the series in stimulating discussion and sharing ideas (on the problems of the elderly living at home, working with volunteers, running social and therapeutic groups, and setting up street warden schemes and educational projects). The second option would be to run a further series of meetings, perhaps in conjunction with local elderly people, to explore some ideas and concerns further – for instance we might learn more about welfare rights or ways of helping those facing death. The third option would be for the group to take further an actual piece of work. The minutes indicate that at past meetings members have been interested in the idea of appointing a coordinator of schemes for the elderly which might then be expanded. Whether or not such an appointment by a multi-disciplinary steering/management group might be appropriate, members identified several possible areas of work. These included setting up further movement therapy groups, exploring the possibility of developing a neighbourhood visiting scheme, a well-pensioners clinic or a home insulation project, and organizing a programme of outings for the elderly which met the needs of more people than was felt to be the case at present. This latter suggestion was linked to the idea of buying a minibus for use by groups in the area.

If it is decided that this group should meet again, perhaps in the autumn, for discussion purposes or to undertake some sort of project, I believe that it is now important to consider the contribution which local elderly people may have to offer. This issue, like the others outlined above, will be discussed at the forthcoming meeting, which we hope you will be able to attend.

In the event we recognized that, though we had lost some members along the way, the experience of meeting regularly with other local workers to share common concerns had been invaluable. Not only had we gathered and recorded much useful information but we had risked exposing and being challenged about our ignorance and prejudices. We no longer felt that we were working in isolation on intractable problems. Indeed, so sure were we that we could do something to improve the lot of the elderly locally that we reported back to the Community Forum that we were going to continue meeting in order to produce some proposals for change.

THIRD PHASE: FOCUSING

For the next phase of the work the group sought the assistance of the local social services team manager, who was a member of the Community Forum. He was interested in promoting community social work and agreed to help the Group to develop a shared sense of purpose and an awareness of the issues involved in initiating dialogue with local older people about needs and services. Recognizing an alignment of common interests, he agreed in particular to come up with a series of attitude measurement scales and to facilitate their use. The attitude scales (which have been included in this book as Figure 10.3) focused discussion and provoked some lively debates, especially around the issue of consultation.

During this exercise a key change took place. Group members came to a shared understanding that some of the problems associated with caring for older people might be to do with 'experts' and professionals imposing their solutions in the form of services upon people whose needs, experiences and perceptions they only partly understood. As we looked more closely at this idea we realized too that, as grass roots workers in under-resourced community services, we lacked the power to influence policy-making. In the context of cut-backs and given the rhetoric of community care, we discussed whether a way forward might be to engage older people themselves in these efforts – to ask them how they saw 'the problems' and what they wanted in the way of services – before developing some shared user/worker initiatives locally. By the end of three demanding sessions we had reached agreement about the next step. We would invite local senior citizens to join us for a discussion about their experiences of growing older in this particular neighbourhood. Thus as a result of a change in the way the group perceived the role of professionals we moved into the fourth phase of the group's development, and consciously shifted from a professionalizing type towards a more empowering type of approach.

FOURTH PHASE: ENGAGING

We put considerable thought into who should be invited and how. We knew from our discussions of Christmas treats that some people got all the invitations and some none, and we knew from our session on 'the invisible elderly' that we were only in touch with a minority of pensioners. Moreover, many of those we knew were frail and housebound with failing sight and hearing. How could we enable them to take part fully – to hear and be heard? Our series of earlier meetings stood us in good stead to deal with these dilemmas because we had reached some understanding of the problems facing older people, and we had established a firm shared commitment to open up a dialogue with them. Between us we were in touch with a cross section of older people spanning an age range of some thirty or so years, including some who were fit, bedbound, supported, isolated, council tenants, owner occupiers, in receipt of means-tested benefits and members of local pensioners' groups. We decided that a personal approach was more likely to produce a response than a written invitation or posters advertising a public meeting. We agreed to contact a variety of individuals and organizations we knew, and we did a role-play to give us confidence and establish a clear understanding of how we intended to 'sell' the invitation. We agreed to provide transport and lunch and to act as enablers in the discussions. We would pay particular attention to those with impaired hearing and would act as escorts for those with limited mobility. The organization of this event benefited considerably from the multi-disciplinary nature of the Special Interest Group. The community centre warden approached the local community association for support and, as a result, free accommodation and lunch were provided. Volunteer helpers served the meal and the transport was obtained through our contacts with the social services volunteer drivers' scheme. Attention was paid to small details, like checking that the toilets were accessible and clearly signposted and that every newcomer was welcomed and introduced to others present.

We drew upon the skills of the social workers present to structure the event and promote small group discussions and, by briefing them beforehand and providing pens and paper to record a summary of the issues raised for display on the wall, were able to give everyone an idea of what other groups had discussed. People discovered that what they thought was a personal problem was in fact shared by others. Many had had similar experiences – of feeling lonely, isolated, vulnerable and immobilized. And many had similar concerns: 'heating costs money' and 'the chiropody services are poor or non-existent'. Moreover, ideas for change bubbled up: 'more day care is needed', and 'a local newspaper could help to inform people about what's going on in the district'. Any doubts which workers may have harboured about the ability of senior citizens to consider the issues and express their views were dispelled once and for all when two women had a stand-up disagreement about the notion of the deserving and the undeserving poor. We had succeeded in opening up the dialogue not just between workers and users of services but, just as importantly, among the older people themselves to such an extent that fifteen out of the thirty pensioners present kept their drivers waiting to queue up and leave their names to be included in the next meeting. The group had not thought as far ahead as that but its occurrence was clearly a foregone conclusion. We had, however, previously agreed that afterwards each worker would take responsibility for gathering feedback from each person whom they had initially attracted to the meeting. In this way we established that for thirty 'visitors', mostly elderly but including one or two younger Age Concern members, and for fifteen workers, the occasion had been a success. As a social event and an intellectual and participative exercise, it had been enjoyable and productive.

Following this, a summary of the issues and ideas as transcribed on the wall charts was sent to everyone who had attended. Seven broad areas of concern were discernible: loneliness, isolation and not having much to look forward to headed the list and these were linked with such topics as social activities, insecurity and vulnerability, mobility and maintaining independence. Comments had also emerged about financial circumstances and knowing about what was going on. The notes included a final comment echoed by many people that 'we have really enjoyed meeting one another today – maybe we should do this more often. It's important that things should change as a result of our discussions and not just stay the same.' Clearly workers and elderly residents in the neighbourhood shared views about the problems and were keen to do something about them.

FIFTH PHASE: PARTICIPATING

The Special Interest Group met again to evaluate progress and invited those who had given in their names at the end of the last meeting to attend a planning meeting. We decided that since we wished for dialogue and participation it was important to share not just the next event itself with local elderly people but the organization and structuring of it too. Six weeks later many pensioners joined us again for a working lunch. We broke up into small discussion groups and asked each to select a topic from the seven previously identified and to consider whether at the next meeting we should concentrate more on the problem itself or on possible solutions. By the end of the session it was agreed that a small group of pensioners, serviced by one of the workers, should form the planning group for a much larger-scale event which should address itself to solutions. It should be widely advertised and aim to draw in as many pensioners as possible. Another letter documenting our progress went out to all those with whom we were in contact, asking them to share its contents with others, and we put a brief article in a local community magazine. We hoped that these would stimulate discussions in pensioners' groups in the community and within residential units as well as between pensioners and their carers, and in this way prepare the way for the next event.

At this point the nature of the group changed. First, the planning group decided that the Community Forum's Special Interest Group on the Elderly should be renamed the Special Interest Group for the Elderly. Substituting 'on' with 'for' was significant. Second, some planning group members began to act as representatives of those community groups to which they belonged. At an earlier meeting we had asked people whether they were in touch with local groups for older residents and in this way we had identified potential contacts, including someone who was actively involved with the city-wide Alzheimer's Disease Society and others who attended groups which we did not know existed. Thus we developed channels of communication with a wider range of active elderly people while maintaining ones with housebound and isolated people who were known to the statutory services. Third, we made links with a pensioners' group which had just started in another part of the city. As a GP-attached worker I had been involved on a consultancy basis with this group's initiatives in running educational workshops and, when the Special Interest Group decided to do the same, we drew upon their experiences.

Over a period of nine weeks the planning group provided transport and met at different venues – the lounge of a block of sheltered flatlets and later in members' houses. We remained loyal to the original principles of participation and accessibility and the group continued as an open one. It was finally decided that we would run a one-day event on health issues and worked in sub-groups to organize the programme, publicity, finance, food and transport. We co-opted on to each of these groups someone from among the original workers' group to service and resource the members. The social services department district manager helped with fund-raising so effectively that the group soon had a grant of several hundred pounds for future activities; the community centre warden made facilities available for paperwork, phoning and organizing the transport; the voluntary help organizer drew upon her contacts to swell the ranks of the food squad; and one of the local vicars took the members of the publicity sub-group to a local resource centre to produce posters.

The local residents had taken note of some of the key elements in the structure and organization of the meetings they had attended and proceeded to replicate these in planning the health day as an information-giving event and a social occasion. It took place at a previously neglected end of the district in a church hall recently provided with a ramp and adapted toilet. Two speakers gave short presentations on health issues of particular significance to older people – chiropody services and continence management. In addition, members of organizations with a health focus were invited to set up information stalls around the room. Representatives from the Health Education Council, Age Concern, the Community Health Council, the Disability Rights Service, the Alzheimer's Disease Society and a local Women and Health Group attended and laid out displays of literature. The teacher from the local junior school brought along some oral history materials so those with relatives or friends suffering from memory loss became aware of a valuable resource for stimulating recollections. We also invited a keep fit club to provide a demonstration of their exercises with modifications to the routines to encourage participation by those present.

The event ran from 10.00 a.m. – 4.00 p.m. but people could come late and/or leave early as they wished and transport was laid on throughout the day to fit emerging needs. A hundred people attended, each of whom paid a small registration fee to cover the cost of notifying them of future events, but we made no other charge. We kept records of their names and addresses and those of their escorts. We asked everyone how they had become involved as a way of checking on the effectiveness of our communication systems and of monitoring the extent of our developing networks. On arrival each person received a programme which included a sentence of explanation about the Special Interest Group and an invitation to initiate and maintain links with us in the future through a list of named contacts on the planning group. We also gave out information sheets prepared at our request by Age Concern, which outlined the range and functions of health and social services for older people with brief details of contact points.

In retrospect, the successful organization of this health day proved to be a key event in developing the self-confidence of the elderly local residents involved. Following a review of how it had gone, they began to plan further activities using the by now familiar pattern of working in sub-groups and taking into account elements which had proved problematic, such as the difficulties of enabling people with hearing impairments to participate fully. Each subsequent occasion, which was attended by about eighty people, was designed to incorporate participation, enjoyment, and information gathering and sharing. Reports were given to the Community Forum, usually in the shape of notices about forthcoming day educational events and feedback on them. While the original group of professionals had been superseded, committed members who had not moved to new jobs continued to participate in these activities, by promoting them among local older people and contributing their skills and knowledge when needed. Most importantly, the Special Interest Group continued as a self-sustaining participatory vehicle for change, involving both elderly residents and professionals in defining needs and seeking to meet them.

Records from this period show that a community staff nurse was to be appointed at the local clinic with a brief to reach out to older people and to offer them a new service which was to be 'sensitive and responsive to their needs'. At the same time the local primary health care team considered setting up a screening service, and ideas about 'well-pensioner clinics' began to emerge at Special Interest Group events. The fifteen women who had told the Women and Health Group representatives that they would be interested in a pensioners' health course were approached to implement this by a district nurse who was attached to the social services office as part of her training as a social worker. Within the Community Forum, discussions took place about how best to encourage and support workers in other agencies who wanted to develop collaborative relationships with other groups about service provision. Document 7.2 is an extract from my notebook.

Document 7.2: Extract from notebook

Maybe we could offer a safe thinking ground to workers unused to sharing power, control and decision-making to enable them to take risks and enter the dialogue, so that, for example, the decisions about screening services and the community staff nurse's new role are made through discussions with potential and future users of those services. It is likely that we shall use the Community Forum to raise these possibilities and develop our ideas further.

This is indeed what happened and eventually some of us who had been involved from the earliest days with the Special Interest Group set up a group for groupworkers who were keen to develop their skills in cooperation with others practising in the area. We also launched a twelve month neighbourhood continence management action research project.

EVALUATION: ONE YEAR ON

In the course of outlining the background to this case study, I indicated that it had been written from my perspective as a participant observer, but that it had also been authenticated by some of those who were involved in the work. I pointed out that this account is focused on an intervention phase which was preceded by substantial research and action. With hindsight it is clear that a rather more rigorous approach to the research aspects might have been adopted at the time if formal evaluation had been accorded a higher status, resources had been allocated specifically for this and the value of the work had been more fully recognized as worth disseminating. As it was, energies predominantly went into promoting and sustaining the change initiatives.

However, a year later I undertook an exercise to evaluate progress and to record developing ideas about future directions for the work. Documents including minutes of meetings, records of attendances at day events and newspaper reports of these were examined, and discussions were held with a range of participants in groups and individually, a few of whom offered written as well as verbal comments. I drafted a summarizing paper for discussion entitled 'The Special Interest Group: Achievements and Directions', and I conclude this case study with an analysis of its key elements and some commentary on the action research project as a whole.

As its title indicates, the paper was both backward and forward looking and it addressed issues of process and of outcome. In process terms, it identified mechanisms for change, including the group's open planning arrangements, its five sub-committees of local people and professionals 'working in tandem', and six 'ingredients of success' which had been incorporated into 'group happenings': companionship; enjoyment; a change of style from other neighbourhood groups for older people; information giving; intellectual stimulation; and provision of lunch. It looked at the range of events mounted and in preparation, and, as the following extract illustrates, it identified not only who had become involved but, just as importantly, who was excluded and what was lacking:

Document 7.3: Extract from 'achievements and directions' paper

The open planning format:
- includes stalwarts who are pensioners and members of local pensioners' groups;
- includes a number of older and younger helpers who come as volunteers and/or Age Concern members and who have been drawn in because of their skills and interests, e.g. as handicraft 'experts', through the Women and Health group and residents' association and as volunteer drivers and fund raisers;
- has lost some of its early members, perhaps because information about planning meetings has usually been passed on verbally rather than formally in writing by a secretary;
- lacks male pensioners;
- lacks a direct input from frailer housebound people;
- has failed to draw in older people from the black and Asian communities;
- lacks a regular input from the domiciliary health services.

The paper also identified functions which in future the Special Interest Group could fulfil, based on developing understandings of met and unmet needs and the possibilities for responding to these by working across agency and geographical boundaries to capitalize on initiatives in other quarters:

Document 7.4: Extract from 'achievements and directions' paper

[The group could] attempt to enrich the programmes of local groups for older people, for example by:
- increasing awareness, among organizers and members, of resources such as communication aids, games equipment and tutors;
- making resources more accessible through the provision of finances and directories of 'useful contacts' e.g. pianists, people who run reminiscence and movement to music groups, horticultural and art therapists;
- encouraging the building of links between different groups to share interests, problems and facilities such as meeting rooms and transport.

Finally, this evaluative document identified some possible ways forward for the Special Interest Group and inevitably these were defined in terms of processes rather than outcomes. Presciption of outcomes was not the task of the facilitator; nor indeed was it possible within the context of such an action research project. The paper posed questions to be addressed by various interested parties and individuals and, for example, incorporated the following:

Document 7.5: Extract from 'achievements and directions' paper

For the professional staff there is the dilemma of whether to maintain a high or low profile: whether to encourage the group to go in a particular direction or to promote self-determination in a very open-ended manner; whether to 'go with' a slower 'learning by experience' or to try to achieve rather more tangible goals more quickly by placing certain problems and some possible solutions on the group's agenda. The availability of resources, such as worker time, may be a determining factor but a crucial point seems to have been reached within the Special Interest Group in terms of the nature of the relationship between recipients of services and paid staff. What philosophical and practice position do workers wish to adopt? Do the professionals wish to see through the launching of this group as a consumer initiative or is the notion of dialogue, developed in recent work together, still important? What are the implications of each for future roles within the group?

From this extract it becomes clear that, in terms of our typology, at this point in the life of the project, workers faced the challenge of repositioning themselves 'back' in the professionalizing type or moving more radically into the empowering type, with all the uncertainties that entailed.

CONCLUSION

I want to conclude this case study by making some comments about the action research as a whole, the initial aim of which was to mount a demonstration project to improve local services for older people through the mechanism of bringing together professional workers in an inter-disciplinary planning group. In the event the key method used by this group to generate change was to involve local elderly residents and carers in a joint endeavour. Evaluation must therefore consider: first, to what extent the group was successful in involving elderly people; second, what the key elements were in securing their collaboration and ensuring its continuation; and, third, what the outcome was and whether services were improved. In terms of the first two, the account shows that older people in significant numbers became involved and remained so over a prolonged period of time. Strategies of engagement were developed and, when they proved successful, they continued to be deployed. Examples of this are the six 'ingredients of success' identified for running events. However, it is less easy to address the third point concerning outcomes. In attempting to evaluate these, it is important to understand clearly the grounds upon which claims are made and to place them properly in context.

In matters of social life it is never easy to establish causal relationships and this is especially difficult where action research is concerned with generating change in organizational and community settings. This is a point which is also highlighted in case study 1, which describes the tensions arising from two apparently contradictory requirements: on the one hand to facilitate change by shifting ownership from researchers to participants through a process-led approach, and on the other to provide the employing bodies with evidence of the effects of the intervention of the action researchers in the form of a list of 'tangible outcomes'. In this case it is possible to say that the Community Forum spawned a splinter group which in turn worked in partnership with local older people to mount a series of day educational events which were attended by some eighty or so pensioners, including some from residential establishments. Newspaper reports and poems spontaneously offered by participants, recording the impact of new ways of working on the quality of their lives and in terms of helping them to solve problems in caring for others, stand in their own right as testimony to change associated with the Special Interest Group. But the purchase of a community minibus might have happened anyway – although increased awareness through the work of this group of the impact of immobility on the lives of older people certainly influenced the decision to purchase a vehicle with a tail-lift. And the recruitment of a graduate with an interest in history to work from the community centre might have resulted in the establishment of a local history group regardless of whether others were engaged in the development of related educational, leisure and therapeutic activities for older people. However, it does seem reasonable to suggest that such an initiative may have been more likely to emerge and to be positively received and nurtured in this environment and among local people and staff actively opening themselves up to new possibilities in the community care of older people.

While I would therefore not wish to suggest that the achievements recorded here are ascribed exclusively to the work of the Community Forum and the Special Interest Group, it is clear that some of them were undoubtedly causally linked and others were informed by initiatives taken in the area by residents and professionals. This, then, is the basis upon which the final evaluative document is presented. It consists of a couple of poems by retired women who, in writing spontaneously about the impact which the project had had on them, point to its value both in helping them to solve personal problems and in enriching the quality of their lives.

Document 7.6: Two poems by members of the Special Interest Group

Retirement

I have reached that rather peculiar age
No longer to work and to receive a wage
The time has come when I must retire
Put up my feet, relax by the fire.

I am afraid for me that isn't the life
A mother and grandma – no longer a wife
The chores of my home are now greatly reduced
So a new way of life must now be deduced.

I visited clubs for those now on pension
Here of life was an entire new dimension
'Please sit in the circle', 'Here's a nice cup of tea'
All strangers around, but friendly towards me.

Next call – Bingo – 'Eyes down, let's have silence'
The atmosphere mildly excited and tense
I disliked it intensely, was bored immensely
Is this my future? Stand back, think sensibly.

From this dissatisfaction arose a new venture
With friends and young helpers began an adventure
'Alternative Interest for the Elderly' now was conceived
There is more to life! I was not deceived.

A series of workshops we nervously acclaim
The lunches at any rate, shot us to fame

Benefits to claim, health and self-care
Happy, successful, hard work is repaid fair.

The World Health Organization at University of Keele
The next big adventure the cards had to deal
A great experience, really enjoyed, I can now admit
Lectures, workshops, discussions and would they all fit?

It didn't stop there, that wasn't the last
Experiences come, new, unexpected and fast
'Will you talk on Mercia[1] to the Coventry retired
Of your actions and interests, and how they were fired?'

Now my days are so full, no time to spare
But to be honest, without help, we wouldn't dare
To take it all on, so many thanks are due
To the younger volunteers and professional helpers so few.

Thank You

For involving me in SPIGE
And in the Health Group too
I'd like to take this opportunity
Of saying 'Thank you'

For the advice and talks you gave me
About my sister when I knew not what to do
For all the friends the Groups gave me
Again I say 'Thank you'.

NOTE

1 Mercia is Coventry's local radio station.

Case study 4
Progress and procrastination – using a project group to implement changes in service provision for people with disabilities

INTRODUCTION

This case study focuses on consultancy work with senior managers of a social services department, and bears comparison with the first case study of action research with senior managers at a district general hospital. Both provide an illustration of action research within the organizational type, in a context in which, under pressure of time to implement government policy, an action researcher was brought in as an outside consultant to help with a problem as defined by management. In both cases senior managers procrastinated at crucial points and undermined the potential of the projects to facilitate change and improvement. In both cases too there was a tension between the senior managers' espoused concern to empower less powerful groups and what happened in practice. Comparison of the two situations underlines the point that a crucial precondition for success in organizational action research may be the preparedness of senior managers to offer their support to an action research way of working, which includes their involvement as participants in the change process. This particular case study also underlines a point made by Halsey over two decades ago that a possible context for action research is 'to "get something done" in response to a recognised social problem', but that such a project might also be seen as a 'diversionary approach', in which 'the project serves as an opiate to placate political pressure for more radical change; the major assumption is that one knows what should be done, but one cannot or will not do it at the moment' (Halsey 1972: 166–7).

BACKGROUND

This case study is drawn from action research undertaken in a local authority to consider the needs of adults with serious physical disabilities requiring accommodation and twenty-four hour a day care. In particular the work was concerned with assisting the senior managers of the social services department to determine the future of Hillcrest (not its real name), the council's only residential facility for such local people.

The department had previously engaged the services of a professional association to assist with other aspects of its residential services, and then extended the consultancy to address provision for those adults under pension age with severe physical and sensory impairments. Following initial negotiations, it was agreed that I (Meg Bond) would undertake a one-year, three-phase project to examine options for existing and potential residents and for the buildings, and to oversee the implementation of changes associated with residents deciding to move out or to remain in the unit. My role would be as an outside researcher working under the auspices of the professional association.

The project can be seen as an example of policy-making research linked to the management of change through the medium of an action research strategy. As the researcher I was in a position to propose the action research strategy and, as part of this, only agreed to accept the brief on condition that a project group, chaired at senior management level, should be convened from the outset to provide an arena for discussion and a vehicle for change. In focusing on the micro-processes influencing my role as a change agent, the case study illustrates the contribution that may be made by an outside researcher in taking care of the issues of process underpinning the enquiry and action components. In doing so the case study also underlines the importance of problem-setting as part of problem-solving.

This study serves, to some extent, as an example of failed action research in that the senior managers responsible for commissioning it did not adequately resource the initiative in terms of staffing over the project's lifetime. Moreover, having insisted on almost impossible deadlines they then blocked progress at the transition from first to second phase. Flying in the face of their previously supportive stance and without warning or explanation, at this point they so procrastinated about authorizing research funding for, and therefore progress to, the next phase that they effectively destroyed the momentum for change. By the time they decided several months later that it was 'all systems go', participants no longer trusted the department's commitment to the project. As the researcher, I shared this view. The reneging by senior managers on agreements about timescales and deadlines had seriously compromised my position, and my carefully established credibility as a change agent had been so thoroughly undermined by this that my position no longer felt tenable. Since the room for manoeuvre had also narrowed considerably, in terms of options still available for residents and for the site, I resisted pressure to undertake further work unless senior managers shifted their position in line with their public declarations of cooperation. This was a challenge they were unable to accept, so the programme of action research remained in abeyance.

In deciding on the appropriate stance to adopt during these negotiations, it was necessary for me to take account of both my own position and that of the professional association I represented. We had been engaged as an organization partly because of our reputation for standing firm about rights of residents and staff to be consulted on, and directly involved in, decisions which affected their living and working conditions – that is, a reputation as an organization able to bring about negotiated change. This had given us acceptability among the different interest groups involved with

Hillcrest and weight of influence in working towards change. It was important that this reputation should be protected. After the project had lapsed, feedback spontaneously offered by a number of key players, including some who had been disappointed by the lack of further engagement, indicated that our reputation had not been undermined by the way things had turned out.

THE CONTEXT

The terms of reference for the study were outlined in a research brief, which is reproduced below.

Document 8.1: Research brief

A feasibility study will be undertaken to investigate the range of alternatives to traditional residential care for local adults under pension age with severe physical impairments, and to identify the practical implications of operationalizing appropriate options in relation to meeting the needs of those currently living in Hillcrest and determining the future of the land and buildings. The researcher will work with and service a project group chaired by the relevant senior manager which will be established at the beginning of the project. Its role will be to coordinate developments, promote discussion and implement changes in the light of the study findings.

The project will be conducted over a twelve-month period and in three interrelated phases. Reviewing the situation of current residents and maximizing their independent functioning will take priority in the first four months, but as some people make decisions to remain in the unit so changes will be introduced to improve caring practices there. These changes will be carried forward into the second phase which will span the next four-month period, during which it is anticipated that some people will be assisted in moving to alternative accommodation. At the same time attention will be paid to the needs of potential applicants for this type of local residential provision and also to other uses to which the building might be put. The final stage, lasting a further four months, will allow for evaluation of these wider needs and options for the facility, as well as evaluation of residents' moves to more independent living schemes and of the changes introduced in caring practices in Hillcrest.

An interim report will be drafted based on the first stage of the work and the researcher will submit a substantive report after eight months for discussion by officers and councillors. At this point permission will be sought from them to resource and continue the study into its final stage.

Changes in legislation, in social care policy and in the systems for funding local authorities and places in residential homes had led the social services department to rethink its need for expensive long-stay care provision in a purpose-built unit. The prolonged uncertainty associated with deciding the establishment's future had contributed to its running down. It was underoccupied and therefore disproportionately expensive to operate, maintenance work on the buildings had not been undertaken and staff who had left had been replaced by temporary workers.

Nationally there was much uncertainty about how care for very dependent people could be provided, financed and organized, given the shift in emphasis towards community care and privatization in a time of economic recession and resource constraints. Politically there was also an increasing rhetoric about promoting independence and consumer choice, and about the need for professionals to take more account of users' views.

Having for some time ceased to admit new applicants into long-stay social services provision, and having enabled less dependent and more confident people to move into their own accommodation, this cash-strapped authority was faced with a difficult problem of knowing how best to look after those adults with severe physical disabilities and high care needs who remained in Hillcrest. If appropriate accommodation and care could be made available and they all agreed to move out, resources currently allocated to institutional care could be freed to support them in their own tenancies. A few purpose-built units were coming on stream in the near vicinity, but they were limited in number and suitability, the necessary funding to cover living and caring costs was not readily available and could not be guaranteed on a long-term basis, and staffing resources, currently deployed in Hillcrest, were uncertain.

Without financial support and carers no one could survive, so no one could move out. But until several people moved out no caring resources could be released from Hillcrest, and until everyone moved out there was no opportunity to draw upon the capital resources tied up in the building. In the situation between the extremes, the unit costs of caring for a dwindling number of heavily dependent people were rising, draining resources from care in the community and placing increasing pressure on the local authority to disregard the wishes of those wanting to remain at Hillcrest and to place them, however unwillingly, in alternative accommodation.

For residents to decide to move elsewhere was an enormous once-and-for-all decision to make, especially for those who had lived in institutions for most of their lives, who had few contacts outside and whose verbal communication in many cases was restricted. Being able to make an informed choice on such a matter depended directly on understanding what was on offer and determining whether it was viable in their particular circumstances. But, as already indicated, what was available was far from clear, and no real opportunities existed to test the viability of different, more independent, living arrangements before a commitment was given to accept them.

Residents who wished to consider moving out were therefore in a position of interdependence with those who were uncertain about this or who wished to stay, and in turn their room for manoeuvre was tied into that of the social services department, which had reached something of an impasse in this matter. In such a situation their rhetoric of choice was in direct conflict with the exigencies of budgetary constraints. In the past, *ad hoc* and piecemeal approaches had been adopted to help individuals with disabilities to obtain a tenancy and a package of care, to find a temporary replacement for a departing member of staff or to postpone essential building repair work. But the social services department had eventually concluded that a more concerted effort was now required to resolve the question of the future of Hillcrest and of those currently in residence. This in turn had implications for the local authority's services to other local people with severe physical disabilities who might in the future need such adapted accommodation and intensive care.

TIMESCALES

Of crucial importance in this action research project was the issue of timing, which was to some extent dictated by government requirements for local authorities to implement in some haste aspects of the 1990 National Health Service and Community Care Act. Over a period of a month, the local authority agreed proposals for the researcher to start work immediately on a four-month first stage with activities overlapping into the next of two further four-month phases. These deadlines were extremely tight but were set by senior managers who, nevertheless, themselves instantly defaulted on arrangements to meet the researcher and to provide vital background documentation. This caused several weeks' slippage at the start.

Further delay followed an initial meeting with key senior managers while they identified project group members and, by the time work eventually got under way, there were a mere eight weeks to go before a progress report was to be submitted for typing. It was to signal to senior managers completion of the work identified for the first stage and the transition into the second phase. It was the point at which payment was due for the first block of research, during which financial terms for the remainder of the work were to have been finalized.

In the event these financial arrangements were not carried through. The senior managers involved with the project put off making the first stage payments, and agreeing the second stage, until, as they said, they 'had had a chance to read the progress report', which took them several months. By this time the situation had so altered that continuation was impossible without a re-negotiation of roles and purposes. The social services department managers were unwilling to accept this and the study was therefore set aside.

This account highlights an aspect of doing research which may be experienced as puzzling and indeed frustrating. Points of beginning and ending are seldom clear-cut and it is essential that allowance is made for this in allocating time to do the work. Equally important is the maintenance of a diary or log (Ely *et al.* 1991) from the opening through to the closing of negotiations. In this case my recording of early events subsequently enabled me to recognize and trace back to my own earliest dealings with senior managers, patterns of behaviour which were used to obstruct the progress of the project. Thus, it was instructive to turn up log entries which predated any direct contact with residents and Hillcrest staff and find evidence there of managers behaving towards subordinates and residents in ways which mirrored their style of interaction with me.

PROBLEM SETTING

As with all research enterprises there is a crucial early stage in which the researcher is challenged to identify in more or less precise terms the question(s) to be addressed. At the time I started work on the research brief the situation outlined on pages 151–2 was far from clear. The following extract from a research memo written at this time was an attempt to clarify aspects of the situation:

Document 8.2: Extract from research memo

In talking about Hillcrest, reference has been made by two senior managers to the fact that it will *not* be closing. Previously I have been told that no decision has been made that it will close or that it will remain open. But it has been stressed that the current situation of uncertainty cannot continue. 'Not closing' can of course mean a number of things, including remaining open:

1 long-term under social services control and providing a service for local authority admitted users and staffed by local authority employees;
2 long-term under the management and control of the local authority and others such as the health authority and/or a housing association and/or a voluntary organization;
3 long-term under entirely new management;
4 short-term with a view both to changing its designation and to transferring management and control fully or in part to other(s);
5 short-term with a view to moving out all remaining residents and selling it off.

The phrases 'long-term' and 'short-term' can also imply different things, especially given the shifting sands of local government and public finances. We need to be clear whether long-term, for instance, means:

1 until all present residents die;
2 within the foreseeable future and given the present balance of political control both nationally and locally;

3 for the next defined number of years;
4 for any open-ended period beyond the end of this financial year;
5 not short-term (where this is defined as within the current financial
   year) but not beyond the end of the next financial year.

This may not be an exhaustive list of alternative definitions but it offers
a starting point for us to begin to clarify our understandings.

There is also the matter of establishing whether the sponsors'
and gatekeepers' versions of the current situation tally with the
perceptions of others and with, for example, written documentation.
In negotiating the brief for this study, senior managers had talked
about reviewing plans and paperwork about clients' needs for
care and accommodation and about identifying options for the
future as well as a strategy to implement changes. They implied
that assessment work had been undertaken already and that changes
could to some extent be planned in advance. It subsequently
emerged that neither of these held good.

No essential needs assessments had been carried out with any
residents and, while it was clear that ultimate responsibility for
deciding the future of the unit as such lay with elected members
and officers of the local authority, so tight were the alternative
housing and staffing deadlines that members of the project group
had no choice but to 'go with' developments. They quickly discovered that the situation could not be held static while they
explored options, and the pressure to find out and act immediately
in individual cases led them to concentrate on some possibilities to
the exclusion of others. In other words the action components
were closely associated with the enquiry aspects of the study right
from the very first day and, once the project group picked up the
reins, there was little time to stand back and refine the details of
the research questions.

DATA COLLECTION

Recognizing that Hillcrest was operational round the clock, I
interspersed office-hour visits to key people and places with a
number of overnight stays at the unit. Assuming a participant
observer role I thus developed a sense of what was going on in the

lives of residents and the shifts of workers during weekdays and nights, at weekends and over a public holiday. The building was rambling and set in open space in a poor, densely populated area and I came to understand the vulnerability felt by night staff when hot weather caused people to leave open ground floor windows. In the small hours with lights turned down in corridors, the burglar alarm offered little protection and it came as no surprise to hear the night shift of only three women expressing fears for their own and residents' safety. I realized that it was important that these should be taken into account by senior management in any future plans for staff deployment or building alterations. Had I confined my visits to office hours and only conducted formal interviews it is unlikely that I would have reached this level of understanding so quickly.

Data collection was of course a key component and one that was ongoing throughout the life of the project. The kinds of data collected included: an organization chart of the social services department, proposed documents about the department's current and proposed services to people with physical disabilities and relevant papers about the provision of services through community care from the research and development officer, and plans and photographs of the units potentially available to Hillcrest residents from the occupational therapist on the project group. I also visited a number of people in the statutory and voluntary/self-help sectors in order to understand better local provision for care and accommodation and to see for myself some of the available options. I shared these activities of data collection with different people 'in the field', including the occupational therapist, a community nurse and senior staff members of Hillcrest. Working in consultation and in cooperation with the project group, we collected and generated material, for example on demand for and provision of services and on staff training needs. This in turn led to a blurring of identities between those who in other models of research might have been differentially labelled as researchers and 'research objects' (Mies 1993: 68), 'subjects, respondents or informants' (Johnson 1990: 10).

This way of proceeding might be criticized as flawed in that those with a vested interest in the outcomes of the research are put in positions where, in the course of collecting sensitive data, it might be tempting for them to behave in a less than objective manner. For instance, someone like the senior staff member at Hillcrest who was asked to gather information about patterns of staff training might have been inclined to screen out evidence which did not reflect well on the organization's human resource development policies. On the other hand, this person's knowledge of the system might allow him or her to spot discrepancies or gaps in information, the significance of which an outside researcher might initially fail to identify. Here an example of this was an entry in a file suggesting that a care assistant had done a first aid course but that crucial updating had never taken place so the certificate was no longer valid. However, even projects set up within the strict conventions of academic research are not immune to challenges of reliability, validity and credibility as regards their methods of data generation. None is problem-free, but an approach built upon thinking critically and creatively when collecting and analysing material and reporting openly on these activities is likely to counteract poor practice.

Another point is the dual usage to which collected evidence can be put. From the research point of view the occupational therapist was 'a key informant' and could provide plans and photographs to supplement knowledge gained in site visits to analyse the facilities available in adapted accommodation. But she was also part of the action/implementation team and as such she was heavily involved both in assessing residents for transfer to independent living schemes and in allocating units. Two aspects of the project's brief were to maximize residents' levels of independent functioning and to improve caring practices. On these counts I had discovered that residents who were being asked to express preferences about future living arrangements had little access to hard facts about the tenancies on offer. Professionally, 'normalization' is a guiding principle in caring work with dependent people and comparison, for example, with what able-bodied house hunters would routinely do when seeking a suitable property highlighted the shortcomings in the information available to the Hillcrest residents. Indeed, because they were wheelchair users and some of the buildings were not yet finished, there were major problems in arranging site visits. The provision of maps, plans, models, photographs and written and taped descriptions held an enhanced importance which had not been recognized. This finding of the research was therefore acted upon immediately and the occupational therapist worked with other members of the project group to put together displays of information to enable residents to make better informed choices. This led in turn to residents using their expert knowledge of their own needs to suggest small but significant modifications to the buildings, the importance of which the architects and builders had failed to recognize. Charting the emergence and evaluating the adoption of changes such as these and then considering their potential transferability to other situations could then become the focus for subsequent research activities.

Another aspect of data collection which was shared between the researcher and project group members concerned information about adults with severe disabilities and their needs for care and accommodation. It was necessary to build up a profile of current residents and also of those local children, teenagers and adults living with families or elsewhere who might at some point need Hillcrest-type facilities. Information of this kind could be drawn from, for example, population statistics, special school rolls and lists of those receiving or applying for related services such as transport to day care and grants for housing adaptations.

As far as the current residents were concerned, biographical information in considerable detail was needed by the social worker who was responsible for putting together the multi-disciplinary assessments that would enable service providers to begin to match their needs for care and accommodation with available facilities. It was therefore decided that an assessment form would be designed to serve the research and action components of the project. Residents and their advocates/relatives were to be able to see and use this form and it was to include biographical facts and information about personal and health care, and about functional abilities. It was to indicate people's views on their current situations and their wishes for the future. Because it had the potential to be used before and after decisions had been taken and implemented about moving to alternative accommodation it was a key evaluative tool. As time went on essential elements of the forms were extracted, summarized in charts and set against emergent information about accommodation options to give overall snapshots of progress to date. These in turn served the twin purposes of action and research. They featured in the collectively written interim report submitted to senior managers at the point of transition between the first and second phases of the project, and project group members used their copies to stock-take on progress within their individual areas of responsibility.

MANAGING THE ACTION RESEARCH PROCESSES

In making the decision to adopt an action research approach to this study, I placed the issues of process at its centre and recognized that mechanisms had to exist for the dissemination and implementation of ideas if change was to take place. The project group was a key vehicle. The next extract gives a further example of my role in paying attention to the processes of research and action, and more specifically in conceptualizing options for their management. It is taken from documentation written just as it became clear that the project group meetings were being set aside. It records possibilities which had been explored up to that point on the assumption that the action research was to proceed as planned, and also spells out some of the anticipated consequences of suspending project group meetings.

Document 8.3: Extract from draft interim report

The processes of consultation and change
One model for moving forward was to have been based upon small groups involving 'significant others' – one of potential stayers, one of potential leavers and one of potential users. These three groups would have been coordinated through some sort of project group-serviced planning forum which would have drawn in representatives from 'outsiders', initiated requests for information and run a series of larger debates. This model would have taken as essential the continuation of the project group, in some form, in order to coordinate its spawned activities.

   An alternative suggestion could best be described as the 'think tank' approach which is modelled upon the House of Commons Select Committee system. Such a proposal would have involved the project group itself bringing on board representatives of the 'leavers' and the 'stayers', both residents and 'significant others', as well as one or two key 'outsiders' from the voluntary self-help sector, to form a Hillcrest Think Tank. This could have held a series of meetings which individuals and groups, with an existing or potential interest in the unit's future, would have been asked to attend, by invitation, in order to talk about their needs for and ideas about services which Hillcrest already does or might in the future provide. A record of 'the evidence' presented and the deliberations involved would have formed the basis for the project group's next report to senior management.

The sudden and unexpected setting aside of the project group's meetings means that within the foreseeable future such consultation is unlikely to take place between users, potential users and service providers about Hillcrest proposals, because the infrastructure does not exist to underpin any such exercise. It is nevertheless within the spirit of the legislation to enable people with disabilities to take initiatives and work in partnership with those providing their care. Tacking the name of a single resident on to the end of a list of project group members is not sufficient on this count.

The department is faced with implementing widespread change at Hillcrest and it is therefore ironic that the research literature and the researcher's experience indicate that such a process may be facilitated by the establishment of open channels of communication and partici- pative styles of working. In other words, if attention is not paid to the process as opposed to the task elements of change, achieving the desired outcome will be hampered by a lack of consultation when this itself could actually become a valuable vehicle for change.

The course now set

In the absence of any consultative or collaborative mechanisms to promote the processes of change, the danger is that attempts to meet the Hillcrest deadlines will be professionally dominated and task- orientated. This is not intended to underestimate the respective contri- butions of individual members of staff but merely to indicate that their already difficult jobs are likely to become that much more so without the arena which project group meetings provided for co-ordinated planning and action. Some project group members are continuing to meet to identify models of care for those intending to move out and to look at mechanisms for managing and delivering these. These staff are committed to holding fast to a principle which has informed the project group's work from the outset, namely that residents should be set up, not to fail, but to succeed in their transitions to more independent styles of living.

Further work is being done as quickly as possible on other named issues. It may be that stock-taking in the light of this report would allow some further discrete steps to be taken from among the following suggestions:

- the groupwork mentioned above might be undertaken;
- information on costings and unmet need might be sought;
- current staff allocation and rostering could increasingly become informed by a small group living approach;
- staff meetings and training sessions could aim to prepare workers to operate more flexibly within more independent living arrangements;
- some meetings could be scheduled periodically to update staff, residents, their relatives and advocates on the department's thinking and progress.
- some deadlines could be set and publicized for the time by which the department intended, for example, to have drafted proposals for submission to the Social Services Committee and to have made at least some short-term decisions about the future of Hillcrest.

If such steps were to be taken, the researcher believes that the department would be making an active and positive contribution to the management of uncertainty. In her judgement the need for this at Hillcrest should not be underestimated in the current climate of widespread internal and external change.

CONCLUDING COMMENT

I stated earlier that this study served as an example of failed action research. From my point of view it was less than successful on two associated counts. First, it remained unfinished in that the planned programme of work was brought to a premature end with the result that a formal evaluation of ideas and developments never took place. The interim writing-up phase concluded with submission of a progress report but never went on to a dialogue about its contents and messages, or to planning and establishing agreement among the participants about the next stage of the action research cycle. Second, because of the uncertainty about proceeding further, at the time it was deemed diplomatic to avoid pressing for wider publication of any parts of the report in case this jeopardized negotiations.

Such studies may also be criticized as being too situation-specific and therefore as producing findings with limited scope for generalization. The work recorded here is inherently limited in that it was unfinished. But my involvement for even a short period of time alerted me to the unrealized potential which lay within this project to contribute to the wider debate about the transfer of very dependent people from long-stay institutions to independent living arrangements. Where managers are seeking to promote such transfers they may need to allow people to move gradually, with long-term 'cushions of support' provided in the form of access to ongoing respite care, further rehabilitation and temporary or permanent readmission to residential care (Phillips *et al.* 1990). At the time the 'cushion of support' concept was not one which we had come across elsewhere and to have explored it and then written it up might have made a useful contribution to the literature. Similarly, scope existed to investigate further the extent to which, in such a scenario, key players have and can exercise real choice about outcomes.

One last point is worth making. Evaluation of this action research project as far as it went requires more than the recording of my perspective on events. The premature termination of the work reduced the opportunities available to seek out the perceptions of others, but a telling piece of feedback emerged from the pages of the social work press. A contact at Hillcrest let me know that a personal account of developments had been accepted for publication in the 'Soapbox' section of *Social Work Today* (Anon. 1990). Written anonymously, the article suggested a fair measure of agreement between its author, who had been a key informant, and the researcher in terms of problem analysis. The person who wrote it had not had access to the interim report, but nevertheless there was clear evidence that common understandings had been reached about the nature of the problems and about the importance of issues of process in finding ways to move forward.

9

Case study 5
Changing medication practices in a home for older people

INTRODUCTION

This case study describes an action research project undertaken in a local authority home for older people (Bond 1990). The project focused on medication practices and grew out of my (Meg Bond's) concern as the recently appointed manager that large quantities of drugs were being distributed, daily and unchecked, by unqualified and untrained staff to passive and dependent elderly people, who had low expectations for their health care and limited understanding of the benefits or side-effects of the medicines they were taking. Errors frequently occurred and no mechanism was in place to monitor or review individual medication regimes or the home's systems of drug distribution and storage.

The study is interesting as an example of insider-generated action research of the organizational type. Exploring problems encountered by a manager attempting to change the work practices of an established work group, this case study touches on the classic problem of 'resistance to change' which has preoccupied managers and academics for decades, including of course Kurt Lewin, the acknowledged pioneer of action research (Roethlisberger and Dickson 1942; Lewin 1946; Lupton 1963). However, it was also informed by a professionalizing agenda concerned with improving the quality of life of older people by changing accepted medication practices. It exploited commonalities of interests among participants, was concerned with practical problem-solving at grass roots level, and was undertaken without any additional resources being made available by the wider organization.

The account indicates the range of research tools that were used to collect the data and highlights ways in which care staff were drawn into the project to gain their cooperation and commitment to the introduction of improved practices. It illustrates how an initiative for change along one dimension of caring – the distribution and consumption of medication – opened up opportunities within the unit for further action research initiatives on other fronts.

Finally, the case study shows how, as a front line worker and manager of the establishment, I was able to exploit my relatively autonomous position to initiate change in a systematic way. But this freedom to act was also associated with a distancing from and disengagement by senior management, which in turn served to undermine sustained implementation of the project's findings and their more widespread dissemination.

THE SETTING

The setting for this study was a neglected public sector residential establishment for forty-two older people situated in a shire county in the Midlands. It had been purpose-built seventeen years earlier close to the centre of an elegant town, but people came to live there from a wide area of the neighbouring countryside as well as from two other towns, though significantly not from the Asian communities in the immediate locality. Over a long period older people, whose applications for residential care had not been accepted elsewhere, and staff who had had to be redeployed, had been directed towards this particular home, which in consequence

had become a 'dumping ground' for rejected and dejected residents and workers. Its reputation was not enhanced by its downtown position by a busy road on the edge of a housing estate, with litter and dogs fouling the unfenced lawns. Inside, bare walls and uncarpeted floors combined with dim light bulbs and frayed curtains to create an atmosphere of seediness made worse by the smell of unmanaged incontinence . . . Care staff acknowledged they would not wish to live there themselves or seek admission for someone close to them.

(Bond 1993a: 13)

The care staff's attitude was significant because the local authority had a policy of providing institutional services to people on a neighbourhood basis, and as most workers, including me, and some of their ageing relatives lived in the home's catchment area, this unit was the staff's place of work and for many their local residential facility. Besides this important but previously under-recognized point of common interest, during the twelve-month period of the project, women outnumbered men by twenty-eight to twelve in the resident group and by twenty-eight to two in the staff group. Most of the care staff were over thirty years old, many had histories of ill-health themselves and several were responsible for the care of sick relatives. In embarking on this project to examine medication practices and to heighten awareness of the significance of these in the maintenance of health, there was therefore an explicit intention to exploit a common interest among residents and female care staff. From the outset it seemed that by working on a health issue which mattered to staff in both their private and their professional capacities the action research could be seen as doubly relevant, resistance to it might be reduced, and staff might become committed to implementing improvements.

RESEARCHER ROLES

As manager of the home and initiator of the project I could 'fix' access to documents and 'informants'. For one thing, in undertaking it I was merely doing my job, but even so there were still considerable constraints. With no resources available from elsewhere and existing staff fully stretched, the exercise had to be carried out in my 'spare time' and with the help of a volunteer, a newly qualified sociology graduate/social worker. Neither of us had any prior pharmaceutical knowledge. We had to fit the project work into our other commitments over a period of several months, while the records upon which much of it was based remained in constant use, so it was not possible to operate from a single set of baselines. As residents became ill and recovered so their medication altered, and the exercise itself led to some changes as we took steps to correct errors and eradicate dangerous practices.

The first extract from our working documents (Document 9.1) consists of the notice put up on the home's information board after a period of discussion with staff. It explains the role of the volunteer as a collector and analyser of data from documentary sources within the home and as a participant observer in relation to routine medication practices. It defines her as a resource person in relation to the care staff, exploring the related literature and presenting findings for further consideration. It also indicates the direction in which the initiative was likely to go – the action component(s) – without prejudging the outcome(s) or foreclosing on any options.

Document 9.1: Notice board item

[The volunteer] has agreed to look at the pattern of drug-taking among residents – who is prescribed what, for what, and over what period of time. She will be looking at how we record medication and how we give it out. She will be getting information about drugs and dispensing in residential homes. She is not a pharmacist and she is not going to tell us what to do! She, with our cooperation, is going to build up a picture of what goes on here which she will give to us – she'll prepare some material for us which we can then use in discussions with the district pharmacist and with Mr Z [our community pharmacist], both of whom have agreed to advise us on our practices. In addition we will be able to use the information in talking to doctors who might usefully think about reducing prescriptions for minor tranquillizers, for instance.

The volunteer was introduced as such to residents, relatives and other health and social care colleagues, and in functioning as an 'honorary' member of staff for the periods of data collection she operated within the normal parameters of respect for persons and matters of confidentiality. As an outsider and 'a student type', as one person put it, she posed relatively little threat to those care staff whose 'drug rounds' she observed. Evidence for this came, among other things, from the fact that errors in distributing medication occurred unabated in her presence. Her willingness to spend hours in the home deciphering records, working round staff in examining documents and discussing patterns emerging from our analysis won her many friends.

At the outset our combined ignorance, pharmaceutically and procedurally, publicly cast us as learners in relation to established senior members of staff who traditionally 'put up the drugs'. Later, as we sought advice from pharmacists, doctors and nurses about problems and poor practices, staff began to tap our growing knowledge base and were encouraged to think more critically for themselves about medication issues. Senior colleagues were invited to bring forward any prescriptions which they perceived as problematic and two long-standing staff members offered to make an inventory of the contents of the medicines cupboard. This proved to be unfortunate in terms of recording for research purposes because their shame at what they found in terms of forgotten and outdated drugs led them to get rid of many bottles of pills without noting down their contents. But we coped with this by labelling it as part of the action phase since it implied changes in staff attitudes, and in discussing their methods of disposal we learnt significant information about questionable practices on this count.

RESEARCH ACTIVITIES

The volunteer began by examining the medicine book kept for stock control purposes and the records of all individual residents, which included notes written daily by care staff on a Kardex, case files including medical records (but not GP NHS records), sample prescriptions and individual medication profiles containing details of drugs prescribed. There was no system in place for recording the actual consumption of medicines even though many residents took a combination of different drugs several times a day. The volunteer also observed the task of 'putting up' the day's drugs, that is of re-dispensing them from separate containers into a single uncovered pot labelled with the person's name for each resident.

Throughout this period we identified relevant articles, books and pamphlets. Interestingly, almost nothing had previously been provided in the home. For example, an internal health and safety policy document had a mere eight sentences on 'use of drugs' and included a reference to a departmental procedure manual, but the latter was not in evidence at the start of the project. We drew heavily upon the most recent edition of the British National Formulary (BMA 1986), Parish's (1985) *Medicines: A Guide for Everybody*, the invaluable Derbyshire Health Authorities' (n.d.) *Pharmcare* pamphlets prepared by Rivers, and Blair's (1985) *Know Your Medicines*. All these were made readily available in the home. We also frequently sought and unfailingly received help and advice from our neighbour, the community pharmacist.

When we had collected our material, we invited staff from two other local authority residential establishments to join us for a meeting with the district pharmacist to discuss our responsibilities and practices in administering residents' medication. A summary of our findings and deliberations was put on display in the home as a stimulant to further discussion, learning and progress. A senior member of staff was designated to assume responsibility for implementing and consolidating new and better practices. She was also delegated to draft an interim paper on the system of drug administration for reference in the home and for discussion within the local authority, though in fact senior management never at any stage showed any interest in this project.

We did not view this paper as the definitive statement. Indeed it recorded practices, like re-dispensing, which we intended to change because by then we had seen for ourselves how the separation of 'the medicine from the label written by the pharmacist' (Blair 1986) increased the risk of error. We were keen to incorporate recommendations from the Pharmaceutical Society's 1986 report on medicines in residential homes and to look at the costs and benefits of different equipment to facilitate the administration of drugs from original containers. But in the meantime, with continuing and numerous staff changes, we wanted to make sure that the system we had in place was adhered to and that as far as possible errors were excluded. And we wanted to open up the issues for debate within our local authority: hence the need to produce a paper.

In the event this task took many months. Lacking secretarial support, it was a casualty of prolonged staff shortages and the reduction of those of us who remained to survival strategies. This confirmed how influential had been the contribution of the volunteer who had provided commitment, objectivity, a disciplined approach, writing and presentation skills, and a crucial extra pair of hands.

CAPTURING DATA IN A CONTEXT OF CONSTANT CHANGE

We employed three techniques to obtain a picture of the consumption of medication in the home. First, on one day early in the project, when I was the 'duty officer' responsible for 'putting up' the drugs, we counted and analysed all preparations dispensed to residents. Such a snapshot could obviously be repeated at intervals and provided one measure of the quantity and range of drugs consumed by residents. On a subsequent count, and following an initiative to assess and improve residents' dietary intakes, the consumption of laxatives (initially by six out of the thirty-four residents then taking medication of any kind) had stopped altogether.

Second, we examined and compared for consistency all available information on every resident's medication regime. This allowed us to develop individual profiles of medication regimes and to expose to scrutiny recording practices on the part of the home's staff and of health care professionals including doctors, receptionists and pharmacists. The next extract from our working documents is an example of the summary of one such profile which we prepared for discussion with colleagues and which led them to hypothesize explanations for the discrepancies that were all too evident from the material.

Document 9.2: Mrs B's medication records

Mrs B's repeat prescription ordered over the phone was for four items: fenbid (an anti-rheumatic drug), thioridazine (a major tranquillizer), nitrazepam (a benzodiazepine used principally as a sleeping drug) and dothiepin (a tricyclic anti-depressant). The label on her new bottle of dothiepin tablets stated '75 mg as directed' so we had to look up our records to find out what the dosage should be. Our paperwork provided the following confusing information which the resident herself was unable to clarify:

Information available about Mrs B's dothiepin

21.3.86	Personal file opened on admission	No information ever recorded
Undated	Kardex	} 25 mg × 2 at night
4.4.86	Individual medication record	
30.4.86	Stock control book entry of script ordered	25 mg × 1 at night

5.5.86	Individual medication record	} 25 mg x 1 in the
6.5.86	Kardex	} morning
2.6.86	Stock control book entry of script ordered	25 mg x 3 daily
5.6.86	Label on bottle in current use	25 mg { 1 morning { 2 at night
	Label on new bottle	75 mg as directed

Observations made by the volunteer suggested that it was not unusual to take delivery of drugs labelled to be taken 'as directed' and in this case it was likely that this would have been interpreted as 75 mg x 3 daily (i.e. 225 mg in total). However the many entries in her individual medication record and the Kardex system suggested that he may only have intended her to take a single dose of 25 mg.

Third, we took advantage of the need periodically to order repeat prescriptions to explore resident's, GPs' and staff's different understandings of each older person's health status and the relevance to this of her or his prescribed medication regime. This entailed a shift from a quantitative to a more qualitative approach to data collection and as part of this we observed and participated in the processes of obtaining prescribed drugs for all residents on an individual basis. As the following two case studies illustrate, this was an area of the project where the action research approach made a powerful impact. It served to raise and develop awareness of the extent of the problems facing us and prompted staff to begin to change their behaviour in relation to medication regimes.

Document 9.3: Two case studies

Miss A
Miss A was partially sighted, diabetic, very overweight and barely mobile. Her regular repeat prescriptions included daily doses of pericyazine (a major tranquillizer), mianserin (a tetracyclic anti-depressant), glibenclamide (an oral anti-diabetic drug), digoxin (a drug to treat heart failure), and Aldactide (a diuretic), with dorbanex added, as necessary, to treat constipation (the last has now been taken off the market). She also used the antibiotics chloramphenicol ointment and soframyacin as well as Melolin dressings and Tubigrip bandages.

When we came to examine her records it emerged that we had no information about what was wrong with her except what we could deduce from her prescriptions. Although Miss A readily agreed to allow the manager to ask her GP to enlighten them both about her health so that the staff could better meet her needs, the doctor was enraged by this request. He wrote across the home's medical records in large red print, 'Diagnosis is a confidential matter between doctor and patient' and then threatened to make a complaint to the local authority about the incident. Miss A did not feel strongly enough to assert herself independently to insist that the doctor shared any information with her, so her records remained blank about what was wrong with her.

This lack of information had potentially serious implications given that the GP did not do regular check-ups and the monitoring of her well-being was therefore left by default to the staff of the home. The project had alerted us to the fact that older people on long-term multiple drug regimes are vulnerable to adverse reactions. In particular Miss A was taking the combination of digoxin and a diuretic which the literature suggests increases the likelihood of unwanted side-effects occurring (Hurwitz and Wade 1969) and calls for speedy reporting of any such symptoms to the physician (Jackson 1989). The doctor's failure to help us to understand more fully Miss A's medical conditions and the intended and unintended effects of the combination of drugs she was taking constrained our ability to recognize, and therefore to report, symptoms which may have suggested side-effects.

Mrs C

Mrs C was a heavily built seventy-five-year-old woman who moved slowly about the home, where she had lived for eighteen months. Her medication had not been documented on admission and no information was available on her medical condition, though she often complained of feeling generally unwell and indeed she died during the period of the study. By the time her drug regime came under scrutiny she was apparently taking the following:

- 60 mg mianserin at night (a tetracyclic anti-depressant);
- 25 mg thioridazine thrice daily (a major tranquilliser);
- 50 mg orphenadrine thrice daily (closely related to an anti-histamine drug, this lifts the mood and relaxes spasm of skeletal muscles);
- one Feospan capsule twice daily (an iron salt used to treat anaemia);
- 100 mg Cetiprin twice daily (used to treat urinary incontinence/frequency but now discontinued);
- two paracetamol tablets when required (a mild pain reliever).

A repeat prescription was requested by phone for all these drugs except the paracetamol, which was still in plentiful supply. Cetiprin was omitted without any explanation. We had no reason to believe that the doctor had necessarily taken an informed decision about this. He had not seen Mrs C since the issue of his last repeat script, he had not told her or us that the Cetiprin should be stopped and as far as she was concerned her condition remained unchanged. We phoned the surgery and a further script was sent but this time for a course of Septrin. We consulted our reference material and the pharmacist and learnt that Cetiprin, which was then used to treat urinary incontinence/ frequency, was a different drug from Septrin, which is an antibiotic used to treat infections. Had Mrs C's urinary incontinence been associated with a urinary tract infection such a script might have been appropriate. Indeed, the advice of continence advisers is that the treatment of urinary incontinence should normally seek to exclude infection as the cause before proceeding with other forms of treatment. But in this case the doctor had not asked for a sample of urine for testing, and Mrs C was not complaining of any new symptoms which might have indicated an infection and worsened with a delay in receiving treatment.

Again a member of staff phoned the surgery only to be told by the receptionist that the latter was unable to clarify the situation from the patient's records because the GP had made no notes on them about any of the foregoing. Eventually another prescription arrived for Cetiprin but again we had to seek the help of the pharmacist because essential dosage instructions had not been included. Leaving aside the obvious issues of poor medical care, this case illustrated the scope which exists between the surgery and the home for errors to occur in the ordering of drugs and highlighted the importance of meticulous accuracy and attention to detail by residential staff at every stage of the process.

TAKING STOCK OF FINDINGS AND IMPLEMENTING CHANGES

The findings which were discussed with colleagues were of two kinds: numerical and narrative descriptions of aspects of the home's medication practices, and case studies and 'emergent themes'. The extract that follows is taken from materials prepared for the feedback session shared with colleagues from two other local authority establishments who had become interested in replicating the processes of our action research project and in learning from our findings.

Document 9.4: Findings

Resident/medication profile and overview

During this study there were forty residents in the home, twenty-eight of whom were women over seventy years of age, including ten over ninety. There were also twelve men, eleven of whom were in their seventies and eighties, while the twelfth was coming up to retirement age. The medical care of these permanent residents was shared among nine different GP practices comprising some thirty doctors. One practice had a single resident on its books while four practices had responsibility for six to eight residents each.

On a sample day thirty-four of the forty residents (85 per cent) were taking medication regularly. Of these, twenty-two (65 per cent) were registered with doctors in seven different practices who provided repeat prescriptions on request but did not visit routinely to keep medication under review or to carry out check ups. The remaining twelve residents (35 per cent), and two others deemed not to need any medication, were seen at about six-weekly intervals, usually by the same two GPs from two different practices, who kept their medication constantly under review.

Dispensing within the home: contents of the drug cupboard and distribution processes

In the course of this project we examined the contents of the 'dangerous drugs' cupboard where we had been surprised to find multi-vitamins alongside diconal (a narcotic pain reliever), both in the names of long-deceased residents. On other shelves of the main cupboard we found opened and unopened containers of medicines well past their shelf life. There was no clear separation between household and prescription-only medicines, or between those for internal and for external use. We came across eye drops which had been forgotten because they were not administered at meal-times and the system was too inflexible to incorporate anything outside the usual drug rounds. We discovered tablets left behind by residents who had been admitted to hospital without staff seeing the value of sending their medication with them. And we observed the potentially dangerous practices of filling almost empty bottles of tablets from new ones and of sharing medication among different residents.

Re-dispensing drugs from the pharmacist's containers in the cupboard into a drug-round pot for each resident was characterized by disorder. Initially the re-dispensing was done by transferring drugs once daily from a muddled collection of original containers to a number of poorly labelled and apparently disorganized pots in four trays, with a pot for each resident taking medication on each drug round. Observation of this process of re-dispensing revealed that staff did not give it priority over everything else while carrying it out, as urged by pharmacist Peter Rivers (Benson 1986). The drugs, which later in the day became someone else's responsibility, were 'put up' at one of the busiest times of the morning shift in a room frequently full of activity, with the member of staff concerned responding to every interruption.

Emergent themes

A number of disquieting features are apparent from the case studies:

- the way in which lack of diagnostic information can disadvantage staff in developing an understanding of residents' medication and their responses to it;
- the frequency with which repeat scripts are issued without any re-evaluation of the person's condition;
- the scope that exists for errors and misunderstandings between home and surgery;
- the way in which errors can be compounded when staff overlook the importance of accurate record keeping and doctors overlook the importance of issuing scripts which leave no margin for misunderstanding;
- the way in which the medical ethics of clinical judgement and clinical confidentiality may be invoked in a manner which thwarts staff's attempts to act responsibly.

Changes which we initiated were designed to make improvements in these areas. As a first step we moved the 'putting up of the drugs' to a quiet room and to the quietest time of the day, and we insisted that in distributing them, account should be taken of pharmaceutical advice (e.g. aspirin to be taken with a long drink). The chaos in the boxes and trays was replaced with simple alphabetical ordering, which then interestingly highlighted that spelling was a problem for some staff. This was of course a significant handicap when it came to dealing with unusual drug names written illegibly on scripts or half-heard over the phone.

It proved much easier to change relationships with local pharmacists than with residents' doctors. Thanks to the assistance of the district and especially the community pharmacist we slowly began to make sense of the data which we were collecting and to establish a programme of change. We introduced a defined procedure for the administration and storage of medication which was scrutinized and approved by the district pharmacist and was to be followed by all care staff. This was written up by the senior member of staff who assumed delegated responsibility for oversight in this area. We introduced some important changes, such as refusing to accept scripts from GPs with imprecise instructions, and instead of making last-minute phone calls for repeat prescriptions we sent monthly typed letters to each surgery and kept copies of what items had been requested.

We then turned our attention to the institution of regular assessment and review procedures for every resident, including a health and medication component. We planned to change to a system of administering drugs to residents direct from the containers supplied and fully labelled by the pharmacist, to encourage self-medication with the necessary individual lockable facilities being made available, and to promote these changes through a continuing programme of education.

It was clear that such a programme had to be founded upon two basic assumptions: first, that errors are inevitable but that reporting them immediately, correcting them, dealing with their consequences and taking steps to avoid their recurrence are the hallmarks of good caring practice; and, second, that a little knowledge can be dangerous but the skilled professional carer needs to develop a spirit of enquiry and to learn enough about medication matters to be in a position to know what she or he does not know and when she or he needs to obtain advice.

The project indicated that there was considerable scope for running courses about health and medication issues within and across establishments, and for promoting learning from opportunities which arise in the course of day-to-day caring. A challenging but potentially highly effective approach to this is to set up health courses jointly for residents and their informal and formal carers.

Often we resourced staff with specially tailored information packs, as when we ran sessions on dementia and visual loss with help from the Alzheimer's Disease Society and the local specialist voluntary agency for the blind, respectively. We took out a subscription for the supply of *Pharmcare* pamphlets and ordered back copies. We turned a disused walk-in linen cupboard into a resources room, which was well used by care staff, who sometimes asked for extra copies of written materials so that they could take them home.

RESISTANCE AND INDIFFERENCE

Resistance to such changes became evident among senior staff and care assistants, all of whom were involved at some time or another in giving out medication. Some staff had great difficulty in acknowledging that, for example, prior to administering drugs prescribed for use 'when needed', like the painkiller codydramol, they should discuss with a resident her or his wishes and requirements rather than giving out a tablet as a matter of routine. In fact this whole area of caring practice was exposed as one in which staff expressed quite markedly traditional 'warehousing' and controlling attitudes towards residents, and the old guard battled to preserve these in the face of initiatives for change. On one occasion a revengeful care assistant remained silent about a senior staff member's failure to make available the lunch time tray of drugs, and when I discovered the 'oversight' two hours later, it appeared that neither a single resident nor any member of staff had asked about the missing drugs. Other workers on duty had colluded in turning residents and their entitlement to receive their prescribed medication into pawns in a power game. A different but related aspect of the struggle for power surfaced when a resident was given double the dose of her breakfast time tranquillizer 'to shut her up' so that the morning staff could have a quiet shift.

On the other hand there were signs that things were beginning to change for the better. A care assistant who accidentally gave a resident the wrong tablet immediately reported the matter and then took an active part in its follow-up in terms of monitoring the person's progress and analysing how such an incident could be avoided in the future. Others made increasing use, personally and professionally, of the available reference material and there were instances when staff made strenuous efforts to strike a better balance between encouraging residents to take medication prescribed for them and accepting the legitimacy of the residents' refusal to do so.

Reference has already been made to the discussion and dissemination meeting set up with and for colleagues from two nearby establishments. This arrangement developed as a result of networking among kindred spirits; at no point in the life of the project did senior management display any real interest in our activities or findings. The home was one of a sample of four visited in the area by members of the Social Services Inspectorate in the course of a national review of the extent to which government advice on arrangements for health care in residential homes for elderly people had been implemented. The inspectors arrived with a senior member of staff from 'headquarters' and they spent a considerable amount of time interviewing me in a room where the walls were covered with charts displaying some of our findings. But these aroused little comment and were not sufficient to prompt the staff member to invite us to contribute to a working party, which we later learnt he had convened, to examine medication practices in establishments caring for older people across the authority. In spite of this we submitted our interim paper on the modified system of drug administration operating in the home and invited comment as we prepared to introduce further changes. We received no response.

Such a lack of interest was, it seemed, the other side of the coin of freedom to act and easy access. It served as a reminder that action research, which was seen as 'top-down' from the perspective of those living and working within the unit, was perceived as 'bottom-up' by the wider organization. It had cost the social services department no extra money but by the same token it had no sponsors. No one outside had a vested – indeed any – interest in its outcomes and it was left to personal commitment to get the findings disseminated more widely.

DISSEMINATION

In the event the material was published through the Social Care Association (SCA) (Bond 1990) and through this route the findings were made accessible first and foremost to front line practitioners. The report appeared as a 'practice paper' monograph after considerable discussion with the series editors about how our publication might be so written as to address simultaneously the interests of care staff, managers and policy makers. Our view was that we might contribute in some small way to bridging the frequently identified theory–practice divide if we could narrow the distance between what those at the top and those at the bottom of caring organizations read. In taking such a position with reference to the medication study there was a consistency of thinking that grew out of the action research approach, which had been adopted because of its problem-solving potential as 'applied research'. The paper was therefore written in a straightforward style and set the project and its findings within the context of other relevant studies and policy changes. While it offered some pointers towards good practice these were couched in the form of questions rather than instructions and followed some critical comments about the limitations of routine adherence to procedures. The final documentary extract below is designed to give a flavour of the monograph's style.

Document 9.5: Extract from 'practice paper'

Thinking staff in residential establishments caring for older and often confused people must constantly be troubled by questions like:

- To what extent is this person's state of health made worse by their medication?
- To what extent do we have a responsibility/right/duty to interfere on their behalf by, for example, insisting on asking informed questions of their doctor?
- How can we contribute towards this person's well-being without over-stepping the mark in relation to the doctor's professional territory and the person's rights to be self-determining?

Adherence to departmental guidelines on the control, storage and administration of medicines is necessary but it is not sufficient to ensure good practice. Staff need to recognize that administration of psychotropic drugs, for instance, may be functional for staff but dysfunctional for residents; that care staff can influence the prescription of hypnotics through their contacts with GPs; that the social interactions which characterize long-term care may be as influential as the written record in determining the administration of drugs of this kind; and that once prescribed, drugs may rarely be discontinued (Wade *et al.* 1986). Such findings from the literature are unlikely to surface in procedure manuals but they are the justification for and should underpin any basic programme of staff education.

Good practice demands that staff effectively negotiate the fine dividing line between accepting a resident's right to be self-determining and a medical practitioner's duty to act professionally, without allowing either party to override/deny the other's perspective. Doctors do not always differentiate between the traditional function of a nurse carrying out medical treatment orders and the role of social care staff operating outside the hospital hierarchy within an ethos promoting independence and self-determination. Residents may lack skills in assertiveness or may have lost the ability to express themselves coherently or to negotiate effectively on their own behalf. It is in this context that residential staff need to intervene and to strike a balance between a *laissez-faire* approach and over-reaching their own professional boundaries. The following pointers towards good practice may help them in this daunting task.

- Are staff aware of the extent of drug taking among those they care for, both individually and collectively?
  (a) What are the commonest drugs?
  (b) What are they used to treat?
  (c) What are their possible side effects?
- Does the home run a programme of activities which enables residents and staff to learn about health issues?
- Are residents empowered to discuss their health and medication with their GP and to have them regularly reviewed?
- Do staff have ready access to clearly written reference material to promote their knowledge of and interest in medication issues and the maintenance of good health?
- Are there agreed guidelines for the administration, storage and control of residents' medication and are these guidelines approved by the district and/or community pharmacist?
- Are there integrated records for all residents which show:
  (a) when they last saw their GP?
  (b) when their medication was last reviewed?
  (c) what conditions are being treated?
  (d) what medication they are taking?
  (e) changes in their health?
- Is this record taken into account at residents' reviews?
- Do residents take their medication with them on admission to hospital, together with a letter from the home explaining what is known of their medical condition and medication regime?

CONCLUSION: ONE RESEARCH PROJECT LEADS TO ANOTHER

In terms of the typology (Table 3.1) the project had the potential to have spiralled into other action research types. It might have spiralled into the experimental type by, for instance, using what was learned to design an experiment to test out the findings elsewhere, perhaps by attempting to reproduce the type of change experiment pioneered by Lewin (1946). In fact a shift to a professionalizing type did come about by locating the problem as one of professional standards of care and disseminating the findings of the case study through a network of critical practitioners. It might also have been possible, given the continued commitment of care staff to the project and the greater involvement of senior managers, to put the findings in the hands of recipients of the service and to have shifted incrementally to the kind of empowering approach adopted in case study 3 for working with older people in the community.

Dissemination of the findings of this particular cycle of action research was an activity that stretched over a prolonged period largely because negotiating and preparing a manuscript for publication is time-consuming. But more immediately and within the home the project outlined above generated other ideas for further work.

First, the analysis of drug taking patterns pointed to a significant use of laxatives, consumption of which potentially could be modified by dietary changes. Recognition of this was a key factor in my decision to approach the local authority's nutritionist to help in mounting a six month action research project to analyse and improve the home's provision of food and residents' nutritional intakes. I obtained the services of an undergraduate student doing a course in nutrition who carried out laboratory analysis on a sample of residents' meals and complemented this quantitative research with several weeks' participant observation of food preparation, distribution and consumption. We engaged the cooperation and participation of residents, some relatives and staff, initially to gather the data and subsequently to introduce changes. A key vehicle for this was the establishment of a reminiscence group which explored residents' and cooks' recollections of vegetable growing, cooking and eating, and later took responsibility for influencing the decision-making within the home about meal times and menus.

Second, the recognition that there was no system in place for reviewing residents' medication regimes, combined with the discovery that several had been prescribed drugs for eye conditions, led us to look more closely at the prevalence of sight loss among residents and at the staff's abilities to respond appropriately to this:

> It was clear that we, as a staff group, needed to enhance our knowledge and understanding of these issues and [with] some urgency I approached the local Association for the Blind to enlist the administrator's help in running a short course on visual loss for all the staff. First, we distributed a short questionnaire designed to establish the base levels of knowledge from which colleagues were practising [and then organized and evaluated a training programme using taught and experiential approaches to learning] . . . To transfer the learning from the structured part of the course into improved caring practices with residents (and in some cases with relatives and friends) we arranged for a number of specialist assessments to be undertaken. Interested older people were invited to visit the low vision aids clinic and the mobility officer discussed teaching orientation skills to one woman resident and her keyworker. We also embarked on a phased programme of admission with another elderly person recently registered as blind, and we planned a redecoration of the building taking into consideration the needs of those with impaired sight. Running these initiatives in parallel proved particularly valuable for consolidating participants' learning. The assessments involved residents and staff over a number of weeks and offered opportunities for staff to extend their technical knowledge and practise their new skills.
>
> (Bond 1993b: 24–5)

Each of these initiatives was therefore a direct spin-off from the initial action research and each involved a further series of research, implementation and evaluation activities. The reporting phase for the nutrition project included the preparation of a report for use by other units within the social services department, while that for the visual loss project involved submission of an article, quoted above, to a social work journal widely read by practitioners and managers in the field of social care.

Part III

Working from a
project perspective

10

Toolkit

INTRODUCTION

The toolkit presented here has been assembled from tools and devices which we and others have found helpful as part of the mechanics of preparing research proposals, thinking about research problems and formulating possible strategies. The chapter is not intended as a substitute for further reading, or as a way of avoiding some of the important theoretical questions about choice of research methodology and strategy. Nevertheless, we believe there is value in attempting to find ways of demystifying some of the research thinking processes and of encouraging consideration of the micro-politics of projects.

There are six sections to the toolkit. The first is a self-assessment questionnaire which has been adapted from one we use on a management module for MSc students, all of whom are full-time health care professionals. It is designed to assist with thinking about the research problem and the context of a proposed piece of research. It draws on practice wisdom, your own knowledge of the setting in which you work and your own networks, actual and potential. It also prompts you to consider ways in which you might be able to generate qualitative and quantitative data from everyday activities to help in analysing the problem and context, and includes practical suggestions for ways in which you might undertake some fact-finding. Read in combination with Chapter 4 and the case studies, it may help you to identify similarities and/or differences between specific case studies and your own work situation. The second section is a summary of groupwork guidelines for intending facilitators of staff development programmes such as that with ward sisters described in case study 2. The groupwork guidelines, which are informed by the groupwork literature and practical experience, include a list of other materials which intending facilitators might find helpful. The third section provides examples of ethical guidelines. The fourth aims to help with diary keeping. The fifth presents material on evaluation and suggestions about a portfolio approach, and the sixth section provides an example of the use of attitude scales.

SELF-ASSESSMENT QUESTIONNAIRE: THINKING ABOUT THE PROBLEM AND THE CONTEXT

Question 1   What is the purpose of the proposed project?

Question 2   Why is it important to do something about this situation at this point in time?

Question 3   Why do you want to initiate such a project?

Question 4   Is there a problem (that is, an expression of a need for change) and, if so, who says there is?

Question 5a   You might now want to pause and consider what the problem (or problems) might look like from different points of view, and whether or not there is likely to be a consensus among the different individuals or groups involved that there is a problem. Chapter 4, which considers the process of preparing a research bid, and Chapter 5 (case study one), which explores the micro-politics of relationships between researchers, sponsors and other stakeholders, might be helpful here.

Identify the players (stakeholders) (tick as many as appropriate).

1   Management   [ ]
2   Sponsors (such as RHA)/policy-makers   [ ]
3a Users/patients/clients (through complaints, patient
     satisfaction surveys)   [ ]

3b Interest groups (such as MIND, The Patients'
    Association)/unions   [ ]
4   Practitioners   [ ]
5   Opinion makers (media/general public)   [ ]
6   Purchasers   [ ]

Having constructed the list of 'players', you might want to consider the context in which the problem has emerged and the interest groups involved in relation to the 'action research typology' in Chapter 3 (Table 3.1). You may find it helpful to identify what particular action research type, or combination of types, is suggested by the particular problem and context. For instance, the demand for change might be managerially led in response to government pressure to 'do something', but the problem itself might have emerged from user groups, whose actions may be led by values which are at odds with managerial ideology. The typology could also help you in thinking about your position, and about to what extent you might need the assistance of an outside researcher or someone with specialist skills in designing experiments or in groupwork.

Question 5b   Identify the position of the players using Figure 10.1.

Question 6   What, briefly stated, is each interest group's perspective on the problem, including especially any differences within each group and/or whether a group(s) does not see it as a problem (for instance, 'patient participation' may be more of a problem for professionals than for patients)?

Question 7   Using the information from the above questions, list the stakeholders in rank order according to the power they hold, with the most powerful at the top.

Question 8   What is the nature of the power of each of the stakeholders? Use the lists below to consider the difference between 'power to' and 'power over' in relation to each of the stakeholders.

Power over   *Power to*
  Resources   Cooperate/say no!
  People   Disrupt/support
  Access   Close off/open up
  Permission   Deny/recognize
  Time   Make life difficult/make life easier
  Places   Marginalize/centralize
                        Whistle blow/cover up

Question 9 What is your relationship to each of the stakeholders and how might this oblige you to take their view or allow you to act independently?

[ ]   None
[ ]   Employee
[ ]   Peer/colleague
[ ]   Boss/manager
[ ]   Supplicant (if bidding for money for research)
[ ]   Client/patient
[ ]   Friend
[ ]   Relative
[ ]   Other

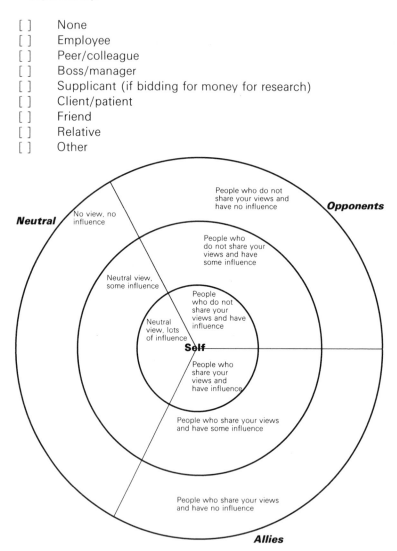

Figure 10.1 Mapping exercise: spheres of influence of allies, opponents and neutrals

Question 10   What is the problem as you see it? Describe it in your own words.

Question 11   Are you able to identify causes of the problem or say anything about what *you* feel lies at the heart of the problem?

Question 12   Are you able to identify causes of the problem as the other stakeholder(s) see(s) it, or say anything about what *they* feel lies at the heart of the problem? Link this to the interests of each of the stakeholders.

Question 13   Are you able to list different viewpoints about what the nature of the problem is? (Look for things such as one group locating the problem in another group, or 'blaming' or 'scapegoating'.)

Question 14   By what means might you do some fact-finding about the problem?

[ ]   Talk to people about it
[ ]   Read policy documents
[ ]   Find out what happens elsewhere – make phone calls, use your
        network
[ ]   Cognitive mapping (Eden *at al.* 1983)
[ ]   Force field analysis
[ ]   Review academic literature/professional journals
        (what is written about the problem in literature?)
[ ]   Observation – go and see for yourself
[ ]   Diary keeping
[ ]   Analysis of records
[ ]   Think about contributions that other groups and stakeholders
        can make (have you excluded anyone who could give you
        valuable information?)
[ ]   Form a project group and make alliances with others who share
        your views

Question 15   What evidence of the problem do you have?

Letters of complaint
Information from formal evaluation (questionnaires, interviews)
Financial information
Research findings (in-house and/or by outside agencies)
Low morale
Exit interviews
Expressed dissatisfaction
Uncooperative staff/clients

Statistical information, e.g.
    re-admission rates
    absenteeism
    sickness and absence
    turnover rates

Question 16 How might you generate evidence of different kinds, quantitative and qualitative, to help with problem definition and analysis? This might include drawing on the appropriate research literature, using information from a diary kept systematically over a specified time period, and/or collecting numerical data of various kinds. It might also include conducting your own questionnaire survey, such as, for example, on job satisfaction.

Question 17 What sources of information are available to you to help with the above? Think about individuals you work with as well as documents or written evidence.

Question 18 Do you need specialist skills such as financial, statistical/or research expertise? If so, who can you go to for help? Do you need an outside person?

Concluding comments

Having worked through some of these questions you might well feel that the problem is beyond your scope to change single-handedly. It may be helpful to use the map (Figure 10.1) to identify individuals who might be interested in working with you in a project group, including others from different professional and user groups. It might also help to re-formulate the problem in a way which makes it manageable by going back through the questions and answering them again, but this time trying to focus in on the problem or look at it more broadly. It may be that you could identify more clearly who the different stakeholders are, what different interests are involved, or what may be at the heart of the problem. Or you may have focused too broadly and at too general a level. In our experience the problem tends to be become more complex rather than less as the analysis progresses. We have found Eden *et al*. (1983) particularly helpful in identifying ways of assisting with thinking about problems in organizational settings, and Mares *et al*. (1985) in addressing community-based needs research.

GROUPWORK GUIDELINES

Introduction

Action research, as a collaborative venture, has an affinity with the practice of groupwork since action researchers work with both formal and informal groupings of people to promote their shared endeavours. Lewin's work, for example, took for granted, explored and exploited the dynamic possibilities within groups; subsequently, where aspects of social life have come under investigation within the experimental type of research, the use of groups and control groups may be a central methodological feature. Our case studies cite several examples of groups being brought together, and the following guidelines were generated as a result of one of these initiatives.

The groupwork with the ward sisters in case study 2 took place in the context of a project which moved from the organizational and professionalizing types towards the empowering type of action research. When the project came to an end, two possibilities emerged. One was that the action research should be written up for dissemination among ward sisters facing the transition to ward manager status. The other was that those who had been our collaborators would take from the action research process ideas and techniques which they could employ and adapt for use with their immediate colleagues. They began to think in terms of further programmes of education and change on their wards and more widely within the hospital, thus recognizing the potential for generating other cycles of action research. For both of these purposes, it was decided to draw out from our shared enterprise points which would make explicit some of the steps that had been taken in running the group. The guidelines that follow are the product of this exercise, but may be used to inform work in other settings.

Our intention in including them here is not to spell out the essence of doing groupwork; nor do we pretend that the knowledge and expertise deployed by experienced practitioners can or should be distilled into a list of 'dos and don'ts'. That would be to reduce a valuable and demanding form of practice to an unrecognizable and quite unrepresentative state. Nor can we begin to do justice here to the very substantial literature which exists on the theories, skills and scope for groupwork – and while social work and social care staff have in the past made more use of it than nurses and therapists, there are signs that, where opportunities can be created, professional carers more generally are recognizing its potential in terms of therapy, education and collective action.

Our aim is to illustrate some of the issues a novice action researcher would benefit from addressing when considering the idea of using groupwork as a strategy for progress. This may have the dual merits of, on the one hand, demystifying the approach and thus making it seem 'doable', while, on the other hand, indicating where further reading, preparatory work and assistance might prove beneficial.

Factors to be considered by facilitators

Planning
When planning to act as (a) facilitator(s) in a staff development programme of the kind undertaken with ward sisters in case study 2 consider:

1 The membership.
    - Who decides who is to attend?
    - Are ward sisters to select themselves?
    - Will they be instructed to attend?
    - Will they be invited?
    - Do potential group members already work closely together as colleagues or do they merely know each other?
    - Will each member give a commitment to attend all the sessions and be enabled to do so by his or her line manager?
    - Will new members be admitted during the life of the group or will it be run as a 'closed group'?
2 Pre-course preparation with each member. What contact should be made beforehand to explain the purposes of the programme to likely participants? (This presents an opportunity to gauge interest, explain your involvement, gain cooperation, explore participants' own agendas, allay any latent anxieties and identify any obstacles in the way of their attendance.)
3 The venue. Is the setting both comfortable and functional? (A setting which gives cues about staff having time out is likely to promote progress. To meet away from their normal place of

work with allowance made for travelling, protects staff from the daily demands upon their time and attention. It encourages them to step outside their normal and perhaps entrenched patterns of behaviour and interaction, and frees them to step back and take stock of their situations. It opens up the possibility of exploring new ways of seeing and doing things in an unexposed setting.)

4 Practical arrangements.
- Is one room enough and is private space needed for small group work?
- Can interruptions from outside be prevented except in emergencies?
- Can staff have access to a phone should they need to make or receive calls in an emergency?
- Is a flip chart or overhead projector available?
- Can refreshment or meals be provided to fit in with participants' needs?
- How are the costs of the programme in terms of staff time, staff cover and running costs to be met?

5 The length and timing of the programme.
- How many sessions do you need?
- How long should each one be?
- How far apart should they be spaced?

6 Concluding the developmental programme.
- At the end of the programme is the group to continue to meet? If so, where and in what form (e.g. a social meeting at someone's house or a peer group meeting at work)?
- Is the group going to 'report back' to manager(s), to staff, or to both?
- How might you use the information you have gathered and generated, for example, to do something about a particular problem or implement an improvement?
- Where do you go from here, individually and as a group? What kind of further development and training needs have you identified and how might these be fulfilled?

It is helpful to decide these matters in advance, perhaps at an initial planning meeting with participants. This will allow group members to clear their diaries to accommodate their commitment to the group and will make explicit to their organization their unavailability for normal duties. It also enables members to tailor the group's agendas to the time available. If, as often happens, more development needs are identified than can be met within the existing programme, an evaluative session at the end can allow participants to work up a bid for a further series of sessions or for additional learning opportunities.

Getting started

At the outset of any such programme it is essential to spend time with participants clarifying expectations, purpose and ground rules. It is easy to assume, sometimes wrongly, that because people work in the same hospital or community setting, they know each other and all get on well. On the other hand, it is important not to underestimate the substantial knowledge base and experience which they share, by virtue perhaps of long-standing employment within the health authority and of residence in the locality. Introductions need to encourage participants to feel in control of the sharing of selected personal and professional information about themselves while at the same time allowing them to introduce different aspects of themselves from those which are more commonly known about. In this way group members can become more fully themselves at work and begin to draw upon fresh resources and other aspects of their personalities.

The facilitators will need to spell out the thinking behind the setting up of the programme, its purpose(s) and their role(s) within this. Even if time has already been spent discussing such issues, the purpose(s) need(s) restating and, if necessary, renegotiating. It is essential that any expectations (e.g. a written report to senior management or verbal feedback in staff meetings) and any recognized constraints (e.g. that there are resources to cover only a set number of sessions) are made clear. All participants need to check their hopes and fears on these counts and discuss any differences between them. This part of the groupwork is about building up trusting relationships among members. A sense of trust is an essential prerequisite for the development of good working relationships. If it is not engendered and maintained throughout the group's life, little progress will be made in terms of either individual or collective learning.

Agreeing some ground rules at the outset and ensuring that they remain appropriate and influential is another component within the process of involving members in the programme's agenda, giving them maximum control over how it is conducted and creating a secure environment for the promotion of learning and growth. It is useful to pay some attention to the following points when drawing up ground rules:

1 Confidentiality. Are members free to say anything they wish regarding the content of the sessions to anyone outside the group?
2 What kind of recording is to be made, either during or after group sessions, and what is to be done with any written material? Does someone other than the facilitator(s) need to write up notes? Should this responsibility be rotated? If notes on the sessions are prepared and distributed in the subsequent week will this enable anyone absent through illness to be updated and at the same time enable group members to chart their progress?
3 How will the beginning and end of sessions be signalled, and the time in between be managed? Is there a need for a timekeeper? Should this responsibility be rotated?
4 How will the group decide what to talk about at each session? Does someone need to act as chairperson or 'prompt' when discussion starts to drift or get out of hand?
5 How can the group enable those who are shy or unsure of themselves to have some 'air time' and those who are vocal not to dominate?

Ice-breaker games
1 Take it in turns to say what you would have been doing had you not been attending today's session. Name one thing you are sorry to have had to miss doing because this meeting took priority and one thing you are pleased to have avoided.
2 Work in pairs with a member of the group you know less well and share details of a recent incident or event which gave you pleasure. It could be one that touched on your professional or your personal life. When feeding back to the group each person should recount the essence of her or his partner's account.
3 Work in pairs to find out something about each other that you have in common. It could be a hobby, an aspect of your life

histories, a pet hate, a dream for the future. Identify exactly what aspects of this topic you experience in the same way and also how you differ. Decide together how you will share your findings in a one-minute feedback slot to the group.

The 'life' of the group

Groups go through stages. To begin with, participants will be unsure of what to expect and they will need time to get going as a group and to sort out how they are to proceed. Settling into a way of working results from and contributes to members recognizing and establishing areas of agreement and difference. Especially in the early part of a group's life it may seem that members are not very focused. For example, they may not stick closely to topics previously identified for consideration or they may find it too difficult to make decisions and, even when they do, they may not act upon them. This is to be expected because the groupwork setting is a test bed for the development of new and different ways of working. It is essential, therefore, to have faith in the process of allowing people with shared interests to use their own resources to find a way through difficulties, to solve problems and to generate fresh ideas.

Within this the role of the facilitator is important. Her or his task may include:

- Encouraging everyone to have a say and to listen to other's views;
- Providing a sense of direction by getting people started, by time keeping, by asking clarifying questions, by providing intermittent summaries and by making links between what has transpired in different sessions.
- Achieving some kind of balance between, on the one hand, the exchange of ideas and opinions and, on the other hand, the presentation of information.

The task of the facilitator is not to teach or train but rather to ensure that the processes of learning and working together take place. The facilitator is concerned more with how participants interact – encouraging, supporting and challenging them – than with determining the content of their discussions. Although the two of course cannot be entirely separated, if the facilitator pays attention to group processes the group itself will take care of the product.

Ending and moving on
As any group proceeds, participants usually develop some sense of belonging. For some people, sessions such as these may provide one of the few opportunities to work together collaboratively and to experience a strong sense of trust and self-esteem. In order to minimize the feelings of loss and isolation which may be associated with the ending of the programme it is important from the outset to recognize the time-limited nature of the enterprise and to plan ahead for closure. This may be done by reserving the last session for: (a) evaluation and for saying goodbyes; (b) looking beyond for opportunities to meet again, for example for a reunion meal and/or for a further one-off or series of sessions to evaluate subsequent developments and/or plan another course. Some participants might make commitments to work more closely together, actively seeking out ways to do this when they return to their workplace, and some might seek more regular informal contacts with each other. In taking such steps, group members will be carrying forward, into their daily practice, mutual support mechanisms which are likely to be sources of sustenance in managing and implementing changes addressed during and generated within the staff development sessions.

Concluding note

The following is a list of materials we drew on and have found helpful. There are further sources of references for workers wishing to develop basic skills and to extend their repertoire of knowledge, including, for example, the journal *Groupwork*, published three times a year.

Further reading

Butler, S. and Wintram, C. (1991). *Feminist Groupwork*. London, Sage.
Elgood, C. (1990). *Using Management Games*. Aldershot, Gower.
Ernst, S. and Goodison, L. (1981). *In Our Own Hands: A Book of Self-therapy*. London, The Women's Press.

Henderson, P. (1989). *Promoting Active Learning*. Cambridge, National Extension College.

Mullender, A. and Ward, D. (1991). *Self-directed Groupwork: Users Taking Action for Empowerment*. London, Whiting and Birch.

Preston-Shoot, M. (1987). *Effective Groupwork*. London, Macmillan.

Vernelle, B. (1994). *Understanding and Using Groups*. London, Whiting and Birch.

WEA (North West District)/Health Education Council (1986). *Women and Health Teaching Pack*. WEA Publications Department, 9 Upper Berkley Street, London W1H 8BY.

EXAMPLES OF ETHICAL GUIDELINES

We have placed considerable emphasis on the active role of participants in the change processes, and we would agree with Roberts that:

Drawing on the active contribution of citizens to research is a necessary way of ensuring that policies which arise from that research can in a meaningful and effective way be connected with the lives of those towards whom they are directed.

(Roberts 1992: 190)

With this aim in mind we have included examples of working documents. The first of these is adapted from a standard ethical protocol, the second was drawn up by Fogg (1988) for use in a study of nurse education, and the third by Lund (1992) for a study on services for incest survivors. Each of these illustrates that the kind of protocol drawn up is another reflection of your position in the typology (Table 3.1), including an organizational type (Document 10.1), a professionalizing type (Document 10.2) and an empowering type (Document 10.3). In action research the preparation of protocols might be seen as an opportunity to draw up documents collaboratively with participants, and to keep such documents under review. For instance, Fogg's was used as the basis from which a negotiated agreement was drawn up by Lund for a case study about the provision of services to incest survivors. In terms of our typology her small-scale research, using the life history approach, was positioned within an empowering type and included additional elements which reflected this, which are included as Document 10.3.

Document 10.1 is a standard ethics protocol. We would argue that it is not sufficient for the interviewer simply to read it out and then expect the respondent to sign as it suggests. The respondent might justifiably feel anxious about signing anything, particularly at an early stage when the interviewer may be unknown to him or her. In our view it would be better to give the respondent time to read and re-read the protocol for himself or herself at his or her own pace, and to negotiate any additions or changes to it with the researcher. We would also recommend that the respondent should have a signed copy of the form as a record.

Document 10.1: Standard ethics protocol (adapted from McCracken 1988: 69)

(To be read by interviewer before the beginning of the interview. One copy of this form should be left with the respondent, and one copy should be signed by the respondent and kept by the interviewer.)

My name is _____ . I am a principal researcher/ researcher/ research assistant on a project entitled:

_____

This project is being sponsored by _____

at _____

I am/ _____ is the contact person/person in charge of this project and I (he/she) may be contacted at this phone number _____ should you have any questions.

Thank you for your willingness to participate in this research project. Your participation is very much appreciated. Before we start the interview, I would like to reassure you that as a participant in this project you have several very definite rights.

First, your participation in this interview is entirely voluntary.
You are free to refuse to answer any question at any time.
You are free to withdraw from the interview at any time.

This interview will be kept strictly confidential and will be available only to members of the research team.

Excerpts of this interview may be made part of the final research report, but under no circumstances will your name or identifying characteristics be included in this report.

I would be grateful if you would sign this form to show that I have read you its contents.

_____ (signed)

_____ (printed)

_____ (dated)

Please send me a report on the results of this research project (circle one)

YES   NO

Address for those requesting research report _____

(Interviewer: keep signed copy; leave unsigned copy with respondent)

Document 10.2: Principles and procedures – participants' rights (from Fogg 1988)

Thank you for agreeing to see me to discuss aspects relating to your nurse training. The following information outlines your rights in the interview. Please feel free to discuss anything you do not fully understand.

You have the right:
1 To be fully informed of the purpose of the research.
2 To be able to terminate the interview at any stage.
3 To anonymity.
4 To ask for information to be changed or recalled to you as the interview progresses.
5 To know who the audience will be, i.e. who will be receiving my research project.
6 To have your comments and any information safeguarded.
7 To have your views objectively reflected.
8 To express your opinions on the research.
9 To discontinue the tape recordings at any stage of the interview.
10 To negotiate the content of the interview.

Document 10.3: Agreement between S and Jenny Lund (from Lund 1992)

Jenny will share the transcripts of the tapes with S.

Jenny will give all the tapes to S after she has transcribed them for her to use or dispose of as she wishes.

Four interviews have been agreed but if, by mutual agreement, it is felt further interviews are necessary these will take place by arrangement.

If S should need to contact Jenny at any time in respect of the research she is at liberty to do so. She has Jenny's work and home telephone numbers.

DIARY KEEPING

We have found diary keeping useful in a number of ways as: a place to deposit emergent 'facts'; a wall to bounce ideas against (dialogue with self); *an aide-mémoire*; a running record of events; a linking mechanism for ideas, including those from the literature.

The following is adapted from material prepared by Julie Repper, at the University of Nottingham, following which two examples from diaries are included as illustration of the points raised.

The use of a diary as:

- *A chronolgy of the research process* from first ideas, to contacts, to interesting literature. How ideas develop, what influences them and what constrains them. How you feel about the situation, what people tell you and when, how this fits into the development of the project. What role are you taking on at the moment and how do others see you – as an insider or outsider, a helper, or what? What does it feel like at the moment during this phase – do you feel blocked and unable to move forward or are things going well for you? What are others doing and what kinds of relations are being established (including tracking the process of maintaining them)? What appear to be the consequences of particular actions or events (including tracking them over time)?
- *A form of field notes* to generate data. For example, in attempting to describe and understand the implementation of a particular strategy, or to analyse and assess the environment, you make field notes about what happens on which day, how this fits with previous activities, what they mean to you, what people in that situation said to you, how this compared with others' views,

how you felt, how it related to the literature, ideas raised for you in terms of understanding the situation, or in highlighting new ideas for research, or new directions to explore.

- *A means of assessing your own performance*, i.e. as a reflective diary, showing the extent to which you are perhaps applying a particular theory to practice or implementing practical ideas. Here the very fact that you are personally evaluating your own practice relies upon your ability to reflect accurately not only what happened but also what this meant, what you were thinking at the time and whether there was opportunity for a more effective mode of action.

- *A means of evaluating progress* by using diaries you and/or others have kept, e.g. by participants keeping a record of what happened after a particular change was introduced or of how you and/or they felt over time about a particular problem, whether your or their ideas changed and in response to what kinds of events or interventions. The diaries of patients, clients, users, families and/or carers are a means of generating data about their impressions, experiences and changing views of health and/or social care. For example, diaries of women maintained throughout pregnancy give a unique insight into their feelings, concerns and experiences of antenatal care. Another example of diaries kept to evaluate services comes from health education, where clients are asked to record specific health-related behaviour during a course of education or anxiety management. Thus they assess for themselves any changes in their responses and behaviour, and the researcher has a means of evaluating the effectiveness of the programme from the person's point of view.

The next two documents are from diaries currently in use. The first, predominantly made up from field notes, is associated with work on a patient satisfaction survey undertaken in outpatient clinics. The second is taken from Pat Walton's personal log written in connection with research into the experiences of non-abusing mothers of sexually abused children. While the focus of this second document is the process of research, both diaries show evidence of capturing feelings and emerging ideas.

Document 10.4: Diary extract 1

Outpatients' clinic, 24 November

8.45 Examined notice board in waiting area – sister is named but so far not in evidence – consultant given full title, registrar anonymous, nurse in charge only identified by initial and surname but widely known by first name and is the driving force. Patients number more than twice those in adjacent clinic: 45 to 19. Details about approximate waiting time left blank. Impressions conveyed? Deliberately? By default? Computers working today.

Survey in hand about patients' waiting times. Asked by nurse-in-charge if we wanted our names added on as part of the procedure. Thought about it – decided not to – no point for us or them – but clinic to note our presence on returns lest data is skewed. Unlikely but will protect their interests.

10.35 Announcement by nurse-in-charge to assembled patients in waiting area 'Mr X's patients – we're running $\frac{3}{4}$ hour late. A bit more than that for new patients. I've got problems but we're doing our best. Sorry about that. Sorry too that I'm not interested in Mr Y's patients'. (n.b. 'I've got problems' – explore.)

10.40 Care assistant again to patient – 'Are you alright darling?' Presence of staff and her engagement seems appreciated by patients – but false intimacy. Voice raised to draw attention to behaviour. Will start to count occasions when this happens – I'm so irritated by it as unprofessional behaviour that maybe I'm at risk of over-emphasizing.

Document 10.5: Diary extract 2 from Pat Walton's log

12 March Finally typed paper on Focus Groups. Feel I could manage this method – if ever I find a sample of mothers! Feeling very tired. [A colleague] also enthusiastic about helping me run the groups – will provide tape recorder.

17 March Aware today how little formal time is left – new waves of panic about no 'sample' yet. Meg thought my Focus Group paper quite useful. Hope I can use it. Meg says writing up 'dead ends' explored is still interesting for methodology chapter. Don't know if [informant] would approve of his being a 'dead end' – hope he's not!

Still struggling with – whether I 'go for' a case study which I think I could achieve – but probably will stand little chance of achieving anything much for the 'mothers' – or whether I take a risk and use the policy group to carry 'it' forward – attempt the more difficult – too difficult? route of research by questionnaire – two major stumbling blocks...

Diaries are also useful as part of a portfolio approach to evaluation, since they provide a means of assessing progress and of tracking the course of events over time, and may assist in pinpointing factors which may have contributed to change and improvement.

Figure 10.2 has been developed for research students on an MSc programme, to assist with diary keeping during their research year. What it does is to make a distinction between a 'today' and 'tomorrow' diary, and to underline the way in which during the course of diary keeping the thinking process may shift back and forth between inductive and deductive ways of thinking and working with data.

Further reading

Burgess, R. (1984). Keeping a research diary, in J. Bell *et al.* (eds) *Conducting Small-scale Investigations in Educational Management* London, Paul Chapman.

Ely, M. with Anzul, M. *et al.* (1991) *Doing Qualitative Research: Circles within Circles*. London, The Falmer Press.

Corti, L. (1993) *Social Research Update 2: Using Diaries in Social Research*. Guildford, Department of Sociology, University of Surrey.

EVALUATION

We agree with Stufflebeam and Shinkfield that 'The most important purpose of evaluation is not to prove but to improve... We cannot be sure that our goals are worthy unless we can match them to the needs of the people they are intended to serve' (Stufflebeam and Shinkfield 1985: 151). In looking at the issue of evaluation we have also found Beattie's approach helpful, particularly his incorporation into a four-fold map of goal and process-focused approaches (Beattie 1991: 230). We agree that the 'choice of strategy is likely to be bound up with much broader considerations relating to power and knowledge... most notably... basic orientations about what

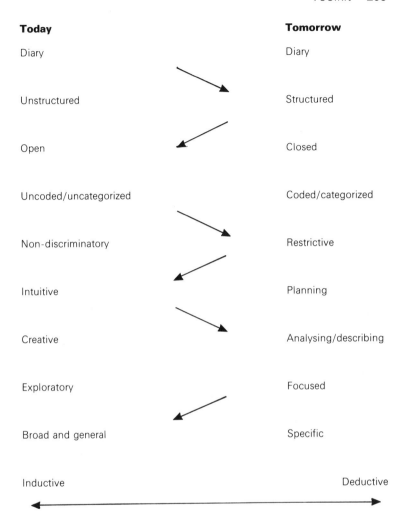

Figure 10.2 Today and tomorrow diary
Developed by Julie Repper and Elizabeth Hart, University of
Nottingham 1993

counts as 'reliable knowledge' ... [and] fundamental dispositions as regards the exercise of political power, swinging between paternalist and participatory philosophies, and between individual (or private) and collectivist (or public) processes' (Beattie 1991: 80). As action researchers we would also agree with Beattie that evaluation needs to be an integral part of any project, not an 'add on', and that it should be addressed at the outset and conducted in an ongoing and frequently reviewed manner. Beattie argues that no one approach to evaluation can be expected to meet the different interests and requirements of different stakeholders and audiences and proposes a 'portfolio' approach: 'The portfolio would constitute a cumulative open-ended file of all sorts of information, qualitative and quantitative, a "mixed bag" representing the broad sweep of work in the project. It would be a resource, to be raided and edited and put together in different ways, in different formats, for different audiences, for different occasions' (Beattie 1991: 81) Beattie (1991: 230–1) defines six broad categories of 'portfolio' constituents, which we have adapted and listed below, and have incorporated into Table 10.1 to indicate their use in each of our case studies in Part II:

- *basic work records* – attendance, costs, diaries, logs, minutes, memos, workplans, activity profiles;
- *needs database* – local health statistics, local survey findings, practice reports, interviews;
- *project file* – time charts, curriculum vitae of project workers, job descriptions, agendas and minutes of meetings, research diaries and activity logs;
- *audits* – summaries of feedback sessions from users/clients, consumer satisfaction surveys, letters of complaint and/or thanks, evaluation and free comment sheets;
- *follow-up data* – learning contracts, action plans, pledges/pleas, digests of follow-up surveys;
- *external monitor* – press cuttings, testimonials, conference presentations, publications.

Table 10.1 Portfolio evaluation constituents of case studies

	Case study 1	Case study 2	Case study 3	Case study 4	Case study 5
Basic work records	Minutes Memos Questionnaire Costs Attendance at meetings	Diaries Activity profiles	Attendance records Case records Activity profiles Minutes	Staff rosters and job descriptions Resident needs assessment forms Minutes, memos	Stock control book Kardex Resident profiles Medication profiles
Needs database	Interviews Nurse staffing statistics Patient throughput	Staff rosters Patient throughput	Local needs information Agency records	Numbers on waiting lists for services Population statistics Interviews	Requests for repeat prescriptions Requests for literature
Project file	Agendas Minutes Research diaries	Job descriptions Agendas Minutes Research diaries	Funding bids Agendas Minutes Service directories Research diaries	Minutes Agendas Working papers Research diaries	Charts Minutes Interim procedural notes Research diaries
Audits	Summaries of feedback Letters of complaint Press cuttings	Summaries of sessions Evaluation forms	Feedback information Letters Evaluation sheets	Complaints Letters Press cuttings	Feedback from carers
Follow-up data	Action plans	Action plans	Action plans	Action plans	Action plans and resident reviews
External monitor	Conference presentations Publicity, including press cuttings	Groupwork guidelines Conference presentations	Press cuttings Poems Letters Radio interview	Letters Journal articles	Publication

Further reading

Smith, G. and Cantley, C. (1985). *Assessing Health Care: A Study in Organizational Evaluation*. Milton Keynes, Open University Press.
Cheetham, J., Fuller, R., McIvor, G. and Petch, A. (1992). *Evaluating Social Work Effectiveness*. Buckingham, Open University Press.
St Leger, A. S., Schnieden, H. and Walsworth-Bell, J. P. (1991). *Evaluating Health Services' Effectiveness: A Guide for Health Professionals, Service Managers and Policy Makers*. Buckingham, Open University Press.

ATTITUDE SCALES AND OTHER TOOLS

The use of tools such as attitude measurement scales is perhaps most readily associated with the more experimental forms of practice and it is therefore worth commenting that those included here (Figure 10.3) were developed as a contribution to the professionalizing and empowering forms of action research described and discussed in case study 3. This material was used to promote the development of shared understanding among colleagues from different community care agencies about engaging in work with older people.

In the course of some preparatory groupwork each participant was given a chart and marked his or her personal starting position at a point between 1 and 5, in relation to the five identified ways of thinking about services provided to older people and working relationships with them. Following discussions, the scales were then used again to identify differences between workers, and between personal and agency stances. Finally, comparisons were made on each scale between the perceived current positions of the group as a whole and the positions that members hoped to move towards as a result of their shared endeavours.

Examples of standardized questionnaires which might be used in a similar way to generate data and enhance understandings of a particular problem situation include: *Measure of Job Satisfaction*, which is designed to measure the morale of community nurses and is available from Daphne Heald Research Unit, Royal College of Nursing, 20 Cavendish Square, London W1M 0AB; and, Cooper *et al.* (1988) *Occupational Stress Indicator: Management Guide*. Reviews of rating scales used in mental health can be found in Hall (1980) 'Ward rating scales for long-stay patients: a review'.

Figure 10.3 Special interest group for the elderly attitude scales
Source: Material by John Weeks based upon work done at the National Institute for Social Work

A Consultation

1	2	3	4	5
Asking elderly people for their views is worthwhile as a one-off exercise, just to make sure that our own ideas are not way off target.	Asking elderly people their views is something that we could do at regular intervals during the course of whatever piece of work we decide to undertake.	The initial act of consultation, if we handle it well, might be the first stage in the creation of a regular users' panel of elderly people.	We should make it a priority, before undertaking any particular piece of work, to create a users' panel of elderly people for the purpose of jointly planning that work.	In the membership of the Special Interest Group for the Elderly we should ensure that elderly people themselves always outnumber professional workers.

B The expression of opinions

1	2	3	4	5
Elderly people are likely to be so wrapped up in their own situations that what they say will probably be of little use to us in our planning of services.	Elderly people are likely to find it hard to express themselves, although one or two useful bits of information may emerge.	Elderly people may be able to talk well about their own situations, and so their views are worth gathering, but we should be careful not to generalize from them.	There is no reason why elderly people should not have worthwhile views to express to us, provided we handle them in the right way.	Elderly people are citizens in the fullest sense, and it is our responsibility to provide positive encouragement and help them to express their views.

C Individual and group

1	2	3	4	5
Each elderly person is unique and our services should be delivered to them as individuals.	Elderly people see their problems as being individual and we should work from the same assumption, although we can see some connections between them.	Elderly people are in some situations aware of themselves as a group, and we should recognize that, but they are still likely to gain services by virtue of their individual problems.	Elderly people can be stronger if they get together and press upon us their claims for individual help, and we should encourage them to see and do that.	Elderly people should be urged to combine in order to negotiate with the various agencies both for individual help and for changes in policy and the allocation of resources, which will benefit them as a class of people.

D Preventive medicine versus casualty service

1	2	3	4	5
In the present climate we can only hope to provide a casualty service to those elderly people who come to grief.	In spite of the present climate we should try to ensure that once an elderly person has a problem, that problem does not get any worse.	No matter what the present climate is, we should not only be preventing problems from getting worse, but also ensuring that once an elderly person has overcome a problem it does not recur.	We should be attempting to provide a preventive service which will identify particularly vulnerable elderly people and ensure that they do not get into difficulty.	We should be screening all elderly people in a positive effort to intervene at an early stage with counselling, advice and services to minimize the occurrence of problems.

E Bingo – who knows best?

1

Many elderly people want only more bingo, but we should resist that vigorously, for we know that they need much more worthwhile forms of stimulation.

2

Many elderly people want more bingo, but that is not a very worthwhile form of activity and we should keep it to a minimum in the services we provide.

3

Many elderly people want to play bingo and since it is important to start from some common ground in our work with them, we should tolerate that, but we should nevertheless try subtly to steer them on to other activities.

4

Elderly people enjoy playing bingo and as an activity it gets them out of their homes, it gives them social contact and it helps them to maintain mental alertness, so we should let them play bingo as much as they wish.

5

If elderly people are playing bingo, do you think they will let us have a game?

11

Conclusion: working from a project perspective

In nursing and social work it is often commented that practitioners do not sufficiently use research findings to inform their work. While such a complaint may frequently be made by educators and managers, many health and social care staff, both qualified and in training, also recognize the difficulties of integrating theoretical ideas into their practice. In our years of teaching on health, social work and social care courses and of accepting student attachments in professional settings, we, like many other providers and recipients of training (Mattaini 1992; Harré Hindmarsh 1993), have often struggled to get to grips with the interrelationship between what is written about practice and what is done in practice.

Within nursing this problem emerges, for instance, in a study by O'Connor (1993) on the theory and practice of wound management. Wound care is a key area of work for nurses. It is one where they have scope to act on discrete nursing knowledge and to offer specific nursing advice across professional boundaries. Results from O'Connor's enquiries in a surgical ward showed that:

the gap between theory and practice was a wide one. What emerged was a lack of sound in-depth knowledge among nurses, with practice based upon tradition and difficulty in applying knowledge to practice . . . Although the nurses questioned must have been taught to assess and manage wounds at some stage in their training, they were unable to recall or apply this knowledge.

(O'Connor 1993: 64)

O'Connor goes on to quote a related study by Flanagan (1992), who found that in situations where the nurse's decision was not backed up by the patient's doctor, nurses chose not to make a decision at all rather than to use current research to support their professional judgement.

The nursing profession is deeply troubled by this gap, which is seen to exist between research, practice and theory. In the week when we were drafting this section the front cover of one of the magazines most widely available to nurses, the *Nursing Times* (1993a), carried the question 'The theory practice gap – Why do nurses ignore research?' Earlier in the year, the same journal had introduced a new layout for presenting research. Its announcement went as follows:

Research-based practice is now recognised as the only way forward for nursing, midwifery and health visiting. However the relationship between research and clinical practice can be a difficult one. Nurses undertaking research have complained that hands-on nurses are not always as helpful as they could be when a project is underway – either because they see it as implied criticism of what they are doing or because it appears too abstract to be of practical use. For their part, the practising nurses may resent nurse researchers for their nine-to-five existence, or for being out of touch with 'real' nursing . . . we hope . . . to encourage researchers to think about why and for whom they are undertaking research. We hope it will also help practising nurses assess and, when appropriate, implement the findings of research more easily . . . Nursing research in isolation helps no one. It is only of value when the results help to change nursing practice for the benefit of patients.

(Nursing Times 1993b: 30)

The need to encourage research-minded practice combined with scepticism about research is an issue which finds expression in the social work literature too. Everitt *et al.* (1992: 36) observe that:

Social workers have had little experience of research being used to serve purposes which they would support. They tend to experience it as researchers descending on them for poorly explained and unilateral reasons, or sending time-consuming and apparently irrelevant questionnaires. At the very best, they may have been fortunate enough to encounter researchers who valued their own views and involvement . . . These experiences have been ones of greater co-operation between researchers and practitioners but have still separated research and practice.

Munn-Giddings makes similar points when she reflects on her experiences as a local authority social services department researcher studying aspects of a health authority's community care provision for people with learning difficulties. Having adopted a 'traditional' ethnographic approach, she notes that

many pertinent issues arose from the study which were none too easy to relay back to the staff who at the time I felt were defensive and unwilling to concede the 'blatant truths' with which they were presented. On reflection I have considerably more understanding of their position. At the same time that they were being 'retrained' to move from hospital to community settings, having to follow new local and national policies in [sic] which they had no part in framing, they were also being subject to 'observation' by a researcher who had no clinical experience, informing them that basically they were working to the detriment of their clients! . . . [There] is a fundamental problem in research becoming an 'expert service' disconnected from the issues and services it wishes to explore. Not least is the danger that if the data are not owned by those who can ultimately act upon it [sic] it is unlikely to be directly used. An important dynamic therefore exists between those who purport to explain and illuminate issues and those who are charged with acting upon them. In the context of social work and other social care work there has been a lot written about the relationship of research to policy but there has not been a corresponding interest in the crucial relationship of research to practice.

(Munn-Giddings 1993: 281–2)

The source of these difficulties lies partly in how knowledge is conceived and partly in how such knowledge is generated. We look at this first within nursing and then go on to make some comments about the situation in social work, where a developing interest in practitioner research suggests a way forward.

OBSTACLES AND OPPORTUNITIES: SOME EXAMPLES FROM WITHIN NURSING

Through the new style of nurse training known as Project 2000 and through Post-Registration Education and Practice (PREP) of nurses, midwives and health visitors, the nursing world anticipates the 'production' of 'knowledgeable doers' with a commitment to extending and updating their nursing knowledge base. But this increased interest in professionalization seems not to include the breaking down of barriers between those who practise nursing and those who do research for nursing. The maintenance of such a separation implies to nurses that research into their own work is not something that they are allowed – let alone routinely expected – to do and this in turn is likely to further entrench the practice–theory divide.

The message that nurses should know their place and keep out of doing research in their own right is powerfully expressed in the next two extracts. The first is taken from an article in another widely distributed nursing journal, the *Nursing Standard*, which describes the setting up of a research, ethics and consultancy committee to guide, support and monitor research activities among staff and students in a nursing college. Commenting on the increasing involvement by nurse teachers in further academic study, the authors refer to the committee's promotion of research activity, awareness and knowledge but add:

> One of the initial concerns of several of the committee members was the apparent requirement of a number of pre-registration courses that students undertake projects which could involve them in active research. While it was agreed that the promotion of research awareness on such courses was appropriate, members of the committee felt that it was entirely inappropriate for pre-registration students to be expected or encouraged to

undertake active research. [This was] first because of the possible impact this may have in the clinical areas in terms of the numbers of patients or staff who might be approached with requests to participate, and second because of the very real problem of providing skilled and adequate supervision for such projects. There was, therefore, a unanimous decision by the committee that as part of its consultative role, it should make a formal recommendation to the college that no pre-registration course should either require or encourage students to engage in active research, and that the appropriate strategy was to encourage research awareness and the development of critical evaluation skills. This recommendation was considered by the college and ultimately adopted as the guiding principle for the development of pre-registration course curricula.

(Ghazi and Cook 1993: 30)

Such an attitude has serious implications for the teaching of research skills, especially qualitative methods, which some would argue are essentially unteachable in the accepted sense of the word (Parry *et al.* 1992). Training for careers in the fields of health and social care requires all students to move outside the classroom and begin to put their learning into practice under supervision. Underpinning this are ideas about the interrelationship between teaching and learning which are neatly summed up in the words of a Chinese proverb: 'Tell me and I'll forget, show me and I may remember, involve me and I'll understand.' For those who believe that any real learning only comes about by doing, it is hard to see why teaching about research should be treated differently. As Wright Mills (1959: 199) puts it, 'Merely to name an item of experience often invites you to explain it.'

We are not arguing that all students on all courses should go out and do original research but we are making out a case that teaching about research should include an element of first-hand doing. Contrary to the views implied by the committee referred to earlier, clinical areas are not the only places in which to gather data; nor do patients and staff have a monopoly on acting as informants. Resource constraints might be seen differently if there was an enhanced commitment to both active learning about research and the promotion of critical thinking in and about practice. Moreover, if the teaching of data collection recognized that students have lives outside institutions of health care, they might, for example, practise observation and recording techniques while travelling home on a bus.

OBSTACLES AND OPPORTUNITIES: SOME EXAMPLES FROM WITHIN SOCIAL WORK

As we indicated earlier in this chapter, social work is not immune from these difficulties. Greve (1990: 3) observes that 'Social workers, on account of their backgrounds and personal attributes, and commonly held assumptions about what research is and must be, often lack interest in pursuing research and, moreover, often have not developed research competence.' Writing in a Central Council for Education and Training in Social Work (CCETSW) publication, Whitaker and Archer spell out the problems in more detail:

> Social workers often do not see themselves as researchers or as having the skills necessary to undertake research. Their hearts lie in practice. Their qualifying course may not have included training in research or, if it did, this training may have seemed less relevant and therefore less worthy of their attention than parts of the courses related directly to practice. Some may think of research in stereotyped ways: research is cold-hearted; it exploits clients; it is selfish and self-indulgent; it is expensive, time-consuming and necessarily lengthy; it can only be done by experts who work in universities and other teaching institutions or in special research units; it requires extensive knowledge of the opaque world of statistics; to engage in it may somehow damage sensitive relationships with clients.
>
> (Whitaker and Archer 1989: 12)

These authors go on to suggest that such obstacles to undertaking research may disappear when the parallels are identified between research and practice, and especially when individuals and organizations recognize the problem-solving nature of both. This in turn prompts the suggestion that, as an explicitly problem-focused form of research, action research may then be seen as the methodology of choice for practitioner researchers doing small-scale projects and for managers and policy makers seeking to promote improvement in service delivery through systematic and collaborative programmes of change.

The opportunities inherent in making the links between practice, research and improvement have long been recognized within the field of education and there is a substantial literature which has grown out of the teacher-as-researcher movement (which we outlined in Chapter 2), informed by the writings of, for instance, Habermas (1974) on critical social science, Freire (1972a, b) on education as a weapon for social change and Schön (1983, 1987) on reflexive practice. The emerging interest in practitioner research in the social work and social care sphere is similarly concerned with the making of connections

> between what is happening and what could happen . . . The rationale of practitioner research is that of continuous reform by professionals who have insights and influence in a democratically accountable practice . . . Practitioner research is in both a defensive and developmental relationship with professionalism. Practitioner-researchers want to make the most of both realism *and* idealism, to be beyond cynicism but not as far as utopianism.
> (Broad and Fletcher 1993: 9–12)

In many respects descriptions of practitioner research are very similar to Lewin's (1946) accounts of action research written almost fifty years ago (discussed in Chapter 2). It is our recognition of this that leads us to suggest that the arguments in favour of practitioner research and research into the practice of social work and social care may also be seen as arguments in favour of action research as a potential methodology of choice for exploration, enquiry and problem-solving about the workings of human service agencies.

How might such a strategy be put into practice? We draw first upon the classic writings of the sociologist Wright Mills (1959) about the capturing and development of ideas, and then go on to propose the merits of working from a project perspective.

KEEPING OUR INNER WORLDS AWAKE

Wright Mills remarks, albeit in the gendered language of his time, that:

> A practising social scientist ought periodically to review 'the state of my problems and plans' ... Any working social scientist who is well on his way ought at all times to have so many plans, which is to say ideas, that the question is always which of them am I, ought I, to work on next? And he should keep a special little file for his master agenda, which he writes and rewrites just for himself and perhaps for discussion with friends. From time to time he ought to review this very carefully and purposefully.
>
> (Wright Mills 1959: 197–8)

This is wise advice for professionals in health and social care interested in developing reflexive practice through action research and much of the work described in the case studies (Chapters 5 to 9) rested on such an approach. Wright Mills spells out details about the file or journal, the maintenance of which he sees as 'intellectual production':

> There is joined personal experience and professional activities, studies underway and studies planned. In this file, you, as an intellectual craftsman, will try to get together what you are doing intellectually and what you are experiencing as a person ... It also encourages you to capture 'fringe-thoughts' ... [which] may lead to more systematic thinking, as well as lend intellectual relevance to more directed experience ... By keeping an adequate file and thus developing self-reflective habits you learn how to keep your inner world awake ... The file also helps you keep up your habit of writing ... Under various topics in your file there are ideas, personal notes, excerpts from books, bibliographical items and outlines of projects. It is, I suppose, a matter of arbitrary habit, but I think you will find it well to sort all these items into a master file of 'projects', with many subdivisions. The topics, of course, change, sometimes quite frequently ... Such a file ... is a continually growing store of facts and ideas, from the most vague to the most finished.
>
> (Wright Mills 1959: 196–9)

GATHERING OUR INTELLECTUAL AND STRATEGIC CAPACITIES: WORKING FROM A PROJECT PERSPECTIVE

Wright Mills's use of the word 'project' is interesting and is one that is very widely employed when the topic of action research is under discussion. Lewin (1946: 207), in his paper 'Action research and minority problems', referred to 'the many projects and findings' which were emerging from collaborative initiatives between research institutions and 'action organizations'. The large scale Home Office Community Development Projects adopted the term in the 1970s, as did the Humanities Curriculum Project and another influential education initiative, the Ford Teaching Project (Hopkins 1993). In the area of health care, the *Ward Sister Training Project* (Lathlean and Farnish 1984) is frequently quoted as an example of action research in nursing and very many initiatives developed within the 1980s community health movement were described as projects and informed by an action research approach (Mayo 1975; Nottinghamshire County Council Social Services Department/HEC 1984; OU/HEU 1991). Most recently Titchen and Binnie (1993: 858) have discussed models of action research in the nursing literature with reference to their development of a 'double act' as researcher and practitioner engaged on the Oxford Patient-centred Nursing in Practice 'project'.

In the fields of social planning, social work and social care, Whitaker and Archer (1989: 20–22) address action research in terms of goal-directed 'practice programmes or projects' involving 'successive readings of a situation at pre-specified points'. And while Adams (1990: 42–4) does not use the term 'action research', he implicitly advocates the adoption of such methodological approach for the Children's Society nationally in his chapter on a 'shared enquiry model of research'. He describes this as being based on projects which empower workers and span organizational and geographical boundaries. Adams is attracted by the scope which such a strategy has to offer when used collectively and harnessed 'to respond flexibly to emerging needs', as an 'action generator', a validator of and dissemination mechanism for practice wisdom, and a stimulant to organizational development. In this, like Cohen and Manion (1984) and Halsey (1972), who also write in terms of projects, he recognizes the significance of context for an action research initiative.

It is therefore not by chance that the term 'project' appears frequently in relation to the case studies included in this book. We also find ourselves using it, like Addison (1988) and Bell (1993), in our discussions with nurse and social work practitioners doing dissertations as part of advanced level professional education courses and with managers seeking to improve practice in identified spheres. For us the word conveys a sense of purposeful and planned collaborative engagement in an area of interest which has potential for learning and therefore for change. Changing, which in our view more accurately portrays the dynamism inherent in change, occurs externally, internally and subjectively, and includes developing new and different ways of seeing, interpreting and intervening. The *Concise Oxford Dictionary*'s definition of a project as a 'plan' or 'scheme' should in this context perhaps be taken in conjunction with the definition given for the verb 'to project', which includes references to contriving a course of action and causing an idea to take shape. Such change initiatives concern the researcher as subject, actor and facilitator, and immediately pose questions about how change can and should be measured and evaluated. Project-based thinking, when seen in these terms, not only encapsulates the key components in the action research process but also mirrors the model of daily practice adopted by health and social welfare professionals who employ a problem-solving approach, interweaving activities of assessment, intervention and evaluation. They share this in common with project managers in manufacturing companies and aid agencies (Eggers 1993). A reminder of the inherent value base of a project-based approach may be found in Freire's discussion of the education process as a vehicle for personal and political change:

> For man [orientation in the world] means humanizing the world by transforming it. For man there is both an historical and a value dimension. Men have the sense of 'project', in contrast to the instinctive routines of animals . . . The interrelation of the awareness of aim and of process is the basis for planning action, which implies methods, objectives and value options.
>
> (Freire 1972a: 22–3)

Finally, Fullan (1986: 80), in writing about action research with teachers in mind, discusses characteristics associated with success in 'effective schools projects', and Carr and Kemmis refer to the adoption of a 'project perspective':

> When teachers adopt a project perspective, they will also create opportunities to learn from experience and to plan their own learning. Very probably, they will arrange to discuss their unfolding experience with others. In short, such teachers 'become critical' – not in the sense that they become negativistic or complaining, but in the sense that they gather their intellectual and strategic capacities, focus them on a particular issue and engage them in critical examination of practice through the 'project'.
>
> (Carr and Kemmis 1986: 40)

These authors put forward a way of thinking about doing teaching and curriculum research – a stance – which is directly applicable to the professional practice of front line workers in health and social care settings who, like teachers, have to exercise their judgement constantly in response to the changing demands of practical caring. Carr and Kemmis argue that every aspect of any and every professional 'act' may be regarded

> as problematic: its purpose, the social situation . . . the way it creates or constrains relationships between participants, the kind of medium in which it works . . . and the kind of knowledge to which it gives form . . . Not every act can be thought about this way (it would be too morally and intellectually demanding), but every . . . act *could* be. And so a constant debate is necessary in education to continue the process of examining its frameworks of tradition, expectation and action, and to understand the consequences of different kinds of provision and performance. Only through open and informed debate about these matters can education improve the chances of achieving a just and rational society.
>
> (Carr and Kemmis 1986: 39–40)

Carr and Kemmis describe such a stance as adopting what they term 'the strategic view' of professional practice. This they define as a form of 'consciousness', a way of thinking of work which takes as given four key points. First, educational and caring activities are historically located with a past that influences present practice and a current practice which aims for improvement in the future. Second, these activities are social activities with consequences for both individuals and the wider society. Third, they are intrinsically political as they affect the life chances of people and shape the services available to them. Finally, every act of teaching and caring, every learning opportunity embodied in a curriculum and every experience of seeking and receiving care is problematic. It therefore has the potential to be reflected upon and reconsidered so as to inform future practical judgements and interventions in order to promote progress towards a more rational and just society.

Carr and Kemmis go on to say that to adopt such a strategic approach means that practitioners will submit work and 'unfolding experience' for discussion with others. They will thereby promote 'critical reflection', contribute to the establishment of 'critical communities of enquirers' and strengthen their 'investigative networks' (Carr and Kemmis 1986: 223). Action research with a project perspective stands as the expression of such a strategic approach.

CONCLUSION

Our purpose in writing this book has been to explore the potential of action research to bring about improvements in professional practice and service delivery through collaborative working. By looking at the historical development of this problem-focused methodology in a variety of settings we have sought to draw out some common themes from the literature with relevance to the fields of health and social care. We have concentrated on the application of these ideas to the work of nurses and social workers partly because of their numerical dominance and the key positions they occupy in these sectors, and partly because our material has been drawn from work done by and with members of these groups in particular. We believe, however, that the messages in the book will be of use to, for instance, health promotion staff and others working in institutional and community care settings: indeed, many such workers played a part in the projects featured in our case studies. We hope that by exposing our practice to scrutiny by others we have illustrated some of the opportunities which exist to work from a project perspective and within an action research framework. Our experience suggests that the adoption of such an approach leads workers to pay enhanced attention to the processes of generating change and that this can be challenging, effective and enriching.

References

Abercrombie, N., Hill, S. and Turner, B. S. (1984). *The Penguin Dictionary of Sociology*. Harmondsworth, Penguin Books.

Adams, R. (1990). 'The potential impact of a shared enquiry model of research on the Children's Society', in D. Whitaker, L. Archer, and S. Greve (eds) *Research, Practice and Service Delivery: The Contribution of Research by Practitioners*, Leeds, CCETSW, pp. 42–4.

Adelman, C. (1993). 'Kurt Lewin and the origins of action research', *Educational Action Research*, 1(1), 7–24.

Addison, C. (1988). *Planning Investigative Projects: a Workbook for Social Services Practitioners*. London, National Institute for Social Work.

Aggleton, P., Young, A., Moody, D., Kapila, M. and Pye, M. (eds) (1992). *Does It Work? Perspectives on the Evaluation of HIV/AIDS Health Promotion*. London, Health Education Authority.

Ahmad, B. (1990). *Black Perspectives in Social Work*. Birmingham, Venture Press.

Allport, G. W. (1948). 'Foreword', in G. W. Lewin (ed.) *Resolving Social Conflicts*. New York, Harper and Brothers, pp. vii–xiv.

Anon. (1990). 'Soapbox', *Social Work Today*, 20 September, 34.

Ardener, S. (ed.) (1978). *Defining Females: The Nature of Women in Society*. London, Croom Helm.

Argyris, C., Putnam, R. and MacLain-Smith, D. (1985). *Action Science*. San Francisco, Jossey-Bass.

Bailie, S. H. (1975). 'Community development as a process of emergence', in R. Lees and G. Smith (eds) *Action Research in Community Development*. London, Routledge and Kegan Paul.

Ball, S. J. (1987). *The Micro-politics of the School: Towards a Theory of School Organization*. London, Routledge.

Beattie, A. (1991). 'The evaluation of community development initiatives in health promotion: a review of current strategies', in '*Roots and Branches*': *Papers from the OU/HEA 1990 Winter School on Community Development and Health*. Milton Keynes, HEU/Open University, pp. 212–35.

Begum, N. (1990). *Burden of gratitude: women with disabilities receiving personal care*. University of Warwick and SCA (Education), Coventry.

Bell, C. and Encel, S. (eds) (1978). *Inside the Whale: Ten Personal Accounts of Social Research*. Oxford, Pergamon Press.

Bell, J. (1993). *Doing Your Research Project: A Guide for First-Time Researchers in Education and Social Science*, 2nd edn. Buckingham, Open University Press.

Bell, J., Bush, T., Fox, A., Goodey, J. and Goulding, S. (eds) (1984). *Conducting Small-scale Investigations in Educational Management*. London, Paul Chapman in association with the Open University.

Benson, S. (1986). 'Chemist in the cupboard', *Community Care*, **606**, 24–5.

Blackburn, C. (1992). *Poverty Profiling: A Guide for Community Nurses*. London, Health Visitors' Association.

Blair, P. (1985). *Know Your Medicines*. Mitcham, Age Concern.

Blair, P. (1986). 'Dishing out drugs', *Social Services Insight*, 31 May, 7.

Bloor, M. and McKeganey, N. (1989). 'Ethnography addressing the practitioner', in J. F. Gubrium and D. Silverman (eds) *The Politics of Field Research*. London: Sage, pp. 197–212.

Bond, M. (1982). *Women's Work in a Woman's World: the Home Help Service Re-examined*. Bristol, University of Bristol School for Advanced Urban Studies.

Bond, M. (1990). *Medication Matters: Improving Medication Practices in Residential Homes for Older People*. Coventry, University of Warwick and SCA (Education).

Bond, M. (1993a). 'Mission possible', *Care Weekly*, **265**, 13.

Bond, M. (1993b). 'An illuminating experience', *Community Care*, **966**, 24–5.

British Medical Association/Pharmaceutical Society of Great Britain (1986). *British National Formulary*. London, Pharmaceutical Press.

Broad, B. and Fletcher, C. (eds) (1993). *Practitioner Social Work Research in Action*. London, Whiting and Birch.

Bromley, D. B. (1986). *The Case Study Method in Psychology and Related Disciplines*. Chichester, John Wiley & Sons.

Bryman, A. (1984). 'The debate about quantitative and qualitative research: a question of method or epistemology?', *British Journal of Sociology*, 35(1), 75–92.

Burgess, R. (1984) 'Keeping a research diary', in J. Bell *et al.* (eds) *Conducting Small-scale Investigations in Educational Management*. London, Paul Chapman, pp. 198–205.

Burgess, R. G. (1991). 'Sponsors, gatekeepers, members and friends: access in educational settings', in W. B. Shaffir and R. A. Stebbins (eds) *Experiencing Fieldwork: An Inside View of Qualitative Research*. London: Sage, pp. 43–52.

Butler, S. and Wintram, C. (1991). *Feminist Groupwork*. London, Sage.

Calouste Gulbenkian Foundation (1968). *Community Work and Social Change: A Report on Training*. London, Longman.

Carr, W. (1989). 'Action research: ten years on', *Journal of Curriculum Studies*, 21(1), 85–90.

Carr, W. and Kemmis, S. (1986). *Becoming Critical: Education, Knowledge and Action Research*. London, Falmer Press.

Cartwright, D. (1948). 'Social psychology in the United States during the Second World War', *Human Relations*, 1(3), 333–52.

Centre for Action Research in Professional Practice, University of Bath (1993). *Collaborative Inquiry*, 11, November.

Chamberlain, J. (1988). *On Our Own*. London, MIND.

Cheetham, J., Fuller, R., McIvor, G. and Petch, A. (1992). *Evaluating Social Work Effectiveness*. Buckingham, Open University Press.

Chisholm, R. F. and Elden, M. (1993). 'Features of emerging action research', *Human Relations*, 46(2), 275–97.

Clark, P. A. (1972). *Action Research and Organizational Change*. London, Harper and Row.

Clarke, M. (1986). 'Action and reflection: practice and theory in nursing'. *Journal of Advanced Nursing*, 11, 3–11.

Coch, L. and French, J. R. P. Jnr (1948). 'Overcoming resistance to change', *Human Relations*, 4, 512–32.

Cohen, L. and Manion, L. (1984). 'Action research' in J. Bell *et al.* (eds) *Conducting Small-scale Investigations in Educational Management*. London, Paul Chapman in association with the Open University, pp. 41–57.

Collier, J. (1945). 'United States Indian Administration as a laboratory of ethnic relations', *Social Research*, 12, 275–6.

Cooper, C. L., Sloan, S. J. and Williams, S. (1988). *Occupational Stress Indicator: Management Guide*. Windsor, NFER-Nelson.

Cope, D. E. (1981). *Organisation Development and Action Research in Hospitals*. Aldershot, Gower.

Corey, S. (1953). *Action Research to Improve School Practice*. New York, Columbia University.

Corti, L. (1993). *Social Research Update 2: Using Diaries in Social Reseach*. Guildford, Department of Sociology, University of Surrey.

Coventry CDP (1975). *CDP Final Reports*. Coventry: Home Office and City of Coventry Community Development Project in association with the Institute of Local Government Studies.

Coventry Social Services (1973). *Looking for Trouble among the Elderly*. Coventry: Coventry Social Services.

Cox, E., Hausfield, F. and Wills, S. (1978). 'Taking the Queen's Shilling: accepting social research consultancies in the 1970s', in C. Bell and S. Encel (eds) *Inside the Whale: Ten Personal Accounts of Social Research*. Oxford, Pergamon Press.

Cunningham, J. B. (1993). *Action Research and Organizational Development*. London, Praeger.

Daphne Heald Research Unit (1994). *Measure of Job Satisfaction (MJS) 1994*. London, Royal College of Nursing.

Department of Health (1989). *Working for Patients*, Cmnd 555. London, HMSO.

Derbyshire Health Authorities (n.d.) *Pharmcare* pamphlets prepared by Peter Rivers, Staff Pharmacist, Social Services Department.

East, L. and Robinson, J. (1994). 'Change in process: bringing about change in health care through action research', *Journal of Clinical Nursing*, **3**, 57–61.

Easton, G. (1982). *Learning from Case Studies*. London, Prentice Hall.

Eden, C. and Huxham, C. (1993). *Distinguishing action research*, Working Paper 93/18. Paper presented to the British Academy of Management Conference, Milton Keynes, September.

Eden, C., Jones, S. and Sims, D. (1983). *Messing about in Problems: An Informal Structured Approach to Problem Identification and Management*. Oxford, Pergamon Press.

Eggers, H. (1993). 'From project cycle management to the management of development co-operation'. *Project Appraisal*, **8**(2), 83–90.

Elden, M. and Chisholm, R. F. (1993). 'Emerging varieties of action research: Introduction to the special issue'. *Human Relations*, **46**(2), 121–43.

Elgood, C. (1990). *Using Management Games*. Aldershot, Gower.

Elliott, J. (1978). What is action research in schools?' *Journal of Curriculum Studies*, **10**(4), 355–7.

Elliott, J. (1991). *Action Research for Educational Change*. Buckingham, Open University Press.

Ely, M. with Anzul, M., Friedman, T., Garner, D. and Steinmetz, M. A. (1991). *Doing Qualitative Research: Circles within Circles*. London, Falmer Press.

Ernst, S. and Goodison, L. (1981) *In Our Own Hands: A Book of Self Therapy*. London, The Women's Press.

Everitt, A., Hardiker, P., Littlewood, J. and Mullender, A. (1992). *Applied Research for Better Practice*. Basingstoke, Macmillan.

Farmer, B. (1993). 'The use and abuse of power in nursing', *Nursing Standard*, 7(23), 33–6.

Flanagan, M. (1992). 'Variables influencing nurses' selection of wound dressings'. *Journal of Wound Care*, 1(1), 33–43.

Fogg, D. (1988). 'A study of wastage in nurse education – no way to treat a lady – or man'. Unpublished MEd thesis, University of East Anglia.

Freire, P. (1972a). *Cultural Action for Freedom*. Harmondsworth, Penguin.

Freire, P. (1972b). *Pedagogy of the Oppressed* (translated by M. B. Ramos), Harmondsworth, Penguin.

Frost, N. and Stein, M. (1989). *The Politics of Child Welfare: Inequality, Power and Change*. Hemel Hempstead, Harvester Wheatsheaf.

Fullan, M. G. (1986). 'The management of change', in E. Hoyle and A. McMahon (eds) *World Year Book*. London, Kogan Page.

Ghazi, F. and Cook, S. (1993). 'Monitoring research in a nursing college', *Nursing Standard*, 7(47), 27–30.

Geddes, M., Hastings, C., Briner, W. (1993). *Project Leadership*. Aldershot, Gower.

Gill, J. and Johnson, P. (1991). *Research Methods for Managers*. London, Paul Chapman.

Glendenning, F. (ed.) (1982). *Care in the Community: Recent Research and Current Projects*. Stoke-on-Trent, The Beth Johnson Foundation in association with the Department of Adult Education, University of Keele and the Health Education Council.

Glendenning, F. (ed.) (1985). *New Initiatives in Self-health Care for Older People*. Stoke-on-Trent, The Beth Johnson Foundation in association with the Department of Adult Education, University of Keele and the Health Education Council.

Graham, H. (1984). 'Surveying through stories', in C. Bell and H. Roberts (eds) *Social Researching: Politics, Problems, Practice*. London, Routledge and Kegan Paul, pp. 104–24.

Graham, H. (1991). 'Community development and research', in *'Roots and Branches': Papers from the OU/HEA 1990 Winter School on Community Development and Health*. Milton Keynes, Health Education Unit/Open University, pp. 237–41.

Green, J. and Chapman, A. (1991). 'The lessons of the Community Development Project for community development today', in *'Roots and Branches': Papers from the OU/HEA 1990 Winter School on Community Development and Health*. Milton Keynes, Health Education Unit/Open University, pp. 54–70.

Greenwood, D. J., Whyte, W. F. and Harkavy, I. (1993). 'Participatory action research as a process and as a goal', *Human Relations*, 46(2), 175–92.

Greenwood, J. (1994). 'Action research: a few details, a caution and something new', *Journal of Advanced Nursing*, 20, 13–18.

Greer, S. (1990). 'On the selection of problems', in J. Bynner and K. Stribley (eds) *Social Research: Principles and Procedures*. Harlow, Longman/Open University Press.

Greve, S. (1990). 'The relevance of practitioner research to the quality of social work', in D. Whitaker, L. Archer and S. Greve (eds) *Research, Practice and Service Delivery: The Contribution of Research by Practitioners*. Leeds, CCETSW.

Grieco, H. and Whipp, R. (1984). *Women and the workplace: Gender and control in the labour process*. Work Organization Research Centre working paper, series no. 8, May, Aston University.

Gummesson, E. (1991). *Qualitative Methods in Management Research*. London, Sage.

Haas, J. and Shaffir, W. (1973). 'Fieldworkers' mistakes at work: problems in maintaining research and researcher bargains', in W. B. Shaffir, R. A. Stebbins and A. Turowetz (eds) *Fieldwork Experience: Qualitative Approaches to Social Research*. New York, St Martin's Press.

Habermas, J. (1974). *Theory and Practice*. London, Heinemann.

Hall, J. W. (1980). 'Ward rating scales for long-stay patients: a review'. *Psychological Medicine*, **10**, 277–88.

Halsey, A. H. (ed.) (1972). *Educational Priority: Volume 1, E P A. Problems and Policies*. London, HMSO.

Hareven, T. K. (1982). *Family Time and Industrial Time: The Relationship Between Family and Work in a New England Industrial Community*. Cambridge, Cambridge University Press.

Harré Hindmarsh, J. (1993). 'Tensions and dichotomies between theory and practice: a study of alternative formulations', *International Journal of Lifelong Education*, **12**(2), 101–15.

Hart, E. (1991). 'Ghost in the machine'. *Health Services Journal*, **101** (5281), 20–2.

Hart, L. (1991) 'A ward of my own: social organisation and identity among hospital domestics', in P. Holden and J. Littlewood (eds) *Anthropology and Nursing*. London, Routledge, pp. 84–109.

Hawtin, M., Hughes, G. and Percy-Smith, J. with Foreman, A. (1994). *Community Profiling: Auditing Social Needs*. Buckingham, Open University Press.

Haynes, M. E. (1989). *Project Management: From Idea to Implementation*. London, Kogan Page.

Health Visitors' Association School Nurse Subcommittee (1991). *Profiling School Health*. London, Health Visitors' Association.

Heller, F. (1986). *The Use and Abuse of Social Science*. London, Sage.

Henderson, P. (1989) *Promoting Active Learning*. Cambridge, National Extension College.

Hickson, D. J. (1988). 'Ruminations on munificence and scarcity in research', in A. Bryman (ed.) *Doing Research in Organisations*. London, Routledge, pp. 136–47.

Hockey, L. (1974). 'Research into nursing services'. *British Medical Bulletin*, **30**, 248–51.

Hodgkinson, H. L. (1957). 'Action research: a critique', in S. Kemmis, *et al.* (eds) *The Action Research Reader*, 2nd edn (1982). Australia, Deakin University Press.

Holter, I. M. and Schwartz-Barcott, D. (1993). 'Action research: what is it? How has it been used and how can it be used in nursing?', *Journal of Advanced Nursing*, **18**, 298–304.

Hopkins, D. (1989). *Evaluation for School Development*. Buckingham, Open University Press.

Hopkins, D. (1993). *A Teacher's Guide to Classroom Research*. 2nd edn. Buckingham, Open University Press.

Hunt, M. (1987). 'The process of translating research findings into nursing practice'. *Journal of Advanced Nursing*, **12**, 101–10.

Hunter, D. J. (1990). 'Managing the cracks? Management development for health care interfaces', *International Journal of Health Planning and Management*, **5**, 7–14.

Hurwitz, N. and Wade, O. L. (1969). 'Intensive hospital monitoring of adverse reactions to drugs', *British Medical Journal*, **1**, 531–6.

Jackson, M. F. (1989). 'Geriatric versus general medical wards: a comparison of patients' behaviours following discharge from an acute care ward', *Journal of Advanced Nursing*, **14**(11), 906–14.

Jacques, E. (1951). *The Changing Culture of a Factory*. London, Tavistock.

Johnson, J. C. (1990). *Selecting Ethnographic Informants*. London, Sage.

Kahn, R. L. and Boulding, E. (eds) (1964). *Power and Conflict in Organisations*. London, Tavistock.

Kalleberg, R. (1990). *The Construct Turn in Sociology*, working paper. Oslo, Oslo Institute for Social Research.

Kemmis, S. *et al.* (1982). *The Action Research Reader*, 2nd edn. Australia, Deakin University Press.

Kemmis, S. and DiChiro, G. (1987). 'Emerging and evolving issues of action research praxis: an Australian perspective', *Peabody Journal of Education*, **64**(3), 101–30.

Key, P. L. (1986). 'The soldier and the aborigine: some thoughts on "better management, better health" ', *Hospital and Health Services Review*, **82**(6), 265–6.

Landsberger, H. A. (1958). *Hawthorne Revisited*. New York, Cornell University Press.

Lathlean, J. (1994). 'Choosing an appropriate methodology', in J. Buckeldee and R. McMahon (eds) *The Research Experience in Nursing*. London, Chapman and Hall, pp. 31–46.

Lathlean, J. and Farnish, S. (1984). *The Ward Sister Training Project: an Evaluation of a Training Scheme for Ward Sisters*. London, University of London Nursing Education Research Unit, Department of Nursing Studies, Chelsea College.

Lee, R. M. (1993). *Doing Research on Sensitive Topics*. London, Sage.

Lees, R. and Smith, G. (eds) (1975). *Action Research in Community Development*. London, Routledge and Kegan Paul.

Lewin, G. W. (ed.) (1948). *Resolving Social Conflicts: Selected Papers on Group Dynamics by Kurt Lewin*. New York, Harper and Brothers.

Lewin, K. (1946). 'Action research and minority problems', in G. W. Lewin (ed.) *Resolving Social Conflicts: Selected Papers on Group Dynamics by Kurt Lewin* (1948). New York, Harper and Brothers.

Lewin, K. (1947). 'Frontiers in group dynamics: concept, method and reality in social science; social equilibria and social change', *Human Relations*, 1(1), 5–41.

Lewin, K. (1951). *Field Theory in Social Science*. New York, Harper.

Lewin, K. (1958). 'The group decision and social change', in E. Maccoby (ed.) *Readings in Social Psychology*. London, Holt, Rinehart and Winston.

Lippitt, R. (1968). 'Lewin, Kurt', in D. L. Sills (ed.) *International Encyclopaedia of the Social Sciences*, Vol. 9. New York, Crowell Collier and MacMillan Inc.

Lund, J. (1992). 'Savanna – an incest survivor: an examination of the appropriateness of support experienced by a female survivor of sexual abuse', Unpublished MA thesis, University of Leicester.

Lupton, T. (1963). *On the Shop Floor*. London, Pergamon Press.

McCracken, G. (1988). *The Long Interview*. London, Sage.

McKernan, J. (1991). *Curriculum Action Research: A Handbook of Methods and Resources for the Reflective Practitioner*. London, Kogan Page.

McNiff, J. (1988). *Action Research: Principles and Practice*. London: Macmillan.

Mares, P., Henley, A. and Baxter, C. (1985). *Health Care in Multi-racial Britain*. Cambridge, Health Education Council and National Extension College Trust.

Marrow, A. J. (1969). *The Practical Theorist: The Life and Work of Kurt Lewin*. New York, Basic Books.

Mattaini, M. A. (ed.) (1992). 'Research and practice: bridging the gap', *Research on Social Work Practice Special Issue*, 2(3).

Mayer, M. (1993). 'Action research, history and the images of science', *Educational Action Research*, 1(2), 317–19.

Mayo, E. (1960). *The Human Problems of an Industrial Civilization*. New York, Viking Press.

Mayo, M. (1975). 'The history and early development of CDP', in R. Lees, and G. Smith (eds) *Action Research in Coming Development*. London, Routledge and Kegan Paul, pp. 6–18.

Menzies, I. E. P. (1960). 'A case study in the functioning of social systems as a defence against anxiety: a report on a study of the nursing service of a general hospital', in *Human Relations*, 13, 95–121.

Menzies Lyth, I. (1989). *The Dynamics of the Social: Selected Essays*, Vol. 11. London, Free Association Books.

Meyer, J. E. (1993). 'New paradigm research in practice: the trials and tribulations of action research', *Journal of Advanced Nursing*, 18, 1066–72.

Mies, M. (1993). 'Towards a methodology for feminist research', in M. Hammersley (ed.) *Social Research: Philosophy, Politics and Practice*. London, Sage, pp. 64–82.

Modi, P. and Pal, J. (1992). 'Beyond despair', in FSU *Confronting the Pain*. London, FSU, pp. 60–76.

Morgan, G. (1986). *Images of Organization*. London, Sage.

Morgan, S. (1993). *Community Mental Health: A Practical Approach to Long-term Problems*. London, Chapman and Hall.

Mullender, A. and Ward, D. (1991) *Self-directed Groupwork: Users Taking Action for Empowerment*. London, Whiting and Birch.

Munn-Giddings, C. (1993). 'A different way of knowing: social care values, practitioner research and action research', *Educational Action Research*, 1(2), 275–85.

Nottinghamshire County Council Social Services Department and the Health Education Council (1984). *Mansfield Community Health Project*. Nottingham, Nottinghamshire County Council.

Nursing Times (1993a), 'The theory practice gap – why do nurses ignore research?', *Nursing Times*, 89(32), 11–17.

Nursing Times (1993b) 'Research in practice', *Nursing Times*, 89(20), 30–1.

Oakley, A. (1981). 'Interviewing women: a contradiction in terms', in H. Roberts (ed.) *Doing Feminist Research*. London, Routledge and Kegan Paul.

O'Connor, H. (1993). 'Bridging the gap?', *Nursing Times*, 89(32), 63–6.

Oja, S. N., and Smulyan, L. (1989) *Collaborative Action Research: A Developmental Approach*. London, Falmer Press.

Ong, B. N. (1989). 'Research from within: blurring boundaries and developing new methods?', *Sociological Review*, 37(3), 505–17.

Ong, B. N. (1993). *The Practice of Health Services Research*. London, Chapman and Hall.

Open University/Health Education Authority (1991). *'Roots and Branches': Papers from the OU/HEA 1990 Winter School on Community Development and Health*. Milton Keynes, Health Education Unit/Open University.

Owen, S. (1993) 'Identifying a role for the nurse teacher in the clinical area', *Journal of Advanced Nursing*, 18, 816–25.

Parish, P. (1985). *Medicines: A Guide for Everybody*. Harmondsworth, Penguin.

Parry, O., Atkinson, P. and Delamont, S. (1992). 'Free range or battery laid: doing a PhD in the social sciences'. Unpublished paper for ESRC Postgraduate Education Conference on *Research Training in the Social Sciences*, St. John's College, Cambridge, 10–11 September.

Pasmore, W. and Friedlander, F. (1982). 'An action research programme for increasing employee involvement in problem-solving', *Administrative Science Quarterly*, **27**, 343–62.

Patton, M. Q. (1990) *Qualitative Evaluation and Research Methods*, 2nd edn. London, Sage.

Payne, G., Dingwall, R., Payne, J. and Carter, M. (1981). *Sociology and Social Research*. London, Routledge and Kegan Paul.

Pearson, A. (1992). *Nursing at Burford: A Story of Change*. London, Scutari Press.

Peckham, M. (1991). *Research for Health: A Research and Development Strategy for the NHS*. London, Department of Health.

Pettigrew, A. and Whipp, R. (1991). *Managing Change for Competitive Success*. Oxford, Blackwell.

Pharmaceutical Society (1986). 'Administration and control of medicines in residential homes', *Pharmaceutical Journal*, **236**(6380), 631–6.

Phillips, D., Berry, S., Booth, T., Jones, D., Matthews, J., Mellotte, C. and Pritlove, J. (1990). 'The proof is in the pudding', *Community Care*, **810**, 22–5.

Platt, J. (1976) *Realities of Social Research: An Empirical Study of British Sociologists*. London, Chatto and Windus for Sussex University Press.

Pollert, A. (1981) *Girls, Wives, and Factory Lives*. Macmillan, London.

Porter, M. (1994). 'Second-hand ethnography: some problems in analyzing a feminist project', in A. Bryman and R. G. Burgess (eds) *Analyzing Qualitative Data*. London, Routledge.

Preston-Shoot, M. (1987) *Effective Groupwork*. London, Macmillan.

Prout, A. (1992). 'Illumination, collaboration, facilitation, negotiation: evaluating the MESMAC project' in P. Aggleton, A. Young, D. Moody, K. Mukesh and M. Pye (eds) *Does it Work? Perspectives on the Evaluation of HIV/AIDS Health Promotion*. London, Health Education Authority, pp. 77–91.

Rapoport, R. N. (1970). 'Three dilemmas in action research', *Human Relations*, **23**(6), 499–513.

Reason, P. (ed.) (1988) *Human Enquiry in Action: Developments in New Paradigm Research*. London, Sage.

Reason, P. and Rowan, J. (eds) (1981). *Human Inquiry: A Sourcebook of New Paradigm Research*. Chichester, Wiley.

Revans, R. W. (1964). *Standards for Morale: Cause and Effect in Hospitals*. London, Oxford University Press.

Richardson, A., Jackson, C. and Sykes, W. (1990). *Taking Research Seriously: Means of Improving and Assessing the Use and Dissemination of Research*. London, HMSO.

Roberts, H. (1992) *Women's Health Matters*. London, Routledge and Kegan Paul.

Roberts, S. (1983). 'Oppressed group behaviour: implications for nursing', *Advances in Nursing Science*, **5**(4), 21–30.

Robinson, J. (1989) 'Nursing in the future: a cause for concern', in M. Jolley and P. Allan (eds) *Current Issues in Nursing*. London, Chapman and Hall.

Robinson, J. (1994). 'Research for whom? The politics of research dissemination and application', in J. Buckeldee and R. McMahon (eds) *The Research Experience in Nursing*. London, Chapman and Hall.

Robinson, K. (1992). 'The nursing workforce: aspects of inequality', in J. Robinson, A. Gray and R. Elkan (eds) *Policy Issues in Nursing*. Buckingham, Open University Press, pp. 24–37.

Robottom, I. and Colquhoun, D. (1993). 'The politics of method in public health research', in D. Colquhoun and A. Kellehear (eds) *Health Research in Practice*: Political Ethical and Methodological Issues. London, Chapham and Hall, pp. 47–64.

Robson, C. (1993). *Real World Research: A Resource for Social Scientists and Practitioner-Researchers*. Oxford, Blackwell.

Roethlisberger, F. J. and Dickson, W. J. (1942). *Management and the Worker*. Cambridge, MA, Harvard University Press.

Rose, M. (1978). *Industrial Behaviour: Theoretical Developments since Taylor*. Harmondsworth, Penguin.

Rouf, K. (1989). 'Journey through darkness: the path from victim to survivor', *Educational and Child Psychology*, 6(1), 6-10.

Russett, C. E. (1966). 'The concept of equilibrium', in *American Social Thought*. New Haven and London, Yale University Press.

Sapsford, R. and Abbott, P. (1992). *Research Methods for Nurses and the Caring Professions*. Buckingham, Open University Press.

Schön, D. A. (1983). *The Reflective Practitioner*. New York, Basic Books.

Schön, D. (1987). *Educating the Reflective Practitioner*. San Francisco, Jossey-Bass.

Schwab, J. J. (1969). 'The practical: a language for curriculum', *Social Review*, **78**, 1-24.

Shakespeare, P., Atkinson, D. and French, S. (eds) (1993). *Reflecting on Research Practice*. Buckingham, Open University Press.

Shipman, M. D. (1974). *Inside a Curriculum Project*. London, Methuen.

Shipman, M. (1988). *The Limits of Social Research*. Harlow, Longman.

Smith, G. (1986). 'Resistance to change in geriatric care'. *International Journal of Nursing Studies*, **23**(1), 61-70.

Smith, G. and Cantley, C. (1985). *Assessing Health Care: a Study in Organizational Evaluation*. Milton Keynes, Open University Press.

Smithies, J. (1991). 'Management theory and community development theory – making the connections', in *'Roots and Branches': Papers in the OU/HEA 1990 Winter School on Community Development and Health*, Milton Keynes: Health Education Unit/Open University, pp. 242–57.

Sparrow, S. and Robinson, J. (1994). 'Action research: an appropriate design for research in nursing?', *Educational Action Research*, **2**(3), 347–55.

Spurgeon, P. and Barwell, F. (1991). *Implementing Change in the NHS: A Practical Guide for General Managers*. London, Chapman and Hall.

Stenhouse, L. (1975). *Introduction to Curriculum Research and Development*. London, Heinemann Education.

Stenhouse, L. (1980). 'Product or process: a response to Brian Crittenden', *New Education*, 2(1), 137-40.

St. Leger, A. S., Schnieden, H. and Walsworth-Bell, J. P. (1991). *Evaluating Health Services' Effectiveness: A Guide for Health Professionals, Service Managers and Policy Makers*. Buckingham, Open University Press.

Stufflebeam, D. L. and Shinkfield, A. J. (1985). *Systematic Evaluation: A Self-Instructional Guide to Theory and Practice*. Dondrecht, Kluwer Nijhoff.

Susman, G. I. and Evered, R. D. (1978). 'An assessment of the scientific merits of action research', *Administrative Science Quarterly*, **23**, 582-603.

Tierney, A. and Taylor, J. (1991). 'Research in practice, an experiment in researcher-practitioner collaboration', *Journal of Advanced Nursing*, **16**, 506-10.

Titchen, A. and Binnie, A. (1993). 'Research partnerships: collaborative action research in nursing', *Journal of Advanced Nursing*, **18**, 858-65.

Towell, D. and Harries, C. (1979). *Innovation in Patient Care: An Action Research Study of Change in a Psychiatric Hospital*. London, Croom Helm.

Town, S. W. (1978). 'Action research and social policy: some recent British experience', in M. Bulmer (ed.) *Social Policy Research*. London, Macmillan Press.

Twinn, S., Dauncey, J. and Carnell, J. (1990). *The Process of Health Profiling*. London, Health Visitors' Association.

van Elteren, M. (1992). 'Karl Korsch and Lewinian social psychology: failure of a project', *History of the Human Sciences*, **5**(2), 33-61.

Vernelle, B. (1994). *Understanding and Using Groups*. London, Whiting and Birch.

von Wright, G. H. (1993). 'Two traditions', in M. Hammersley (ed.) *Social Research: Philosophy, Politics and Practice*. London, Sage in association with the Open University, pp. 9-13.

Wade, B., Finlayson, J., Bell, J., Bowling, A., Bleatham, C., Gilleard, C., Morgan, K., Cole, P., Hammond, M. and Eastman, M. (1986). 'Drug use in residential settings' in K. Judge and I. Sinclair (eds) *Residential Care for Elderly People*. London, HMSO, pp. 173-81.

Walton, R. E. and Gaffney, M. E. (1991). 'Research, action and participation: the merchant shipping case', in W. F. Whyte (ed.) *Participatory Action Research*. London, Sage, pp. 99-126.

WEA (North West District)/Health Education Council (1986). *Women and Health Teaching Pack*. London, WEA Publications Department.

Webb, C. (1989). 'Action research: philosophy, methods and personal experiences', *Journal of Advanced Nursing*, **14**, 403-10.

Webb, C. (1990). 'Partners in research'. *Nursing Times*, **86**(32), 40-4.

Weber, M. (1946). *From Max Weber*. New York, Oxford University Press.

Weber, M. (1947). *The Theory of Social and Economic Organization*. London, Oxford University Press.

Weiss, C. (1979). 'The many meanings of research utilisation', *Public Administration Review*, 9 October, 426-31.

Westwood, S. (1984). *All Day Every Day: Factory and Family in the Making of Women's Lives*. London, Pluto Press.

Whitaker, D.S. and Archer, J.L. (1989). *Research by Social Workers: Capitalising on Experience*. London, CCETSW.

Whyte, W. F. (ed.) (1991). *Participatory Action Research*. New York, Sage.

Winn, L. (ed.) (1990). *Power to the People: The Key to Responsive Services in Health and Social Care*. London, King's Fund Centre.

Winter, R. (1989). *Learning from Experience: Principles and Practices in Action Research*. London, Falmer Press.

Woodward, D. and Chisholm, L. (1981). 'The expert's view? The socio-logical analysis of graduates' occupational and domestic roles', in H. Roberts (ed.) *Doing Feminist Research*. London, Routledge and Kegan Paul, pp. 159-85.

Wright, S. G. (1985). 'Change in nursing: the application of change theory to practice'. *Nursing Practice*, **2**, 85–91.

Wright Mills, C. (1959). *The Sociological Imagination*. Oxford, Oxford University Press.

Wuyts, M., Mackintosh, M. and Hewitt, T. (eds) (1992). *Development Policy and Public Action*. Oxford, Oxford University Press in association with the Open University.

Index

DOING YOUR RESEARCH PROJECT (2nd edition)
A GUIDE FOR FIRST-TIME RESEARCHERS IN EDUCATION AND
SOCIAL SCIENCE

Judith Bell

If you are a beginner researcher, the problems facing you are much the
same whether you are producing a small project, an MEd dissertation or a
PhD thesis. You will need to select a topic; identify the objectives of your
study; plan and design a suitable methodology; devise research instruments;
negotiate access to institutions, material and people; collect, analyse and
present information; and finally, produce a well-written report or dissertation. Whatever the scale of the undertaking, you will have to master
techniques and devise a plan of action which does not attempt more than
the limitations of expertise, time and access permit.

We all learn to do research by actually doing it, but a great deal of time
can be wasted and goodwill dissipated by inadequate preparation. This
book aims to provide you with the tools to do the job, to help you avoid
some of the pitfalls and time-wasting false trails that can eat into your
time, to establish good research habits, and to take you from the stage of
choosing a topic through to the production of a well-planned, method-
ologically sound and well-written final report or dissertation on time.

Doing Your Research Project serves as a source of reference and guide to
good practice for all beginner researchers, whether undergraduate and
post-graduate students or professionals such as teachers or social workers
undertaking investigations in Education and the Social Sciences. This
second edition retains the basic structure of the very successful first
edition while incorporating some important new material.

Contents
*Introduction – Approaches to educational research – Planning the project –
Keeping records and making notes – Reviewing the literature – Negotiating
access and the problems of inside research – The analysis of documentary
evidence – Designing and administering questionnaires – Planning and
conducting interviews – Diaries – Observation studies – Interpretation and
presentation of the evidence – Postscript – References – Index.*

192pp   0 335 19094 4 (Paperback)

RESEARCH INTO PRACTICE
A READER FOR NURSES AND THE CARING PROFESSIONS

Pamela Abbott and Roger Sapsford (eds)

This book is a collection of examples of research, all concerned in some way with nursing or the study of health and community care. It illustrates the kind of research that can be done by a small team or a single researcher, without large-scale research grants. The editors have selected papers which show a great diversity of approaches: differing emphasis on description or explanation, different degrees of structure in design and different appeals to the authority of science or the authenticity of empathic exploration. They show the limitations typical of small-scale projects carried out with limited resources and the experience of applied research as it occurs in practice, as opposed to how it tends to look when discussed in textbooks. The papers have been organized into three sections representing three distinct types of social science research – 'observing and participating', 'talking to people and asking questions' and 'controlled trials and comparisons'. Each section is provided with an editorial introduction.

Contents
Section A: Observing and participating – Introduction – Labouring in the dark – A postscript to nursing – Working with women's health groups – Section B: Talking to people and asking questions – Introduction – Leaving it to mum – Planning research: a case of heart disease – Hospital visiting on two wards – How do women and men in nursing perceive each other? – Section C: Controlled trials and comparisons – Introduction – Treatment of depressed women by nurses – Health visitors' and social workers' perceptions of child-care problems – Health and material deprivation in Plymouth – Postscript – Author index – Subject index.

Contributors
Pamela Abbott, Joyce Bernie, George Choon, Robert Dingwall, Susan Fox, Verona Gordon, Nicky James, Mavis Kirkham, Jean Orr, Geoff Payne, Roger Sapsford, Suzanne Skevington.

176pp   0 335 09742 1 (Paperback)   0 335 09743 X (Hardback)

ACTION RESEARCH FOR HEALTH AND SOCIAL CARE
A GUIDE TO PRACTICE

- What is action research and how can it best be understood?
- How can practitioners use action research to deal with problems and improve services?
- What are the different types of action research and which might be most appropriate for use in a particular setting?

This book has been designed for use as a core text on research methods courses at undergraduate and postgraduate level and on professional training courses. It is divided into three parts. Part one traces the history of action research and shows the links between its use in education, community development, management research and nursing. Building on this background the book explores different ways in which action research has been defined and proposes four different types, each appropriate to a different problem situation and context. In part two, five case studies of action research are described from the perspective of the researcher, including case studies of success and instructive failure. Part three is designed to enable the reader to find a route through the maze of methods and approaches in action research by the use of such things as self-assessment and mapping exercises, a guide to diary keeping and to evaluation. The final chapter suggests that by developing a 'project perspective' action research can be of practical benefit to health and social care professionals in promoting service improvements.

Elizabeth Hart is a social anthropologist and course director for the MSc in Health Care Policy and Organization in the Department of Nursing and Midwifery Studies at Nottingham University Medical School.
Meg Bond is a qualified social worker who now combines research in health and social care with lecturing at the Leicester University School of Social Work.

OPEN UNIVERSITY PRESS

INDEPENDENT INTERNATIONAL PUBLISHER

ISBN 0-335-19262-

9 780335 192625

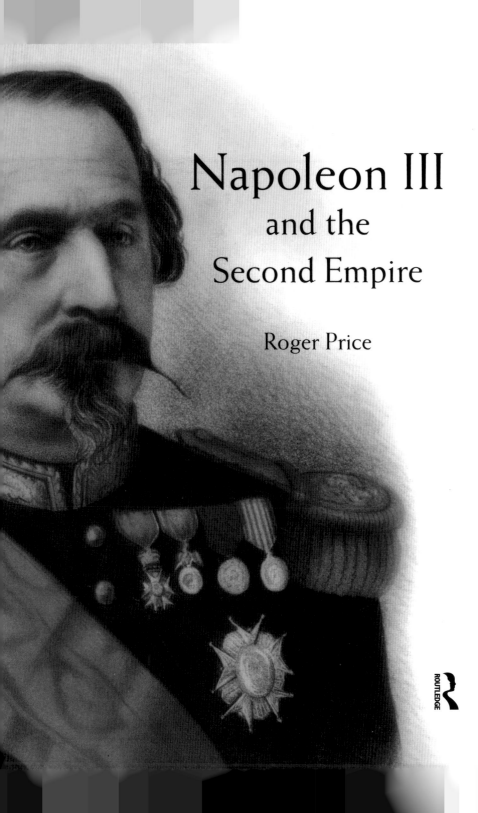

Napoleon III
and the
Second Empire

Roger Price